A

PRISONS OF THE MIND

Prisons of the Mind

OTTO L. SHAW

London
GEORGE ALLEN AND UNWIN LTD

FIRST PUBLISHED IN 1969

This book is copyright under the Berne Convention. Apart from any fair dealing for the purpose of private study, research, criticism or review, as permitted under the Copyright Act, 1956, no portion may be reproduced by any process without written permission. Enquiries should be addressed to the publisher.

© *George Allen and Unwin Ltd., 1969*

SBN 04 157005 7

PRINTED IN GREAT BRITAIN
in 10 on 12 pt Times type
BY NOVELLO & CO. LTD., BOROUGH GREEN, KENT

This book is dedicated to my
generous colleagues: we have all
shared the work.

*It is not thy duty to complete
the work but neither art thou free
to desist from it.*

PREFACE

OTTO SHAW is widely known as an active magistrate and as a member of the council of the Magistrates' Association. Press publicity has occasionally highlighted his magisterial decisions, when he has quite clearly sought to understand the nature of the crime and the criminal rather than to inflict a conventional penalty for the criminal action.

But it is for quite a different reason that I am glad to contribute a foreword to his present book. Those who read its predecessor *Maladjusted Boys* will know of the statistical success that has fortunately accompanied his and his colleagues' work with maladjusted children at Red Hill School, near Maidstone, Kent. Otto Shaw has always disclaimed some of the credit that he and his colleagues deserve for the success of their pupils for, as he is quick to point out, it is he and his colleagues who select the pupils who go to the school, and they select them on the basis of their accessibility to treatment and the likelihood that they will be able to adapt themselves to the methods and techniques used at the school. He is after all, he says modestly, assured of a very high standard of success. Be that as it may, a high standard is achieved and to an extent that is the envy of many similar institutions both at home and abroad.

I have been privileged on more than one occasion to be at the school when the pupils are having their parliament or general council meeting, described in *Maladjusted Boys*. These meetings provide a living experience of the adaptability of a school curriculum and the boys and staff, when a really coherent appeal is made to the children's sense of self-discipline. It is indeed remarkable to see, especially in the case of disturbed children, how law and order of a firm and fair nature, without stress and strain on those who comply with it, can easily be maintained without any idea of punishment or coercion whatever. It is a delight to talk to the pupils, who in their conversation reveal a freedom of expression and thought that many other schools would be wise to copy.

This present book deals with the complexities of human behaviour, and with the real reasons that lie behind many kinds of abhorrent behaviour. Otto Shaw rightly emphasizes the importance of a good family, and the need for the family to show a much better example than is displayed by cultural mass media of today. But in the main, the book is an unemotional and scientific statement. If we are to stop misbehaviour and crime and improve mental health, then first we have to diagnose the cause at an earlier stage in the sufferer's life, and having diagnosed it, treat the sufferer as one deserving of compassion and understanding, rather than of impatience and condemnation. To understand, is to cure. If all readers of the book could see the children for themselves and experience the freedom of the atmosphere within the school, they would realize this is no empty claim.

FRED T. WILLEY M.P.

FOREWORD

FOR those readers who wish to know more about the workings of Red Hill School, *Maladjusted Boys* published by Allen and Unwin in 1965, would be of help.

The school described is a grammar boarding school, recognized by the Department of Education and Science for the treatment and education of maladjusted boys of superior intelligence, whose traditions have been built up over a period of more than thirty years. Without external rules and discipline, law and order has been successfully maintained by the children's own disciplinary court and social committees. It tells also of the special relationships which exist within the community not only between children and staff, but between all the different groups. We have been singularly fortunate in always being able to attract good people for our staff who, having once come to work at the school, appear to find satisfaction in the continuation of their work for many years.

Various homes and different kinds of maladjustment are mentioned and I gave descriptions of the many types of child whom we sought to help. Questions of parentage, religion, sex and the general influence of mass media were all discussed and the book concluded with a note upon the educational aspects of our work, contributed by my very old friend and colleague, Mr Ivor Holland.

An understanding of what is to follow in these pages does not depend upon a reading of *Maladjusted Boys*, but should the reader care to borrow, or, better still, buy the book, he will find the understanding of the rest of these pages made easier.

Case histories are given in this book and, to some, this might seem an invasion of the privacy of treatment offered and given at the school, but the case histories described are disguised in such a manner that no identification could ever be possible, and thus the privacy is fully regarded. Some cases which are mentioned in this book are most disturbed and in a very severely confused condition. Taking as it does fifty-five boys, the school will only accept two or three of these markedly disturbed children at any one time and, remembering therefore that any given moment more than half the children who are living at the school are cured, the pressure upon staff may not be as high as it might otherwise be assumed to be. The cure of children is much helped by the example and activity of the more stable pupils already at the school.

In *Maladjusted Boys* a statistical statement is given as to our cures and failures. Naturally we would prefer that all our geese became swans, but, alas, some of our geese keep to their species. We have been most fortunate in our successes, but our good fortune must reasonably be qualified by the fact that unlike other schools, we choose as pupils whom we agree to take, children who would be most likely to benefit from our treatment and who are not likely to upset the children already at the school. If the same precaution were taken in approved schools, for example, results in such institutions would be better. Perhaps one day we may hope for that improvement.

In those we describe we have purposely used many old cases, the better so to test the permanence of what we regard as a cure. It will be very noticeable to the reader that wherever educational or cognate issues are mentioned we refer to the very high intelligence of our children. Pressure upon our vacancies is enormous and one result of this is the tendency to take children of higher and higher intelligence. Consequently some of our children are within the genius group and with children of that and only slightly less intelligence, it is possible to hope for more co-operation than is likely to be the case where those of dull or only average intelligence are concerned.

Emphasis must be laid upon the fact that in the very intimate details disclosed in these pages, these details are completely private to the adult associated with a particular boy, and in our experiences so far, have never formed the butt of conversation between boys. The preservation of a good and kind atmosphere which respects the privacy and actions of others is one that at all times we seek not only to preserve but to improve. A kindly critic once described us as an oasis of culture in a desert of cupidity. We do not yet deserve that compliment, but one day, if we persevere, we we may be able to say that we have earned that high praise.

OTTO L. SHAW

CONTENTS

CHAPTER I

The Masquerade of Maladjustment

ONCE it was said to me that the chance of understanding a delinquent's motives would distract me from any pleasure in the world and it is true that with the help of imaginative colleagues I have for over thirty years been showing unhappy boys, imprisoned by their own miseries, that the keys to freedom could be fashioned from their own unsuspected happiness. The locksmith was love and his craft creativity; both are often destroyed by others in their infancy so that the process of regeneration, which comes later, calls for patience, understanding and above all an absence of moral judgment.

One of the many baffling influences on youth today is that of organized codes, with their cliché-ridden sayings, promising success, prestige, position, all so well disguised under more flattering and truth-obscuring phrases. How organized Christianity, despite the heroism and pungency of individual priests, manages to fall into the same parcelled cartons of humbug! One of the most disappointing experiences today for a philosophy-seeking youth is the banality of religious discussions on television and the spectacle of the parson trying to be all things to all men in order to receive a spurious kind of popularity.

Provided his congregations are large enough and his publicity self-seeking enough then he feels he has accomplished something which his church requires of him. But all this is so far from the real religious message that should be given. Christ was the greatest star by far when it came to forgiveness but he was preaching an idea, not preaching some abstract saleable commodity of ethics: the idea that love casts out fear.

Delinquency always denotes guilt, and one of the strongest pressures the delinquent experiences is a perpetual need to extirpate his guilt. If only guilt can be removed then perhaps the delinquent act can also be evaded, but this is only possible through love.

Christ never judged morally. He was more inclined to tell judges to put their own houses in order first. If Christ were taken on a tour of the Vatican by the Pope, he would be appalled to see what he had started, or if he attended a crude revivalist evangelical meeting, he would be sorry to see what he had begun, but if he heard a Mother Superior refusing a Jewish child admission to a convent, he would burst into tears.

While I would never have the cheek to compare myself to a religious leader, I know that where punishment will fail to reform a delinquent, understanding, tolerance, goodwill, compassion and charity are likely to succeed.

Controversial weeds flourish in the path of a pioneer and often controversy dims the real motives of those who wish to use punishment. Those who adopt, sometimes in good faith, what they imagine to be the solutions of punishment are those who ensure that our prisons remain full and that our mental hospitals never lack patients.

Worse than that is the marriage which has turned bitter, and which continues in its distorted way to the detriment of the children; the work situation, where misery has crept in; and in the human relationships which instead of continuing in humorous trust are slaves to suspicious doubt.

The further my colleagues and I go with difficult children, the more we realize that punishment is useless, and that our own impatience to succeed with a quick cure and a speedy result is something that must be checked, so that a radical cure for the child's misery can be effected. We seek a solution that goes right to the foundation of the difficulty and rebuilds the child's belief in the faith and goodwill of others.

From our own boarding school experience, we have learnt that to hold a situation is insufficient. We seek not only to understand the child, but to make the child understand himself, so that his relationships with other people may be improved, and the resulting contentment will allow the genius to show itself; he will be able to make a successful marriage which will bear fruit in the happiness of his children. The plea of St Thomas Aquinas was, 'Give me quickness of understanding, capacity for restoring, subtlety of inter- pretation, facility in learning and a copious grace in speaking.'

St Thomas was the forerunner of the psychoanalytic schools of today. It was his ability to see himself as a medium for others' aggressions and love that earned him his title. Today, life is far more complex. His subjects were not confused by cruelty and sadism on television, by sex perversion in the weekly glossy magazines, and by the dreary repetition, day after day, of hatred in the news- papers.

Neurosis, mental ill-health, crime and selfishness, upon which all three are based, naturally existed in St Thomas's time. True in our time they have a greater potential for flourishing; and in our time of vast provocations, the friendly neighbour and the affectionate criticism of a friend are not so easily found. Even so, the barrier between the maladjusted person and friendship is far more difficult for him to surmount today than it was years ago. A genuine outburst of anger at an unpleasant insult or act is understandable to the insulter, and a spontaneous reaction can cause no harm. Bernard Shaw remarked that a blow given to a child in sudden anger did little mischief, and I agree.

I have never yet seen the punishment that has shown the delinquent a better way of life, or the person who can convince the aggressor that society seeks to remove his aggression by showing aggression itself. We have many illustrations which show that, however fairly a child may be opposed and however un- reasonable his demands, opposition only convinces him more strongly of the unfairness of the outside world and creates a position from which no real improvement can be expected. If, instead, understanding is shown and a radical reduction of the child's difficulties is sought, then he will gradually realise that it is no longer necessary to act aggressively.

When the prosecution of *Lady Chatterley's Lover* was launched with maximum publicity, one could guess that we would be likely to hear the word 'fuck' *ad nauseum* in the future. So we have! This is a pity because the word itself is a devaluation of the sexual act. A sexual act is an expression of love and thus an expression of the greatest relationship which can exist in human society. In this respect, as humans, we are different from all other animals, and over thousands of years we have developed a precious and jewel-like act which is now so often degraded by all kinds of associated swear words such as 'fuck', 'cunt' and 'bugger'. Clumsily, one has to use such words even to express one's regret at their existence, but a glance through current fiction shows we no longer have to look far before reading words such as these.

A multitude of strip-tease shops contribute to a far worse situation in London than ever did the murmurings of the prostitutes as they accosted one in the streets of Soho, and this sad sordidity is miserably associated with peripheral criminal activity. By disparaging human dignity the criminal situation can survive. The depreciation of current morality and aesthetics has unfortunately coincided with all kinds of problems with teenagers, the successors of the Regency Bucks, the Hell Fire Club, the Macaronis of the earlier part of the nineteenth century, the dandy, the fop, and the masher, so beloved of Donald Gill, sucking his silver-knobbed walking stick.

When I first meet a new pupil I always ask him if he has ever seen a picture of an ice-berg. Invariably he answers affirmatively, and I then contradict him, causing a dispute which occupies the next few minutes. At last I explain.

'What you are telling me is that you have seen the picture of only the tip of an iceberg, and what goes on under the surface is hidden from you, just as my deepest thoughts are hidden from me.'

It is true of course, that most of our erratic behaviour is due to what goes on unconsciously within us. Much of our behaviour is within our complete control, but at Red Hill School we deal with reactions which are not autonomous, and which if allowed to continue, will be damaging to the person in adolescence or adulthood. We must patiently try to find out what is going on in an uncharted area of the boy's mind. As time goes on, and it is often a matter of several years, we can assemble the curiously fragmented picture we have obtained from the slow exploration of the boy's mind and show him the real fount of his maladjustment.

There is a deal of difference between containing a difficult child and resolving his troubles in such a way that they no longer express themselves because they no longer exist. This is not in any way to gainsay or criticize the devoted and admirable work of probation officers, club leaders and other youth workers. Where such workers have the responsibility for dealing with a difficult child, they very often seek to do it through their own personality or their own capacity for what they hope will be infectious enthusiasm. And while the support of their presence continues, the boy's behaviour improves, but when their assistance is removed, for whatever reason, then the child often relapses to his earlier condition.

Many workers become too involved with the case they are expected to handle. They project their own difficulties into the case and seeing themselves as the subject, feel a sympathy which is always alien to a really radical cure. Sympathy is desirable, but not sympathy of the wrong kind. There is a wealth of difference between a social worker who identifies with the difficult child and the same worker who is able to see the child's difficulties from a distance so that he can disentangle them without becoming himself involved in a vortex of those emotions.

Many factors cause children to misbehave and to carry over their misbehaviour into adult life so that they become charges upon the community, either in institutions or in places of work. The most obvious source of childhoods' difficulties is in conflicts between a child's parents. Too often parents are divorced and although this appears to provide a solution to one aspect of a family problem, in our experience, inevitably it cripples the child in some way. This is not always easily recognized and sometimes the symptoms are not manifest until the child himself is married and visits upon his own children the same disappointments and frustrations that he himself experienced. Demonstrably one often finds in court that the culprit who has more often than not pleaded guilty has a very unhappy family background.

Parents should set a standard of love which children can then emulate and regard as something stable in the whole of life. When one meets a happy, kind and stable person, that person usually comes from a happy united family background, pleasantly removed from the rancours and bitterness of those unfortunates who dwell in a limbo of unfruitful relationships and the consequent terrible confusions this state leaves in its wake.

Another single factor is that which is known as 'spoiling' or inconsistent handling at home, which is also often indicative of bad relations between the parents. Inconsistency to us all, is a confusing thing. We all like to feel we can predict how others are going to behave, and this a child not only likes, but needs to be able to do. Naturally, surprises are always looked forward to with anticipatory interest, but these are expected to be pleasant ones. The sudden emergence of a grumpy, disgruntled father, when a child bursts into the room with some eager information, is so unreasonable if one is hoping for one's child to grow up happily.

The lack of a firm family structure is often responsible for early infantile difficulties and these are later exacerbated by disciplinary and environmental neglect. However, an adolescent also needs a secure family structure; it is often troublesome for a parent to note that a girl can be having fantasies of sexual intercourse at one hour and at the next she will be at the level of playing with her dollies. What the adolescent needs more than anything else is approval. If the family approval of its son or daughter is there, then the adolescent will almost automatically fall into a line of agreeable behaviour. Severity is such a temptation when parents are confronted with what they believe is palpable disobedience and the temptation is greater when their anxiety or uncertainty is based upon their own troubled feelings. While there are plenty of men and women of merit with whom young people can identify, there are also vast numbers of less admirable public and popular figures with whom it is easier for less stable young people to identify. The importance of money in the terms of income of the pop singer and his possession of a Rolls Royce can be held as an index of success in life, and inevitably the unstable personality seeks luck or chance to bring him riches. Thus he is able to persuade himself that there is justification for moral short cuts and idleness. These superficial attitudes rest upon family difficulties, imbalance and discordance.

A petty thief boasts, generally untruthfully, of success. The big thief, usually a professional, keeps quiet about his malpractices. The boaster also regards the evasion of, and brushes with, law and order as the excitement that the more fortunate law-abiding citizen obtains from athletics or academic success, but while one can

22

continue to bemoan the overt acts of the delinquent, none of this argument lessens the fact that only the top of the iceberg of his unconscious mind has been uncovered, and the real basis of the antagonism of the rebellious adolescent arises from the pressures of family neglect. Exhortations, probation, explanation, advice and sermonizing does little for the delinquent especially within a social culture that so completely accepts materialism. The significance of cataclysmic atomic bombing, smash and grab raiders, poor detection statistics and finally the culture in which our country spends a hundred million pounds on gambling every year is quickly seen by the unstable boy as justification for his overt behaviour.

Difficult children not only act like children, but frequently act in anger and frustration, as if they are denying their hunger and thirst for the love which they feel is being unfairly withheld. Whether they are right or wrong to feel in such a way matters little. The fact is that they do so feel, and it is with that feeling we have to deal.

CHAPTER II

The Breast, Drunk
or Sober

ALBERT BROWN came to us not only as an extremely persistent thief but a drunkard, which is not very usual in my experience of difficult children. He stole mainly rum, whiskey and gin from public houses and off-licences, and had been found countless times by the police lying in a state of utter incapability. At first it was often thought he was ill or had had an accident, and whenever he had been found in this unconscious state, he had been taken to hospital. But it was soon realized that all these episodes were preceded by theft from a public house. When he arrived at our school he expressed contrition, and assured us that he had learned his lesson and was going to behave himself now that this chance had been offered, but ten days later he helped himself to the contents of a decanter in my house and was once again rendered incapable. Although the desire to be relieved of this dreadful incubus was sincere, unfortunately like so many neurotics he desired relief from the disability without any real work, understanding or effort on his own part.

His language was filthy; he would decorate the margins of his exercise books with pornographic verses, in which, for instance, 'tit' was rhymed with 'shit', and he would embarrass other boys and members of the staff at the meal table by describing some of the dishes set before him as resembling vomit or shit. Drink, food, faeces and urine were associated and confused in his talk, his rhymes and his vast fund of dirty stories.

We discussed matters with his parents, who appeared sensible and reasonable people, and saw his sister, who had escaped the stigmata of maladjustment and appeared to be a perfectly ordinary girl. Albert seemed likely to have generated all his difficulties for himself, and these were not, as in most cases, caused by deprivation, parental selfishness, parental adultery, or similar kinds of parental mistreatment.

Shortly after the start of his confidential sessions with me, Albert expressed a deep loathing of his father, which seemed to puzzle him as much as it puzzled me. The abhorrence appeared so completely divorced from reason, because his father, although not very imaginative or helpful in dealing with his son (though it is doubtful if any father could deal helpfully with the behaviour difficulties this boy was showing) had done nothing to justify such intense dislike. At times Albert would even admit to having plotted his father's murder.

'One day, Shaw, it got as far as for me to wait for him to come home from work and I actually had a knife I'd stolen, and as he hung up his coat in the hall I was ready to put the knife into his back. Something stopped me; I don't know what it was. I fled upstairs and pretended I had a headache. Actually I was crying, and when my mother came in I buried my face in the clothes and pretended to be angry with her for some reason so she would not discover I'd been weeping. Later I buried the knife at the bottom of the garden, and for all I know it's still there. My God, Shaw, I was nearer to killing him that day than I've ever been to doing anything in my life! Shaw, what's the reason? Why did I do that?'

As the sessions continued, an intense jealousy was revealed, jealousy of the father as the main competitor for his mother's attention. It is useless to pretend, and indeed no cure would have resulted had we pretended, that such jealousies and angers can occur only when verbal expression can be given to them. These perverted pre-verbal conflicts are as real as anything that happens in later childhood years. At a very early pre-verbal age, Albert had formed the idea that the main rival for his mother's lap and for the softness and glory of her breast was this man who came home every night, this person of superior magnetic attraction to whom the mother went, thus 'neglecting' himself. Although this was a completely unreasonable supposition, it nevertheless began to explain something of Albert's addiction to the bottle.

The most important word that we first learn to utter is 'Mummy'. The first muddled sound the infant makes, is a sound beginning with 'M'. Because it is the first sound that the infant makes, it is the sound that gives rise to the most holy word 'Mother' in so many languages. Much proof exists, if proof indeed were needed, that the infant child demands to be handled by its mother, not because it is crying or in some physical discomfort, but because the mere handling by the mother is of a supportive and reassuring kind. The first recognition on the part of the newly born infant is that of its mother's smell and its mother's noise. The noise a mother makes to the baby is always a good thing: the smell a mother has for her baby is always a good scent. Most of us have seen an occasion when an aunt has sought to pick the infant baby out of the cradle; immediately the child sets up a scream, which as instantly ceases when the mother comes and takes her child from the arms of her sister. She did not have 'Mummy's noise and Mummy's smell'. Had she had those two attributes, then the child would not have screamed.

The mother gives her baby food, warmth, security, and all the things that matter to all of us—and throughout all our life continue to matter. As responsibilities of adulthood come to us the substance of our desires changes, but nevertheless the way we deal with adult responsibilities depends upon how we were loved and fed, and upon the very being of the relationship with our mother, when we were infants. Unfortunately, even if the mother is good, proper, fair and kind in all her relationships with her baby, that does not always mean that the baby will grow up without feeling it has been deprived in some way. One of the fundamental problems of maladjustment and delinquency, and one of the fundamental problems in understanding the genesis of these difficulties, is the fact that some children, though brought up in identical ways to other children, can fail where their brethren succeed. Very often one discovers the case of a good mother who has loved and given in utter propriety all that she could properly give to her baby, but nevertheless that baby has turned into the adult who becomes a convict, because he wrongly believes that he was cheated of something at almost the cradle level of his life.

The greatest satisfaction that any baby experiences is drawing milk from its mother's breast. If the baby is fed from a bottle the sensation is much the same because it is given within the aura of his mother's smell and his mother's noise, and from her fond and loving hands, and after the feed is complete the baby is cuddled, warmed and loved by her before being put back into his cot to sleep.

Envy arises in the child if anything threatens his access to the good object, his mother's breast or bottle, the object which gives him food, warmth, comfort and indeed life. If for any reason the child's contact with her breast is interrupted, or is not as secure as a baby would wish it to be, then one has the early seeds of frustration and anxiety: if those seeds are well implanted then it becomes difficult to remove equivalent attitudes in adulthood, because the lack really existed. At the school we have known many cases of children who, in their first few weeks of life, had been tragically subject to the mother's absence in hospital, or had themselves been in hospital, away from her. No doubt these children were well looked after at home or by the nurses in the hospital creche, but however good a nurse or a substitute mother may be, she lacks the essential noise and smell, and other less tangible attributes, that seem to cling only to the real mother, and can never be possessed by even the most admirable and temperamentally angelic mother substitute.

It is unlikely that any drunkard ever attained complete satisfaction at his mother's breast. Every alcoholic is unconsciously seeking that which can in fact be obtained only at that primitive breast level, a satisfaction which he believes, rightly or wrongly, has been denied to him.

Another complication which is so often and so easily overlooked is that the birth of envy in a child gives rise to feelings of guilt. If we are envious we seek to justify our envy, and in maladjusted children or adults this can take a strange form.

It was difficult to show Albert the real reason for his jealousy of his father, for it was buried deep in his sub-conscious mind in a pre-verbal period of his life. He had had the feelings long before he could express them to himself or anyone else, and of course he never will understand them fully.

Within three months his obsession for drink and pornography had disappeared. This was mainly due to our long analytical discussions, for when a person is acting out his fears in interviews there is usually no need for such expression outside. However, because the envy and guilt feelings no longer find expression outside the analytical interview, that is certainly not to say that a cure has been effected. One of this boy's difficulties was that any discussions were merely a substitute; his conflict was being worked out within our relationship, but once this relationship with me ceased his symptoms would return. It took three years for Albert to realize, and fully believe, that his mother did love him, that he had no cause for envy, and that the love was his by right, without having to fight for it.

Albert appeared gradually to be transferring to me his antagonism against his father. One day he admitted to me that, on return from a holiday at home, he had brought back a carving knife with which to kill me and, following his previous ritual at home, had buried the carving knife in the woods of the school. When he understood the basis of his jealousy of me, which was fundamentally the same as the jealousy he had for his father, in this case with regard to my relationship with my wife, he made good progress.

At last he came to the point when he could say: 'You know, Shaw, it's bloody unfair. I'm here at school without any sense of family and you can go home at night to your wife. It's bloody unfair.'

'You do not make it fairer by envying me,' I answered. 'You will not make it fairer by stealing my wife from me and you will not come closer to what you seek by sticking a carving knife into me.'

He understood, and his understanding took the form of a deep emotional experience as it should if the treatment is to be successful. Until the full vigour and violence of the transference situation had been interpreted to the boy, the analysis could not proceed. It is obvious now how closely his foul-mouthed tirades were related to his subconscious belief. It could have been expressed: 'If I cannot have my mother's tit then I'll make certain by turning it all to shit that nobody else gets it.'

Had we sought to rebuke or punish Albert instead of showing that we shared his own dislike of his behaviour, we would not have been very successful in our treatment. His conviction that his father had all the loving milk from his mother was so strong, and he so despaired of ever obtaining his fair share, that he had at first tried to murder his father, and when that failed he tried to ensure that no one else would ever want it by comparing tit with shit, and a dish of food with vomit. Then he could say to himself: 'Me want my mother's breast? How could I ever want that? It's only shit or sick.'

All the time the need for a substitute, the bottle, was so strong that he had to go on stealing it. He had been cheated of it, therefore he would cheat others. He stole it, and drank himself into a stupor, trying to make up for the years of imagined deprivation.

The incredibly stupid assumption of so many people that misbehaviour of this kind is within the boy's control is the biggest impediment to curing such delinquency. Once we understand that as the stammerer does not wish to stammer, the social misfit does not admire his behaviour, we will realize that these delinquents are worthy of the same consideration and understanding. It is easy to tolerate a person with a broken leg, to take him gifts, to give him every kind of attention and consideration. It is much harder to tolerate a foul-mouthed drunken boy even if he is in just as much need of sympathy. As is said in the Koran, the sin has to be rebuked, not the sinner.

Gradually Albert's behaviour improved. He understood he could have love appropriate to his present age in a way that was right for the situation in which he lived. During his holidays at home there was no longer the tension and trickery of getting love by cheating. Naturally when he realized that what he sought could be obtained, there was no need to act it out either in the delinquent situation of theft and foul language, or in the analytic situation in which the analyst had to stand for all those dreadful things the father represented to his son. It is good to be able to record that Albert is now married, and that his two children, aged ten and eleven years of age, are both happy and adjusted.

'One day you will have love and then you will realize that there need be no battle over love,' I remember saying to him in his unhappy days. 'What a pity you are so impatient when Mother seeks to put you back into the cot, and you so mistakenly feel that the source of all goodness and love is interrupted. One day, Albert, you'll know you are only put back to sleep temporarily, and that the love will continue and prosper. You will be married too, and we hope you will not see in your own children the envy you have discovered within yourself.'

It is so true that the emotional relationships we all have with people outside our family reflect the infantile relationship we had with our mother and father, and later with our brothers and sisters. A stable and good family rarely produces those who require treatment in a mental hospital or prison, because in that family the jealousies and rivalries are contained; but this is not always so, as the case of Albert serves to remind us.

CHAPTER III

More Intoxication

BERNARD CHAMBERS was lucky that the objects he stole pinpointed his special condition. He had been charged before a juvenile court for breaking into houses and stealing all kinds of bric-a-brac, but mainly bottles. After two convictions and probation orders for this crime we had been asked to undertake his treatment. Naturally we ignored his dishonesty, as it is useless to tell a boy with this problem that the dishonesty must cease. A maladjusted boy does not cease his misbehaviour merely because he is sent to somebody who is hoping to cure him, so we were not surprised when Bernard continued his dishonesty both inside and outside school. Although we ignored his stealing in any narrow, punitive sense we offered much understanding and compassion, for this can be done without in any way condoning the offence.

Over a period of months we were able to show that we sought understanding without condemnation. After a while the stealing gradually ceased to involve a variety of articles, and was a concentration round objects such as fruit, purses or, more particularly and ominously, bottles of all shapes and sizes. It was when the stealing was almost entirely devoted to these round womb symbols that he was able to attend his private sessions where I could explore the deeper meaning of his misbehaviour.

At first the sessions were typified by irresolution and wasted time, but after long periods of hesitancy and obvious fear there came a time when the boy spoke:

'There is something about myself, Shaw, that I do not understand. At home I have hundreds and hundreds of bottles and I don't know why I've got them. Some of them I keep in my bedroom drawers, some are hidden in the attic, one or two are in an old broken garden shed that my father no longer uses, and some I have buried. Why on earth I collect the things, I don't know; but somehow whenever I see a bottle I've got to pinch it.'

Bernard had a good relationship with a teacher at the school who, on being told of the bottle obsession and happening to be a collector of antiques, suggested to Bernard that he might care to collect antiques himself. The boy then confessed to his interest in different shapes and sizes of bottles.

'Oh, well,' said my colleague, 'I can provide you with things like that. They may take a bit of time to find, but I'll do my best.'

The offer was abruptly refused; and when at the end of the same week Bernard was offered two or three very attractive blue, Bristol glass bottles he refused them.

'I have discovered something else about my silly bottle trick,' he informed me at our next meeting. 'They're no good to me unless I pinch them, or unless I come by them by means of some fiddle. Jack has been offering me some, but somehow there was no point in keeping them. I didn't want them any more than I'd want a piece of coal. I just have to pinch them.'

Apart from the stealing, Bernard's behaviour was reasonably good. He was pleasant in his relationships with other boys, and was quite a useful member of his class. In general he could have been regarded as a popular pupil, but the popularity was decreasing because he felt, and expressed the feeling quite openly to me, that the longer the stealing went on the more he would forfeit people's regard for him. Sooner or later, he felt, all his thefts would be discovered. He worried that he might cease to be satisfied at the theft of mere bottles and bric-a-brac, but would have to go on to other things to satisfy his wretched urge.

A few weeks later the stealing spread to Woolworths. One day, after the inevitable telephone call, we found he had been caught stealing bottles of scent there. Again bottles were involved, but the search for whatever the bottles represented was entering into wider fields. Once a delinquent act is used as an expression of a need, it is extremely unlikely that the delinquency is going to be abandoned merely because of exhortation, pleading or remonstrance from others. If such methods do have any effect, it is almost certain that the delinquent act will be replaced by something even more sinister and damaging to the personality.

Bernard was an accomplished artist who would spend many hours outside the formal art class doing his own oil paintings. One day he wrote an urgent message to me saying he must see me immediately as something of enormous consequence had occurred. He came into the study in great excitement and perturbation.

'Shaw,' he shouted, 'I have discovered that whenever I complete a drawing I always sign it in two places, once at the bottom left-hand corner and once at the bottom right-hand corner. It always struck me as funny, as most artists sign in one place if they sign the picture at all, but I've kept on doing it. In the last two or three weeks, when I've found that I've done a rather, well, not so important drawing I've torn off the two signatures, in some way not wanting people to see what I've drawn.'

I asked him to let me see some of the drawings. He demurred at first, but after a few hours brought them up to the study, and it was immediately clear to me why he had destroyed any evidence of authorship. With seeming disinterest, I asked why he thought he had torn off his signatures from both the left- and the right-hand corners.

'Well, they are not very good drawings, are they? There is nothing really to be proud of that I'd want people to see.'

Each drawing was filled with bottles of all shapes, sizes and colours. At last, he was trying to externalize the nature of his problem.

I asked whether he had any of the torn-off signatures and he produced a dozen or so little triangular torn-off pieces of paper from his pocket. Now his initials were clearly 'B.C.' but he had managed to distort the top semi-circle of the capital 'B' into a kind of test tube shape. The 'C' was written within the lower semi-circle of the 'B', and thus the effect was of a rounded object surmounted by a thin tube-like protuberance.

'Oh dear me, Bernard. What on earth does this look like?' I asked.

33

B

He looked at it and suddenly, after a pause, burst into tears.

'I'm not going to talk to you any more,' he shouted. 'All you think of is filth.'

He rushed out of the study, slamming the door so hard that the hinges rocked. But two days later he came to me again.

'Look, I do want to talk about this,' he said. 'I know damn well that at the bottom of those drawings I have been drawing a tit. It is something I have to hide from everybody else in the world, but I need not hide it from you.'

We then fell to discussing his family, and in the following months he declared his violent antagonism for his sister, and how he sought to get what he thought was revenge, but what I called envy. When he was three he had experienced the mortification of his sister's birth, and the humiliation of being tipped off his mother's lap to make room for this interloper.

'You know, Shaw, I used to make a kind of joke with myself that one day I'd offer to take her out for a walk in her pram and quite accidentally let it slip under a bus. At other times I've had fantasies of taking her for a walk to the side of the canal and lifting her over the railings to see the water in the canal and letting her slip over and drown. I've had thoughts, too, of pushing her over a cliff.'

Dreams had followed in which, night after night, Bernard would think of fantasy ways of destroying his sister. What had this little baby done? She had been born when he was just under the age of three; for those three years he had been the only child in the family, and was not prepared to move up and make room for the next arrival. His parents cannot be blamed for any lack of preparation as it had been no secret that his mother was carrying a new baby and there had been no attempt to disguise the fact that soon there would be two children in the family, and perhaps that a third or fourth might follow. There had been no avoidance of the task of preparing the boy for a newcomer to the house with whom later he would have to share his playthings, and the attention that he had from Mummy. Nevertheless the preparation proved insufficient: Bernard could not withstand the intense envy and jealousy of the newborn child who had, according to his belief, supplanted him in his mother's affections.

When I next saw his parents I obtained Bernard's permission to speak to them about confidential admissions he had privately made to me. They showed understanding and, what is just as important as understanding, imagination without sentimentality.

'You know, you've reminded me about something,' said Mrs Chambers thoughtfully. 'I've never thought of it before because, after all, young married parents know so little about the vagaries of childish behaviour, but I do now see its importance. He cried a terrific amount when his sister was born, and always seemed to be wandering about the house turning over things, opening drawers and cupboards, lifting up magazines to see what lay beneath. He seemed to be going around the house exploring, to make certain there was no fresh discovery that might discomfort him, and he asked me questions about when I was to stop feeding the baby, because I made no secret of the fact that I fed the baby from my breast just as I had fed him. I told him that all babies were fed in the same way, and when they grow older they feed in different ways.'

So the mother went on trying to evade the very thing she ought to tell me. At last she did come to the point, and her information showed how far the boy had been effected by the baby's birth.

'His father,' she continued, 'went into his room and found him feeding his teddy bear. He had always been to bed with his teddy bear which he loved very much.'

'He was feeding his own teddy bear,' I interrupted, 'in the same way that you fed your daughter?'

Mrs Chambers blushed and said, 'No, he was making teddy seem to feed on his own wee wee.'

There was the boy making teddy feed from his own penis. In other words the boy thought the penis just as effective a love object as his mother's nipple. One can appreciate his sense of isolation, indeed desolation, when he had to have a 'make do' nipple of his own with which to feed his own little baby. He could not bear that his mother should have the sole object worthy of such attention; she had the breast, so he invented a breast, a little nipple-like thing, with which he could feed his loved child, the teddy bear. There was a complete supplanting of the mother's position, for the boy could only bear his envy and jealousy by pretending to have the same capacity as his mother to feed and love a child at the breast. The fact that he had no breast was not an obstacle; he could easily invent one, and his anatomical choice was not unreasonable.

35

It was very fortunate indeed that his parents reacted sensibly to the three-year-old's jealousy for, had they not done so, psychosexual fixation at that level would have been far more difficult to remove, and the boy's development into maturity would have been further hampered. Although forgotten at the time of talking to me about his drawings, Bernard's action of feeding his teddy bear had not really been forgotten subconsciously, for in the letter 'B' of his signature was a phallus-like nipple signing all the pictures both on the left and the right-hand side. The pictures are almost exclusively occupied with drawings of bottles. It is needless to add that the bottle represents the feeding of a baby, and the breasts are on the left- and the right-hand sides. Even if he did not have two penes he could fantasy that he had two breasts, but as the two breasts would have been stolen from the mother just as all the bottles had to be obtained illicitly, the evidence of the two breasts had to be torn from the drawing. With great care I explained it all to the boy, adding the story I learned from his mother. Bernard's excitement and pleasure at this discovery was immense. Later the four of us met together and discussed it all again, and Bernard's parents assured him that the envy and fear he experienced were ill-based and need never trouble him again.

The surprising release that he felt in class, the astonishing creativeness he then showed in art and the ability with which he took up a new art, that of music, was remarkable. The unhappy fear had been removed from his life; he could see for the first time that there was no basis for his jealousy, and that his envy leading to murderous thoughts, dreams and fantasies about his sister need never have arisen. His importance, he now knew, was as great as, but different from, that of others in the family. One day soon after these discoveries were made he came to me.

'You know,' he said, 'I still have a sense of loyalty to my silly old bottles, but I think it's only fair to give them away. If there is anybody else here who wants to collect them, let him have them. If not, I'm going to throw them away. But I think I'd like to keep it private because in spite of all the foolishness and silly nonsense I've been going through, those bottles did do something for me. Indeed I expect it was the only damned thing that kept me straight, because if there hadn't been those to fall back on I probably would have gone completely daft.'

The boy left the school many years ago and his marriage is perfectly happy. He is a musician; his creativity is not stolen from his mother nor acted, but is a real talent of his own.

When Charles Duckham came to the school I met him and his parents at the front entrance. From the wealth of detail in the case papers I knew of the boy's thefts and shoplifting, and of particular thefts of money and occasional ornaments from the dresser in his kitchen, but not one item of information in his case history had prepared me for the surprising fact that, once he was in the main hall of the school, he moved sharply round behind me and smelled my bottom. His embarrassed parents apologised and told me that their son was like that. A member of the staff passed through the main stairs at that moment and the boy shifted his interest to that man's bottom. When I said goodbye to his parents he was engaged in smelling the front door bell.

Life with Charles was never without its startling moments for the next few months. We did not wish him to think we considered him a lunatic or such an unstable person that he could not be given the same privileges and outings as others, so we arranged that we alone should take him into town. One minute he would be on all fours smelling the pavement, and the next minute would be embarrassing some stranger by his attention to the man's bottom. His general attitude within the school became more restrained, but at all steps and turns he would be smelling one of the door bells, the covers of his text books, or some other object that happened to attract his attention. Time went by, and although very little was achieved he seemed to come more to terms with his misbehaviour and his follies than we had thought possible.

No real understanding about his smelling was reached until one day in almost chance conversation it emerged that he never actually smelled anything: he inhaled. It was a taking in through the mouth, not a smelling through the nose. At that point an understanding of the complexities and difficulties of his position became more possible.

He had lost his real mother when he was two and a half and a wholly admirable stepmother had married his father a few years later. She had looked after him with consideration and understanding. Unfortunately she was not his mother and no amount of goodness on her part, however admirable, could ever alter that unwelcome fact. A child cannot easily transfer his affections from one person to another just because that person has the dignified title of 'Mummy'. The original Mummy may be a depraved and corrupt being, and the stepmother a benevolent, saint-like personality, but the transference seems only to be accomplished at great hazard and difficulty, and sometimes is never accomplished at all.

Charles had never accepted that his mother was dead and that for all time she, who had borne him and fed him in those early days, would never return. He had therefore been forced back upon some crazy solution of his own. Somehow to him the death of his mother was a disaster that might so easily be repeated. Even if it did not occur in the same or similar form nevertheless a repetition was predestined, and in order to avoid such a calamity he had to build some structure that would not only avoid it but somehow exorcise the first one.

He wanted the two breasts. Theft had been tried, he had stolen various objects which symbolised the missing parts. His good stepmother had offered him her breasts but he had refused them, regarding the lost ones as infinitely preferable to anything nearer at hand. Then he discovered he had two breasts of his own in the shape of his buttocks. They were round, fleshy, warm, shapely, and all the mysterious things that in childhood the breasts seem to be. They were objects of similar curiosity and similar mystery: significantly, they were objects to which other people attach great importance in terms of cleanliness training. Later in life they were objects of a perverted erotic satisfaction. Thus not only had his original mother two round good things, he also had two round good things, and the fact that others would call them buttocks made no difference to their importance. If he were to be denied the two original breasts, very well, he would have the two that he could supply himself.

He told me of the experiments with such objects as test tubes, pencils and toothbrushes inserted anally, and of the special satisfaction he would get from masturbation if at the same time he was able to push some hard object into his rectum. At some stage of his life, after the transposition of the breasts from one place to another had been effected, realizing that it was nothing but a fake and spurious arrangement, he developed the need to test it. The smelling of the bottom, which later turned out to be an oral breathing in, represented the taking of food that he assumed would come from the substitute buttock breasts.

When Charles arrived at the school at the age of twelve years, he weighed nineteen stones. There had been attempts at a diet at home, and sustained periods of medical treatment, but nothing had succeeded in reducing his weight. It has become a byword with us that the fat boy is a boy who lacks some sense of security from his mother. He is a boy who has to be continually feeding himself all the time to assure himself that the object that provides him with food is still alive, and in a position to provide the warmth and consolation he feels he lacks. As such boys are cured, or rather weaned, of their dreadfully dependent position upon the imagined qualities of the mother, so their intake of food becomes more restrained and their weight lowers to normal. Such was the case with Charles Duckham. He came to understand that no matter how avid he was in trying to see breast buttocks wherever he inhaled from all rotund rounded objects he found, he alone could provide the solution to his self-created difficulties. Charles began to realize that security was his if only he recognized it. It took him a long time but, when he had understood it, the need to go about smelling at breast-bottoms and experiencing all kinds of breast sensations by anal games with his own bottom disappeared. He no longer needed to steal the advantage that he thought had been denied him.

All the toleration shown to a difficult child, all the possible understanding, are sometimes insufficient, and unorthodox techniques have to be employed. Charles' behaviour had improved to a certain point, but it was clear that we then faced a brick wall. The boy's silent demand for the missing breast was so intense, and tragic, that it had to be met. I discussed the matter with a female colleague, and, after I had obtained Charles' permission to tell her some of the things that had passed privately between us, she approached him with a suggestion that with the utmost privacy he should be given a bottle every evening. This made it clear to him that the need for his search was appreciated and understood. Charles agreed to the suggestion.

From that night and for the next six weeks, with a secrecy that almost approached a ritualistic significance, Charles was provided with a bottle and thus enjoyed an experience he had regarded as impossible of achievement since the death of his beloved mother. Time would only be wasted in discussing the rationale of such treatment, but either it did work or it cleared the way for analytical work to prosper. Whatever the explanation might be, Charles is now a successful architect with a family of five happy children of his own.

CHAPTER IV

Tics Twitches Stammers

SYDNEY TOWN was three when his father was killed in a railway accident, and his bereaved mother went with her little son to live at the home of her elderly, widowed and highly irascible father. These two people constituted the only family that the three-year-old Sydney knew and when he started to grow up, in default of any other male figure within the family, quite reasonably he used his grandfather as a father. But whatever Grandpa had been in the past, he was no longer temperamentally suited to be a father, or indeed to have any hand in the upbringing of an infant.

When we first met Sydney he was a little over eleven years old, and suffered from a pronounced tic-like movement of his arm and shoulder. This movement was so emphatic that it was quite impossible for him to hold pencil or pen and put them to paper. Consequently since the onset of this severe symptom the whole of his school life and been disrupted. His doctor had prescribed certain sedative tablets, and when these had no effect he was referred to the Child Guidance Clinic. After investigating the case history, and discovering the circumstances in which the boy was living, they wrote to us, and thus he came to the school.

He was a nice boy with pleasant manners, but timid and frightened, and when any courtesy or generosity were shown to him he was overwhelming in his expressions of gratitude. His mother told us the pathetic story of Sydney's life. Lacking money and other resources as she did, it was inevitable that she should go to live with her widowed father. This man was quite well off and readily accepted the responsibility but his behaviour to the small child was beyond all tolerating. From quite an early age Sydney was the target of his aggressive discipline regarding noise, seemliness of behaviour, table manners, times for bed and getting up, with a total rigidity of control to which no child should ever be subjected. Even among the most rigorous days of the Victorian period no child could have submitted to the discipline, and indeed torments, which Sydney had undergone at the hands of his grandfather.

Mrs Town told us that at times life with her father had been almost unbearable. She had survived it by quiet submissiveness and development of hobbies and pursuits that took her away from him, but her little son was open to attack all the time. On one occasion she had a scene with her father in an effort to prevent him waking up Sydney in order to thrash the little boy for some quite small misdemeanour committed during the daytime and just discovered.

In his pitiable misery the boy was at first terrified to tell us of his troubles. When his reserve abated I was able to explain to him that it would be good if he and I were to go in search of the reasons for his tic and, if we were successful, he would then be able to do his lessons well.

Pathetically he interrupted, 'Then my grandfather would be pleased.'

I answered that my hope was to give him pleasure and achievement and if we also gave others the same feeling this was good, but I did not think we could ever reach success if we set out to appease the angry old gentleman. In an attempt to encourage Sydney to talk I explained to him how events could form a chain. As an example I suggested that I might hit a boy (though I would never do so in fact) and that boy, being weaker than me, might get his own back by hitting another boy, weaker and smaller than himself: that second boy in turn would bully a third. The third, lacking a target less powerful than himself, would kick one of the school cats. Later that day I might pass by and stoop to stroke the cat but, knowing from bitter experience earlier in the day that an approach heralded pain, the cat would angrily spit and scratch my hand. I explained to the boy that here was a cycle of events to which I could respond saying that the cat was wicked and should be punished; or, by unravelling the chain of events and studying the nature of every link in that chain, discover that the originator of the sequence was myself.

Demonstrations of the arguments that could arise from such an illustration took a very long time, but the boy did at last understand that he and I could look at the links of the chain of his tic and, if successful in establishing the linkages, could remove it, and show him a different way of reacting to whatever caused the tic. We could release the energies now being frustrated and turn them towards games, hobbies, lessons or other pleasurable activities.

The unravelling and unknotting started, and it was not long before the boy began to talk. He spoke angrily of his grandfather, but after each outburst would be overcome with a guilt that led him at the beginning of the next session to contradict all he had said in the previous one. He felt the grandfather could reach out revengefully and, magically divining what had been said to me, would take some toll of retaliation. Every now and again the boy would interrupt his remarks and anxiously defend himself against an accusation I had not made of disloyalty to his grandfather, but gradually he learned that whatever he and I did and said together within the study was under the seal of secrecy. Just as I would not judge him for anything he said, he too could refrain from any form of self-judgment or self-condemnation. With considerable diffidence and a temporary eruption of stammering he told me that the real thing that his grandfather hated was his very presence in the house because once, in a terrible rage, his grandfather had exploded, 'I didn't want you and your mother living with me. I have finished with children.'

Tears came into the boy's eyes; he blushed and spoke again with a stutter.

'I know really what my grandfather didn't like.'

He then told me how his grandfather had caught him playing with his penis in the bath.

'If I ever see you doing that again,' his grandfather had threatened, 'I will thrash you to within an inch of your life.'

Two or three days later the bathroom door was suddenly flung open and an angry face appeared round the door. Beyond an internal tremble from the boy, nothing more happened; but a week later, again when the boy was in the bath, the grandfather had caught him masturbating. Without even pausing for the child to dry himself, he beat him savagely. So life continued. The boy continued to masturbate and the grandfather continued to beat him for what he considered to be a dreadful sin. At last the masturbation stopped, although the wish to do so was still there. The fear of punishment had dominated the desire for self-gratification but, the wish being there, the hand would inexorably stray towards the forbidden place. The fear of gratifying the sensation would then suddenly emerge and his hand would be spasmodically jerked away from his sexual parts. This was the genesis of the tic-like movement.

Mrs Town had told us it had started with a jerking movement of the hand, and that jerk spread to a spasm in the whole arm which, in turn, spread to something which she compared to St Vitus dance in the shoulder. It was insufficient for us to tell the boy that he could masturbate and that no one would punish him for doing something that is, after all, perfectly natural in an experimental way to all pubertal and adolescent boys, because there would still remain the residual fear of a far more terrible figure than I could ever be, the revengeful, condemning grandfather.

When I studied this case in the light of similar ones I soon discovered that the strength of the child's revenge feeling against the grandfather was as great as the grandfather's apparent hatred of his grandson. However, Sydney would not dare unleash that aggression, and therefore it was expressed to his disadvantage rather than to the disadvantage of the grandfather who started the aggressive relationship between the two. This introversion of aggression is extremely common in such circumstances. Unlike the violent, aggressive boy who can vent his violence and anger, the child who has a tic, or who stammers, is seeking to deal with his aggression internally, not because he is necessarily more generous or more compliant than the nakedly aggressive boy, but rather because he fears the full passion of his aggression if it were once let off its leash. Frequently, tic-like movements are more readily recognizable not as a main symptom which would cause the child's referral to us, but as a secondary manifestation of an inner discomfort.

A boy who has been hated as much as the grandfather hated his grandson Sydney has his own capacity for giving love restricted;

44

and if we are unable to give love to our fellows, they tend to insulate themselves from us and thus our own capacity is even further reduced. The full extent of Sydney's aggression was revealed in an unhappy but so, so convincing manner. He had read in a report of a criminal trial how a son had murdered his solicitor-father. He came to me white and trembling, holding the book in his hand and demanding that I should shield him from the same kind of aggression he feared existed in himself. Reassurance given in these circumstances is more substantial than that given in less urgent cases but, as always, reassurance and support can only depend upon the respect or esteem the child has for the adult who seeks to give him support. Fortunately, by this time, the negative aspects of his relationship with me, in which he had seen many aspects of his grandfather revealed in my personality, had disappeared and he was now able to see me for what I really was, with all my mistakes, with all my imperfections, but nevertheless with all my good will. Despite the shocking nature of this dramatic revelation of his own impulses he was able to withstand the feeling, and so disperse his own aggression against a man who, after all, richly deserved retaliation.

Another boy we cured of a marked tic-like movement of his hand and shoulder had witnessed several assaults against his mother by his father, a man of ungovernable temper with a past history of in-patient treatment at mental hospitals. Whilst wishing to jump to his mother's assistance and, as he once told me, even to kill his father, he realized that any intervention on his part would possibly cause his own death and would do nothing to help his mother. There again, the aggression turned inside the boy, and to prevent his arm snatching a weapon and killing his father it had developed a tic. It is not the tic in itself which is so distressing in these cases, it is the social disadvantage to the child. For example, sitting at a meal he suddenly shoots the entire contents of his plate over the tablecloth or his neighbour. He is always an object of curiosity which sets him apart, and makes it very difficult to win friends. He alone makes these convulsive, jerky movements and he alone has to bear the suffering associated with them and the different class in which it places him from all his playmates.

These tics seem curiously easy to remove, but with the caution born of long experience we are never content with the mere removal of the physical sympton, however delighted the boy himself is. In such cases we pursue the matter to a point where the legacy of hatred and threat of aggression no longer exists in that boy; and that can often take years.

Stammering, however, is most difficult to eradicate. Most of the children we have received as stammerers or stutterers have already been the subject of speech therapy which failed. This is no criticism of speech therapy, which very often succeeds, but we are inclined to suggest that if a child is stammering for unconsciously motivated psychological reasons it is a mistake to attempt to remove the stammer without removing the cause of the stammer. Only if there is some physical cause for a speech impediment can it be remedied by speech therapy.

Before one can really attempt the cure of a psychologically-motivated stammerer one has to realize from the outset that love and hatred can exist naturally side by side. From the time we are born, or from the time we can think, experience and show emotion, anger and rage is as present as is love and harmony. Just as we have a capacity for love, so we have the potential of hate. We have to show the child that there is nothing contradictory in the co-existence of love and hate for the same object.

Thomas Unwin was a thin boy with a slight limp, and with his mouth drooping sideways as if in a thwarted grin. He had a merciless stutter. The main reason for him coming to us was his refusal to attend school even when threatened by the school attendance officer. Indeed, on one occasion when the officer called, the boy had thrown handfuls of pepper in the man's eyes. The school truancy had started at his primary school, almost from the first day he went to school at the age of five and had been maintained with only briefly intermittent periods of attendance until he came to us at twelve. The stutter had started before he was of school age, possibly when he was about four years old, but the queer limp and twisted lip, established by oft-repeated medical examinations as having no physical basis whatever, had gradually developed since he was ten. His relationship with his two sisters, one older and one younger than he by about a year in each case, was good, but the elder of the two girls had begun to show signs

46

of difficult behaviour. She had been discovered weeping for no apparent reason, would be sulky for unexplained causes and, more ominously, she had mentioned delusional visits, from an undefined man and woman who called, she said, unannounced when she was alone reading, or listening to the radio. Unfortunately this girl never received treatment and when we finally concluded the case papers in Thomas Unwin's affair we were informed that his older sister was now an in-patient in a mental hospital.

In the domestic court I and my fellow Justices adjudicate in matrimonial disputes which are generally quite irreconciliable, though we try to give a decision which will improve the total situation rather than add to the dreadful deterioration that has occurred since two people, thinking they were in love, wed. When a separation is agreed upon, a maintenance order is usually made against the husband so that he has to pay a weekly sum to his wife. In a very small minority of such cases the husband states his intention of refusing to pay his wife anything; amongst that small group of people is a smaller proportion who actually persist in refusal and those men go to prison rather than pay maintenance money to their wives.

In such a case the court is powerless to enforce payment, and the wife has to manage on National Assistance or go out to work. What we never hear in court, however, is the effect upon the children of the marriage. An understanding of the full horrors is not necessarily disclosed in court, and indeed their consideration is often irrelevant to the legal definitions that are being sought.

Thomas Unwin's father was given to violent, uncontrollable rages, and as a result of physical attacks upon his wife there had been a legal separation some years before we met the boy. The father was one of those obstinate men who refuse to pay the wife's maintenance and therefore went to prison. When he came out of prison after the third successive sentence for non-payment of the maintenance allowance, Mrs Unwin forgave him and encouraged him to return home. For a few weeks affairs appeared to prosper, but soon the situation rapidly deteriorated and in view of her past experiences she was not prepared to make any further allowance for what was quite clearly psychotic or insane behaviour.

We saw Mrs Unwin frequently, for it was necessary that she understand as much as she could about what we hoped to do for her son. As time passed, she increasingly welcomed the visits in spite of the tiresomely long journey involved, for she gained much psychological support herself. At the interviews she described the family background of this boy and his sisters, and the father's bad-tempered, intolerant abuse and obscene assaults on her were graphically described. She spoke of her husband's sexual assaults, when he would throw her to the kitchen floor and rape her, often when her children, particularly Thomas, were aware of it. Indeed, in one interview she told me that it seemed her husband would only assault her in this devilish manner when he knew for certain that the boy was within earshot.

Despite the stammer that almost prevented any form of communication, Thomas had an amazing verbal facility. This seems a contradiction, but his verbal facility could sometimes overcome the stammer, and when he dwelt upon certain anal and vaguely obscene jokes he was able to speak without impediment.

Referring on one occasion to a boy's meanness, he said: 'He'd bottle a fart and use it again if he could.' Referring to another boy's request for some unlikely object, he said: 'It was like a fart under a grand piano.'

His conversation on such themes was more than monotonous, but his stammer would be abandoned. When I pointed this out to him the jokes upon the subject instantly ceased. I felt perhaps that I had done damage in removing what might have been a reasonable outlet for some pressure about which I understood so little. He told me that one reason he found it so difficult to go to school in the past was in case something dreadful should happen to his mother in his absence. In a spate of conversation, impeded and obstructed by his stammer and stutter at every turn, and assisted sometimes by a written note in which he sought to convey a point which he knew his voice would obstruct, he told me of his fear that, while on the way to school, his father might be attacking his mother. Being a child, he did not readily understand that his father's kitchen assaults upon the mother were sexual, but thought them murderous attacks which put her in danger of her life. In his refusal to go to school he was ensuring that, by his presence, the attack would not occur without some opportunity to dash for help.

I thought his treatment was progressing well until, to my disappointment, he ran away from school. It was only for a day or two, but escapades occurred about twice a week for a period of approximately three months. It was disturbing to us, and it was harrowing for his mother; while he was disappearing from school, we felt more and more incapable of conducting work that needed so urgently to be undertaken with him, and while the boy was appearing at home Mrs Unwin felt more and more discouraged and in what really were not much more than his visits to the school in this very taxing period, I tried to show him that his anxiety over what was happening to his mother, while understandable, was completely irrational and unreal; surely now that his father had gone he could feel more certain of his mother's physical safety. His replies were, in effect, that if it had happened once, it could so easily happen again, and his intermittent presence at home was some kind of reassurance. As I could do little more I could only hope that patient reiteration of the facts of the situation would dissuade his running away, so that uninterrupted work could be resumed. This is eventually what happened; our patience, lack of retaliation and, perhaps, Thomas' realization that we wished to help, enabled him to overcome his fear.

We encouraged more visits from his mother, and her own devotion and willingness to present herself to him as often as she could possibly do so, contributed as much as we managed to give towards the boy's ultimate cure. His running away from us was the same as his truancy at school, but our interpretations had offered a solution which had not risen before. Thomas began to show a far more co-operative attitude to school and said that he would love to be relieved of his stammer and all the other defects he now was aware existed in his relationships with others. He realized that, whatever the causes of the stammer might be, they could only be understood by a proper evaluation of the difficulties of his own background.

'How can I be expected to want to grow up and be a father when I have had such a bad one myself?' he asked.

At this stage other boys began to complain to the staff about him. They spoke of his grumbling attitude and constant denigration of anything they did, and if a boy obtained a higher mark than Thomas in class he was made the target of abuse. They could never understand Thomas's interest in their family backgrounds for, throughout the history of the school, personal and family matters have been kept strictly confidential. It is in fact astonishing how the confidences of the children are maintained by the staff in such a manner that other children do not seek access to those secrets, nor experience pressure to divulge their own. There is a wealth of toleration of other's difficulties and oddities of behaviour, but despite that toleration the provocation given by Thomas to his fellows was intense. Not only would his questions about other boy's fathers be direct, but subsequently in casual conversation he would cross-examine subtly and, imagining he had detected some inconsistency, confront that boy with a hurtful insult.

The same trait was observed in his reference to people outside the school. Any political leader or other prominent person praised in the newspapers would become the target for his abuse: he would describe some imagined crime of that person and, if contradicted, turn the subject quickly to an historical character whose defects were more commonly acknowledged. Nelson seemed to be a special target for such criticism. He would refer to Nelson's amours with Lady Hamilton, attributing the basest motives to Emma, and instead of praising Nelson's naval achievements, occupy himself solely with Nelson's period of unemployment and his extravagant nature with ladies. On one such occasion he referred to Nelson's partial blindness but made a slip of the tongue and instead of using the word 'blind' he used the word 'limp'. Thomas did not notice his mistake but I noted it for future reference.

There would have been no point in trying to show that verbal attacks upon others, instancing his curiosity about their parents, would in the end only exacerbate his own difficulties. Had there been such opposition or clear criticism the aggression would have turned back on himself in feelings of persecution. He had to be regarded as a subject whose analytical treatment must continue, and within the analytic framework frank discussions with him of his aggressive trends, and how he acted them out, would at this stage be the only road to follow. He was partly aware of what he was doing, but he was certainly unaware of any disparity between these forms of social aggression and his comparatively cheerful and pleasant attitude in other spheres.

As the analysis proceeded he learned to accept a surprising amount of responsibility and was bold enough, despite his stammer, to accept a chairmanship of a committee. He identified himself with the school and the community and, although he was still spiky and, if provoked, truculent, he made bad-tempered remarks much less frequently. His difficulties were those fundamentally of a boy who had developed a cynical and sceptical attitude and who tried to protect himself in advance from any possible disappointment or failure, but as this more benevolent phase continued it became possible for him to admit the validity of private criticism in a good constructive way and to realize that his father demon was an inhibiting factor to him in all social and cultural activities.

Although he was still very cynical fundamentally of others good will, the boys were beginning to notice that socially he was more companionable and a far easier person. Much work was currently being done upon the hard vein of obstinancy and we continued to show the special care needed to avoid guiding him into a position from which he could only extricate himself with increased anger. When he did fail to accept the not too high social standards currently expected of him he had the grace to realize it, and in private he would apologise sincerely for his error and seek to prevent its recurrence.

When he was attacking authority, for instance at a committee meeting, he would sometimes realize what he was doing in terms of his father and execute a sudden *volte-face*. The demonic image of his father occupied most of our analytic sessions. At times his stammer would improve, only to relapse again. He understood by now that such a spasmodic improvement was to be expected, as the stammer itself was partly a protection against his horrors and would not finally be removed until his father and mother had taken their real positions in his sub-conscious mind. He understood how deeply he wished to stop his father's attacks upon his mother, and how far his truancy applied to this, but he also knew that the only satisfactory way of stopping his father's attacks upon the mother was to remove the father. This fundamental and ultimate crime he could not accept and his suppressed speech was a suppression of this desire to kill the wicked father. It could have broken out in many other forms but for reasons we do not understand, it happened to be a stammer. True, his hatred of all forms of authority and all forms of parenthood were so intense that it led to other social drawbacks, the limp and the leer, but these were unconscious

51

attempts to antagonize others so much that, having nothing whatever to do with him, they could not come so close to him that he could do them a mischief.

It was a little time however, before we discovered that although his stammer had gone, and although his sense of relationship with others was marked, there were two other factors about which wrongly we had remained content. The English master drew attention at a staff meeting to a curious kind of misspelling Thomas was making in his essays. The misspelling was not ignorance of how to spell a word, but rather the repetition of a consonant or a vowel with a consistent irregularity in the one essay. He had himself drawn the master's attention to this curious factor that had come into his writing soon after the stammer disappeared, and had, in a vague and almost jocular manner, mentioned it as 'a kind of stammer in my English now'. I discussed it with him and he made a remark which included that significant word he had once used before.

He said, 'My English seems to limp.'

'What about your own limp?' I replied. 'You know very well that all the medical examinations of your left foot have never revealed anything other than that this limp of yours is a kind of habit, just as the stammer was a kind of habit, and now you link the word 'limp' with another type of stammer that you have noticed.'

The boy was silent for some minutes and at last said reflectively, 'I wonder what we have found out now?'

I was astonished, far more than the boy could ever have been had he seen what I saw; that the twisted smile had disappeared, to be replaced with an ordinary pleasant smile of his lips and mouth. Despite my surprise I said nothing, but three days later the boy came to me in great excitement and in some fear too, telling me that something extraordinary had happened.

'I was in the bathroom and I suddenly saw my face. Do you know, that damned silly expression has gone now, Shaw? It really has! And one or two of the other boys said so too. One of them said I looked happier. Do you think that is true?'

I said we should hope that its going showed a happier and pleasanter attitude to life than had been the case before.

He answered: 'You know very well I'm happier, the stammer's gone, and now this other horrible thing has gone. It is as if I was not stammering in my words but in my attitude to other people by a kind of frowning or sneering at them instead of laughing and smiling with them.'

Again I replied that what mattered was his happiness and if he felt that happiness and trust in others at last, there would obviously be no need to doubt their motives, and if there was no need for such doubts then there would be no need to put that expression into the shaping of his lips. What had really astonished me was that a configuration obviously involving the musculature of the face to some degree, over many years, could alter so quickly.

Similarly, we did not have to wait for the confirmation of a medical examination to see the disappearance of the limp.

What a dreadful loneliness Thomas must have experienced! Not only a loneliness born of lack of companions, including the companions he had frightened away from him, but a loneliness far more tragic caused by his complete inability to answer his problem and deal with the harshness and rigours of his family life. A person plunged into such loneliness forms false solutions and in that falsity his need and search for love becomes thwarted and twisted just as his lip and the limp were thwarted and twisted. Love and hatred equate, and when the first is disturbed the second can only show a corresponding disturbance.

The only solution to Thomas Unwin's misery had lain within his own mind. When at last he realized that the solutions to all his problems was not a continued regard for his own convenience or an attempt to find all the love within himself and then turn that love back to himself narcissistically, but to live happily with others: he had to learn to love and agree with others. If we had been unsuccessful in that enterprise, not only would we have failed to remove the symptoms which so inhibited all his activities but we would have condemned him to a life of truculent warfare and general emnity which were far graver issues than any limp or stammer.

He now has two happy children and his relationship with his wife, although occassionally assertive, is loving and good. He understands that marriage is more than a partnership, that it is also a sacrament, and this quiet certainty of purpose he has now is something in which he has pride.

CHAPTER V

Splutter of Mother to Son

AN UNDERSTANDING of eleven year old Victor Wells depended upon a knowledge of his mother's curious upbringing. We had a description of Victor in his case papers, and these emphasized an almost complete lack of communication because of his stammer, which was so bad that he often had to converse through scribbled notes. He had a marked dislike of his father and there was a strong suspicion that he played in private with his faeces. But there was no information about his mother, so that is where I started my investigation.

I explained kindly but absolutely firmly to Mrs Wells that she would have to work very closely with us. After the third interview with her, she told me of her own miserable past. 'I was one of those young girls you read about in the paper; who run away from home and are never found again, or get up to some tricks that make the headlines. But I can assure you that in my case you would have read only half the story. You are in fact the first person I am telling it to, and I am only telling it now because I believe you when you say that my son's difficulties are a reflection of family pressures.

'I fled from my own father,' she continued. 'Soon after my mother's death, when I was seventeen years old, he started trying to get me into his bed. I didn't know at first what he meant and when I'd be doing something or sitting down quietly in front of the fire, he'd come up to me and start feeling me. I was old enough at seventeen to know what that meant, but I'd never heard before of a father wanting it with his daughter, and my horror was something that can never be described. Even now, when I am speaking of it to you, it seems like a dream. I worked as a shorthand typist and I would delay coming home in the evening by pretending that I had gone to the pictures, or been doing overtime at the office. I was trying my best to keep out of the house and away from his attacks upon me, but at last it got so bad that one night I woke up to find him getting into bed with me. I won't tell you what he said or what he tried to do, but I rushed out of the bedroom and locked myself in the kitchen. The next day I ran away. I wandered around London without a job, and after a few weeks some probation officer found me; I don't know how, and told me that my father wanted me home and all the usual stuff to the effect that everything would be forgiven and forgotten. I didn't tell the probation officer about the sexual stuff as I didn't think anybody would believe me. Nowadays I know that such things do happen, but to me then it seemed exceptional and unbelievable. But I went home and it was still as bad. Luckily I got a job quickly and soon I found a boy friend and I was determined to fight off the lust of my father. I even thought of quite exact plans of how I could kill him, and although I never actually tried to do it, I kept on pretending to try and work out all the details as if I was going to try that evening or at the weekend. I lived in a kind of hell. I didn't marry that first boy friend but later, when Victor's father and I met, we fell in love and married after a year. I was twenty-two then and my father had died a year before.'

Such a statement not only shows what she suffered, but so clearly defines conditions in this family even before the mother's death. The father's desires arose only when his wife died but that pressure, unspoken, unacted, but nevertheless vaguely present, must have existed in this girl's backbround long before her mother's death.

In Victor's infancy she had somehow inflicted upon him some doubt or disorder arising from her own shocking experiences. Had her own youth been normal, her influence on Victor would have expressed itself in the form of love and gentleness but, as it was, caused him only confusion and calamity. Despite the very real love between Mrs Wells and her husband she was always deeply afraid that the abnormality of her father could be reflected by some mischance in her own husband. On the one hand she sought that non-existent side of Mr Wells, and on the other front she sought an alliance with her little boy as an alternative love object to whom she could turn if the primary tragedy arose again.

We started work on Victor. He was not an aggressive or trouble-some child outwardly, but his very real needs brooked no dis-simulation or evasion. When he could not communicate an idea readily by his voice his periods of frustration would occasion attacks of rage in which he would smash a chair, or his pen, or even strike his own breast or head. In these early days it seemed impossible to find a medium of communication with him which would enable us in the first place to lighten his more immediate need and, in the second place, to remove the disabilities of a fundamentally aggres-sive nature which had occasioned his awful stammer.

He rapidly developed a better and a more studious attitude in his classes, and this development threw further light upon his temperamental difficulties. He was putting up an enormous battle against the carping, obstinate attitude which covered his deep fear of failure, a fear that was being continually highlighted by his stammer and the corresponding impatience of his listener. At a time when in fact both his French and maths were progressing quite well, he went to the two teachers in an hysterical state because he was so certain that he was doing badly. So by assuming that his own failure was inevitable he intensified his own discouragement. The success of another boy, real or imagined, drove him into such a state that he was quite obviously screwing himself down from throwing books at the teacher. A maintaining of our placidity helped him to become more conscious of the irrelevance of his self-criticism and at last an uneasy tranquillity existed in his classroom. With tact on the part of his teachers and an avoidance of all controversial issues, this false tranquillity was all on which we could build.

The next medium where more positive opportunity presented itself was in art where Victor realized that in the creative activity of art no criticism would be expressed of his composition by others and thus he was able to work in a less flustered manner. It was necessary for the art master to find opportunities for praise, and he arranged this so that each successive morsel of admiration was couched in an utterly different form from that which preceded it.

The boy was always highly suspicious of anything that savoured of praise or admiration and therefore the full verbal agility of the art master had to be called into play continually. However, his work was quite genuinely of a standard infrequently found and indeed it formed the basis of one of our several art exhibitions in the West End.

His stammering speech was a curb and obstacle rather than a medium for his creative thoughts, and for speech to be a barrier to thought shows clearly that the speech and its content is something that a stammerer fears and may not express in any naked form through a dread of reprisal. By engineering all that we possibly could in the art room, the music room and in any other creative activity that could be presented to the boy, his general adjustment improved. Although it was far from complete at this stage, he was now able to face problems of the classroom to which formerly he had attached far too great an emotional importance. The desire to break into argument appeared completely to have disappeared, although sometimes, especially when prompted by the frustration of his stammer, he would break down into tearful rage. Another pleasant sign of progress was that, where he could not succeed in stimulating others to attack him, he would often retract his unpleasant comment or gesture with good grace, and then follow it with a clear effort to meet the other boy half-way.

So far, real analytic co-operation had been quite impossible owing to the difficulty of verbal communication. But at this stage, his own efforts having carried him so far in the artistic sphere as to restore some degree of self-confidence and some hope for his future, he wrote to me asking whether he could see me privately for analysis.

What followed succeeded, but rarely in all my work at the school have I been subjected to such a tax upon my patience. The idea that he was seeking to tell me about was so fraught with unconscious feelings and meanings that often his stammer would block communication for more than ten minutes. Later I was able to show him that his stammer was an unconscious attempt to destroy the sessions and thus to destroy me. We were able to bring a real understanding of the social significance of his stammer into our discussions and the further we went with such work, the easier became his speech.

Victor's basic discovery was that he could at last find a way to communicate his ideas and obtain relief from the complexities and often the confusion of those ideas. It was possible to show him that he was colluding unconsciously with his mother in excluding his father, and in that phase his father's presence within the home was that of an intruder. The boy would feel that he and his mother would be happy together without the presence of the father, though this was not, of course, within the boy's own conscious knowledge. Neither, for that matter, was the mother aware that the nature of the unspoken relationship so well suited the shocks and experiences she had felt in her late adolescence. The son and mother, leading a symbiotic relationship, required the exclusion of all others from that relationship.

Unfortunately, if one decides to exclude a father, who is partly responsible for our presence on the earth at all, then that exclusion can only be contrived by incurring the father's hostility, and one of the techniques the boy had adopted to avoid hostility was his stammering. There was no doubt at all that Victor did seek the absence of his father, and in such circumstances the absence is contrived not only by the mere physical expulsion, but by a far more sinister unconscious process, the removal of the father's power. Almost invariably, then, it is a sexual issue that obtrudes into the total position; as we have seen in other cases, one very clear symbol of a father's power and importance is his sexual virility and when the father's exclusion was contrived it was partly achieved by a sapping or a confiscation, and above all a usurpation of his power. Thus we had with Victor an almost total oedipal situation in which, unusual for such situations, the unconscious collusion of the mother was present.

One of the difficulties the boy had to accept was the fact that despite his very real rebellion against his mother's mollycoddling (for her attitude was one of complete protection even to the extent of making decisions for him that three- or four-year-olds normally make for themselves) he nevertheless revelled in it. He would far sooner be over-protected than treated as a growing boy. Now a baby does not communicate with words, but with noises, bodily movements or whimpers. As part of his infantile dependence on his mother, perhaps in the first place wished upon him, but most certainly in the second place enjoyed by him every minute of its practice, he was speaking to his mother, not as a boy, but as a baby. As a baby he could use curiously strangulated sounds because he would not yet have learned a vocabulary. This thesis, provided partly by him and partly by me, was at last understood and the stammer greatly ameliorated.

Now, although great improvement had been effected in his speech, the reasons behind his stammer had not been much affected. The basic envy of his mother, and greed for her, and the aggression against his father, were still active and still conjured the fear of retaliation or anger from his father. During our discussions Victor's stammer would become most pronounced when he had feelings of anger for me. Some interpretation of mine might disappoint him and, instead of viewing the nature of that disappointment in a stable manner, he would feel inwardly that this was another example of the father-analyst attacking him. It was interesting to note the sounds at which the stammer occurred; in every example it was the words of abuse or anger directed at me.

It is almost a commonplace that the stammerer seeks to punish by his words, or by lack of them, the person whom he is addressing. All those who have been in close contact with a stammerer know of the irritation that is felt when the stammerer is impotent to convey his meaning. First comes the desire to assist him by completing his unspoken sentence, and sometimes that desire when yielded to gives rise to a completion which was not what the stammerer had intended, and therefore increases the nature of his anger and aggression to the would-be helper. A second reaction the listener feels is one of acute impatience in which he unconsciously assumes the stammerer is acting the stammer in order to annoy him. This is quite untrue in any conscious form but the listener has come surprisingly close to the truth which is, as has been indicated above, that the stammerer does attack his listener.

Victor saw me as a father, and his guilt about what he had sought to do to his own father led him to fear the retaliatory consequences of anything he said to me. Ease of his torment had now considerably improved his understanding of his father, mother and fellows, and he showed much greater confidence in their good will. Unfortunately if he was put under any stress the stammer could recur in such a way that, although not as severe as hitherto, it could remind his listener of the condition that existed once before.

Victor wanted to suspend his analytic interviews, saying his stammer had almost gone, and left to himself it would go completely. I tried to show him that his stammer was something he could now contain, but containment was not a cure. Demonstrably, as excitement or other stimulus brought it back, it could not be borne, and a lurking beast is best chased to its own oblivion. He saw the point, and after the customary reticence he started telling me about deeper unconscious thoughts that he had not yet revealed.

He told me of his hoarding of faeces, which he kept in little specimen boxes in many well concealed hiding places. With a curious, indefinable suggestiveness he added to his explanation.

'I suppose,' he remarked, 'you know I don't spend much money.'

I replied, 'Like a miser hoards money, so you hoard faeces, only you do both.'

He then explained to me the sexual satisfaction he obtained from putting his finger into his bottom and manipulating it, obtaining an erection and removing some faeces, which then joined the other specimens in his little boxes. He had a terrible fear of discovery, and the feeling that awful punishment would inevitably come to him; but he could not resist the sexual satisfaction he obtained. Many an hour was spent at home in the solitude of the lavatory, and with more difficulty at school in the closets, obtaining the anal pleasure, which to him gave him a pleasure he could obtain in no other way. It would have been as foolish to tell him to stop doing it as to tell him to stop stammering. One had, instead, to regard this interest in his faeces as existent at an even more fundamental level than the stammer.

From his unconscious conspiracy with his mother, caused by the imbalance in her parent's family transferred to her own, had come a curious intimacy. Mother and son could live in complete harmony, but the intruder had to be removed. One way of effecting that was for the boy to disarm his father's suspicions that he, Victor, was a male, and convince him that he had, like his mother a vaginal reproductive part. Such reasoning is not available to a child but it was nevertheless the unconscious reasoning, understanding without awareness, that impelled Victor to adopt his peculiar mannerisms.

So there were two women in the family: he, the fake one, and his mother. His father, confused as to which he should choose, because both could offer the same vaginal orifice, would the more readily, Victor argued, retire to a psychological exile.

The boy himself, by his desire to exclude the father completely from all relationships within his family, had in a sense committed a crime, and he certainly felt that if he was incautious or admitted anything, the crime would be brought home to him. One of his interests when he came to us was reading detective novels, and whenever he could communicate an idea about the behaviour of the detective, it was always the hope that the detective would never solve the mystery. In his personal situation, he could prevent any detective solving the mystery at all because how can a detective do his work if the person he suspects cannot speak? So by a stammer that inhibited verbal intercourse, he was preventing a successful conclusion to the imagined psychological detective's interrogative work.

Many hours were spent during his sessions in discussing and explaining the material he continued to produce about a real masculine part he could play, and about a real feminine part his mother could play. He began to understand that a usurpation of his father's masculinity or the mother's femininity could never be a way of using his own genuine attributes.

The stammerers who come to us are those who have long passed beyond the elementary stage and they are trying to work out their own solutions. Sadly, these solutions often lead to more social awkwardness than the original stammer. Any attempted solution of the stammer without knowledge of those very early psycho-sexual fixations, is not an attempt that is likely to succeed.

The release that Victor experienced both in arts and science subjects in his classroom work was remarkable. With the abandonment of his stammer, whole areas of thought and learning opened to him which hitherto had been hidden behind closed gates. In the art room he was aflame with feelings and afire with thoughts, and from that outburst of legitimate and mature creativity, we knew that the stammerer was at last in charge of himself.

He now teaches at a recognized art school, and as well as being an effective teacher he is an artist within his own right who can sell his productions. No bohemian or crank, he lives a very conventional suburban life with his wife and two children, and is a person who, in control of his own capabilities, will continue within that happiness.

CHAPTER VI

Bed Wetting and Trouser Messing

WHENEVER PEOPLE are frightened, or wish to make a joke about fear, a comparison with incontinence often leaps readily to mind. For example, the expression 'he pissed himself with fear' is very well known, and there are several variations of that sentence. Small children, too, when faced with an attack or verbal condemnation, will occasionally wet their trousers especially if the attack is sudden.

This incontinence from fear is quite a common situation within the animal world. Many of us remember, from visits to the circus, the smell or urine that pervades most of the interior of the circus tent whenever the lion cage is in the arena, revealing the fear the huge beasts have for their trainer.

Bed-wetting, trouser-wetting and trouser-soiling are only too well known, but they occupy the attention of the teacher and parent mainly because of their great domestic inconvenience. The sufferer goes to bed every night hoping he will awake in the morning to discover a dry bed. Too often, of course, he is disappointed and a vicious circle of discouragement is created. A trouser-soiler when asked why he did not go to the lavatory instead of messing his trousers, will reply that he had left it too late, and assert that he was at such a distance from the lavatory that he could not be expected to get there in time to avoid what he hopes he can still regard as an exceptional accident.

If these sufferers came to regard their condition as permanent they would feel that some tragedy, unspoken, undefined but never-theless dreaded, would sweep over them. It was almost a common-place in the army for a new young recruit or newly-married soldier to wet his bed for a few nights after his return to barracks. This is evidence of his fear of being separated from a loving home and parents, or from his new wife. Where there is no fundamental inbalance or neurosis, the symptom clears in a night or two and has no deeper significance.

George Hanfield had been brought up exclusively by his mother. She was a woman who, in good faith, had married a man only to discover a fortnight later that she had been the unsuspecting party to a bigamous marriage. By this time she was pregnant, and within the year George was born. His mother had the anxiety of the illegal marriage, which was grossly increased by the financial difficulties of her position. She had to go to work to support her child, and yet be a mother; and feeling as she did about her own refusal to accept parental advice, she was reluctant to turn to her own home in the early days of her difficulties in bringing up her son. By one shift and another, by part-time jobs, by sharing a flat, she brought the boy up for the first few years of his life. The relationship between them was good and there could be no suggestion that she was doing anything but sacrificing her own convenience to the legitimate needs of her son.

But when he was three and a half, she obtained a residential job as an under-matron in a small preparatory school. She was naturally very worried lest her employers felt she gave more attention to George than she gave to the work for which they paid her, and for that reason her time with him was perhaps curtailed, though her solicitiousness for him increased. In an uneasy battle with her conscience, adjustments to her work timetable and the attention to her work, she managed to survive the battle very well. But as the boy's vocabulary increased and his perception developed he realized that his mother was looking after other small boys besides himself. Soon he began to regard these as competitors for his mother's love and grew to resent her attention to their needs. At such times he would whimper about some pretended ailment.

As the years passed, George's mother found that George had started to wet his bed at night, and to wet and soil his trousers during the day. Knowing little about the reasons for such maladies, she remonstrated with him in a way that seemed reasonable to her, but in fact bore no relation to the true cause. George could only reply that he was not near enough to the lavatory at the time, or that he had drunk too much before he went to bed. So the years passed with no relief in the enuresis and it was only when George was about ten years old that his mother, for the first time, consulted a doctor about George's condition. He attended a clinic as a result, and finally came to us.

It is a pity that Mrs Hanfield delayed so long in seeking advice, although one must admit that even had she sought it earlier, it is unlikely the boy would have been sent for residential care at an age much earlier than eleven. When he first arrived, it was clear that not only did George's lapses upset and terrify him, but there were other factors that caused him to be quiet, withdrawn and even surly in his approach to adults. Intuitively I realized that the basic fact was the absence of his father. At times, he had asked where his father was, and the explanation that father had been killed in the war had been given, and apparently accepted. But when a lie is told an atmosphere is conveyed which in fact contradicts the lie.

Mrs Hanfield told us how possessive the boy had become. On her Thursday afternoon free from work she would get ready to catch the bus for an afternoon's shopping but just at that minute the boy would complain of a terrible headache. She would take his pulse and perhaps his temperature, and sometimes indeed the thermometer did register a slight increase, and she could not disbelieve his statement. It was in fact, the truth and it remained the truth just long enough for her to miss the bus. Then on re-taking his temperature she discovered on several occasions that it had sunk again. But neither the headache nor the temperature went until it was quite certain that her chance of catching the town bus had gone. The boy did not know what he was doing. Unconsciously he was saying, 'This afternoon, Mummy, I must have you alone. All the other days of the week you are with others. Of course I know you look after me well, but just for this one afternoon, I demand your exclusive attention.' The child did not use such words of course, and I only choose such wording to convey the urgency and emphasis of his demands, which induced the psychosomatic symptoms of a headache and a slightly increased temperature.

Our first important contact to influence our character is with our mother's breast. But at the same time we discover there is yet another way of getting mother's attention. No matter what she is doing, if we whine and whimper and demonstrate that we have wet our napkin then she will come to us, clean us, tidy us, kiss us and give us all the noise and tactile impressions that are so fundamental to an infant's well-being. So when some mentally disturbed people feel they have lost mother's attention, either by their own bad behaviour, or by her departure or illness or pre-occupation, then they return to those far off cradle days, when a wet napkin would assure her speedy appearance.

Thus one can understand the unconscious motives of the home-sick soldier and the semi-conscious motives of George who, feeling that he had the right to her attention, would return to the cradle techniques by soiling himself, ensuring that his mother would do for him what he wanted.

At school he had been called 'smelly-bags' or 'shit-pants', and one of the first things one has to accomplish with a child in that socially inferior position is to remove the feeling that he has any responsibility for the smell. In this particular case George was always smelling so inconveniently that we had to make special arrangements, formulating a special timetable so that he was in a class with only two other boys, and spacing the boys in this minute class so widely that the smell was not too noticeable. Naturally we had to do this without George being aware of the reason.

At other times, outside the classroom, his smell led to social ostracism, and so when he came to see me to talk about himself and his problems, I said, 'Come and sit on my lap.' He looked astonished and said, 'But, don't you know, my trousers are messy?' And I said, 'Well, perhaps they might be messy. Mine aren't, so perhaps I had better learn what messy trousers are like.' He then demurred a second time, saying, 'You know I smell, don't you?' 'Well, if that's the wost thing you do, we'll manage to get by. There are plenty of worse things that people do than smell you know. They can be jealous, they can be bitchy, they can spread false rumours and they can do things of that kind which are far more injurious to everybody else than the smell of messy trousers.'

He sat on my lap then, and I was very glad when that interview was over and I could go home and change my own trousers. But I felt that something had been achieved.

65

Over the next few months, George told me of his developing sense of deprivation. Of how he would be in bed at night and hear his mother's voice in the passage and wonder if she would come into the bedroom which he shared with her, or go somewhere else to another boy's dormitory or to the matron's office. He described to me his fear that her voice would disappear into the distance as she set about her work and his joy and relief when that voice became louder and the latch of the door lifted and she came into the bedroom.

Poor George had never been able to grow out of these childish desires, and one reason for his progress now was that he was away from his mother and this anxiety did not exist. The separation also eased his mother's burden of anxiety; she no longer felt the clash between her duties to her son and her obligations to her employer. The letters she wrote to George were excellent in their content, without sentimentality or any effusive promises that could never be kept. But she gave George the assurance that her love for him continued and could never be diluted. She was carrying out our instructions, which seemed needless, because of her own innate understanding.

To George we continued to explain that his technique for getting what he rightly needed and deserved to have was the wrong technique, and would never be able to satisfy his requirements. Continued use of his trouser- and bed-soiling trickery would only remove from him the esteem he so much valued from other boys and adults.

No cure would ever have been effected had we not been successful in showing the boy that his wants were quite legitimate and he was wrong to think he was being denied them, although at times he was being denied an immediate satisfaction of them. He came to understand the reason for his incontinence and its irrelevance to any real solution of his troubles.

We also felt it necessary to explain the motives of a bigamist and the consequences of his mother's personal tragedy. Such explanations were not given in any critical or sentimental spirit, but calmly, as something that had occurred and of which he had the right to know. He soon found that his natural intelligence, ability and interests enabled him to succeed in the subjects that interested him. He saw that his experience, although exceptional, was nevertheless something that could be coped with.

We heard from him some years after he left that he had successfully started a small garage, but it was only very recently when he visited us with his wife and four children that we discovered he was running a very successful chain of nineteen garages. Obviously he had achieved a maturity and independence which we had discerned only with difficulty in the bed-wetter and trouser-soiler he was when we first met him.

Quiet and self-possessed in manner, Harry Ireland was a boy of superior intelligence who, on account of his mother's temperament and chronic illness, had been forced to live an abnormal life for twelve years. He was constantly nagged by his mother, forbidden to take home any of his friends, and had to bear his mother's bitter complaints about her poor health and misdeeds of his father, who had left them to live with another woman. His symptoms at the time we first met him included temper tantrums and soiling his trousers, and these were not unnatural under the circumstances, but he appeared to us to be fundamentally a boy who could react, without any deep therapy, to a good environment. Either because she disbelieved in us, or because of her illness, the mother would not come to see us, but a neighbour of good intention and apparently accurate information accompanied the boy when he first came to school. She told of his misbehaviour when he lived with them for some weeks, but she also emphasized his tragic position and isolation from any real adult companionship, and the significance of his mother's frequent stays in hospital. Although the mother made the most of her illness, she was genuinely seriously ill and very difficult to live with. Whatever improvements occurred in her health were only of a temporary nature and she often had to return to hospital. As his parents were separated and there were no other interested relatives, the boy was very urgently in need of some stable environment.

Living in his mother's house had been a young married couple, who attended as much as they could to the condition of the sick woman. Harry would observe how this young couple looked after their own little boy of two years, and perhaps compared the attention this child was receiving with the lack of attention he was given by his absent, uninterested father and his ill, nagging mother. Harry's schoolwork deteriorated but he gave very little trouble at school: his friends were chosen from the better behaved boys and those who could, I suspect, introduce him to their own homes and give him the comfort and normality lacking in his own. His schemes to conceal the fact that he wet his bed and soiled his trousers were fantastic and varied in their incidence. One could respect his wishes to keep such an affair private, but the smell after soiling denied much success in his concealment. Very often, having soiled himself in the classroom, he had to fake an excuse to leave.

When he came to us, most of his life was dominated by the need to avoid detection of his wetting and soiling, and almost every minute of the day he was formulating some plan to deal with any emergency that might arise.

During the first few months, we spent much effort and certainly a great deal of time, in trying to show him that men were quite different in their attitudes to the responsibilities of marriage than was his father. He expressed considerable surprise that married couples could live in harmony. He had been to my house and to various colleagues' houses and experienced the ready assumption of the intimacies of ordinary social intercourse within a family setting, and his surprise to me was tinged with a bitter regret and sadness. I assured him that his experiences had been exceptional and whatever life had been in the past there was no need to expect a repetition of it in the future. I remember arguing with him that all his misery had been in the first few years of his life as a rather concentrated ration, whereas with most others their misfortunes were spread evenly over the whole of their lives, so that they could be more easily borne. He understood our good will, but at all times the curious concealment and effacement of his incontinence continued.

I felt at last I had to broach the matter and I told him quite plainly that I had noticed his smell, that I knew he wet his bed, that I knew of his diverse expedients to escape attention of these lapses, and I felt the time had come for he and I to try and understand what he was seeking and, if fortune was with us, to try and find better ways of satisfying that search. He tried hard to contradict me and pretend he was not a soiler, but his own innate truthfulness prevented him. So we talked about it and again the primitive desire was for a mother who could be a real mother, who could give, not only demand and take as the poor bed-ridden woman did. He had seen it from the attitude of the couple who lived in his house, with their own child; he had seen it in the families of myself and my colleagues. But it was necessary to insist on the improbability of his experiencing such normal and pleasant attitudes and to accustom him to the idea that, as far as his boyhood was concerned, no matter how much he and I talked about his misfortunes, his mother's health, his father's absence, we could never replace what he had lost. No false promise should ever be made to a child; in one's natural sympathy for a child who has had more than his rightful share of misfortune, it is easy to imply a promise that might not be kept. With such a case as this, it is necessary for the Harry Ireland's of our community to know that their misfortune is something that must be accepted, and that acceptance can be made more bearable if the future appears to justify an optimistic outlook.

At every opportunity we reminded the boy of his high intelligence, his good appearance and perfect health, and gradually the confidence that had been sapped within the home environment showed signs of restoration. After a year, we heard that his mother's health had now deteriorated to such an extent that it was likely she would die shortly. By now, fortunately, the boy's confidence in me and my colleagues was of a sufficiently high order for him to be told that his mother's death might occur at any time. I tried to show regret, not so much because she was going to die but because while she lived she had not been much happier. I asked his permission to tell two members of the staff of his mother's condition, so that there were now at least three adults who were in a position to give sympathy and understanding when the time came.

A week after we had heard of Mrs Ireland's relapse, I was told by the Local Education Authority that she had died. With his permission I told the school at the next community occasion of the death of Harry's mother, asking those boys who believed in prayer to pray for the repose of her soul. I assured the boy that she would have my own prayers too; and he, from the solidarity and committed friendship and support in that public announcement, was able to overcome much of the shock of his mother's death.

We knew he had overcome it by this time, because all the soiling had ceased, and it did not recur even temporarily now. His was a very quick cure. He stayed on to take the usual examinations and finally went to university where he read Engineering. He is now a mechanical engineer, married with two small children, completely happy and adjusted.

We suspected that Iola Jameson's exclusion from his elementary school was not so much because of his incontinence and his truculent behaviour towards the staff, as his mother's almost daily visits when she came to complain in terms of anger and arrogance of the school's failure to deal with her boy. These complaints were usually loudly shouted in front of other pupils as she was advancing down a corridor or into a classroom or the headmaster's office. She refused the school's suggestion that she should visit the child guidance clinic and all she would do, through the intermediary of some acquaintance, was to come and see us. Her interview with us gave a whole catalogue of the boy's vices, but did not mention the one difficulty, incontinence, which we observed so quickly when he came to the school. The other vices she detailed were scarcely present in the boy's behaviour, even from the first day of his arrival.

Amongst the endless chatter of this woman, she did establish the fact that she had been married no fewer than three times. When I asked her to tell me why all three marriages had broken down, she gave contradictory explanations. One was that her first husband was interested in opera, and she was not; so he found some woman who was. Another explanation was that her husband had left her for somebody of superior education. A third explanation she offered was that when she had carefully prepared a meal for her third husband, he flung it out of the window, and then threw articles of furniture at her.

The woman looked to me like a lower class prostitute or a fortune-teller on the sea front. I found it difficult to believe her accounts, but as the story developed we established that not only had she been divorced twice but she had taken at least six or seven lovers, all of these events taking place during the twelve years of her son's life. The boy had been to eight different schools, and in this maelstrom of confusion it is surprising that he had not totally collapsed into some condition from which there could be no return. The present husband was the guard of a railway van. He had a small sports car, which he certainly could not have afforded from his wages, and it became quite clear as the mother's visits continued that he was not a husband but a man whom she was keeping on her immoral earnings.

She visited us, despite our rules that appointments must be made, without the slightest warning. Her tempestuous scenes with her son were always characterized by criticism of some imagined aspect of his behaviour and by promises that she would send and give him all manner of gifts. These visits were extremely tiresome for during the intervals we had been trying to show the boy that there was such a thing as a permanence whilst growing up and there was such a thing as tomorrow being similar to the day before, experiences quite unlike those he had had at home. But the mother's sudden arrivals with promises of generosity and largesse which were hardly ever kept was a disruption to the orderly existence we had hoped to institute for Iola.

There was a double tax on our patience and on the boy's good will. This case had not come through a local education authority, but much against our better judgment by Mrs Jameson's offer to pay our fee; though in fact never at any time during the boy's stay at the school did she pay. There were plenty of reasons advanced for her failure to do so and many promises made that she would, but neither the fee nor even the boy's pocket money ever arrived. She made matters worse by telling her son to say certain things to me which would support her entirely untruthful promise that she would soon be paying the fee. It was such a pity that the boy should be so embroiled in a dispute between us and her: the fact that we would naturally want our fee, however small it might be, was unimportant compared to the welfare of the boy.

To show Iola the truth about his mother's follies was difficult without introducing a vein of disloyalty to his mother, which in our experience is never properly used with maladjusted children. If there is anything amiss the child will know of it. No amount of propagandist intervention on the part of an outside person is going to increase his perception. The sole duty of the educator in these respects is to show where true contentment lies and not where other people have made mistakes. Iola's was not a case where discussion needed to be held with the boy at every step and turn: rather it was a case in which one hoped he would learn, as speedily as possible, that his life until now, with the changes of schools and fathers, was something exceptional. As time went on his behaviour improved, but it was only after about a year that he was prepared to talk about his incontinence.

At this point I held private interviews with him. Words poured out of him in a torrent of complaint; he could never expect to have what other boys had; even Christmas at home was different from other people's Christmas and consisted mainly of promises of presents to come, which of course never materialised. He spoke bitterly about the various fathers punishing him. I recalled, although I did not communicate the memory to him, how his mother had laughed quite cruelly when she once described to me how one of her 'husbands' had beaten the boy in front of her, and how she had derided her son when he had complained to her about the unfairness of the punishment. But although I did not tell him of that, it never-theless showed there was substance in his bitterness and complaints.

It was miraculous that the mother allowed the boy to stay with us because every letter we had from her contained some allegation of her mistrust and dislike: either we were neglecting him in one respect or neglecting her in another, or we had been offensive in the tone of our reply to one of her letters, or we had not been as helpful as was expected by her. Daily we expected her to descend upon us and take Iola away, just as daily we had to dissimulate that knowledge and express confidence that the boy would stay with us, despite our feelings to the contrary.

At long last the boy realized that he need expect no consistency from his mother and her various men friends. At that stage, he realized the impossibility of ever attracting his mother to clean his napkins, because after all, having no interest in him, why should she ever think of coming to clean him? Once that had been accomplished, the soiling ceased. But during that period, of course, there had been substitute mothers, and I well remember the self-sacrifice of our matron of that time who had taken upon herself his personal attacks upon her. He accused her of disliking him, of neglecting his linen, of neglecting himself if, for instance, he had a cold. But all those bitter recriminations were absorbed by the matron as part of her task and, as the boy discovered, despite his insults and vigorous attacks, there nevertheless could be a bond of affection between them, which could therapeutically be regarded as love.

Similarly the same pressures were being applied to the male staff. Under various fathers he had had absolutely no pattern of male authority and responsibility. Consequently men were people who had to be manipulated and tricked into situations for his own advantage. Occasionally too, if the trick had been successful, the men would give him a present; one day he was able to tell me that he was quite certain to get gifts more easily if the men had just had sexual intercourse with his mother. That was a terrible idea for the boy to have about the whole concept of love. I have always been surprised that the bad sexual example to which Iola had been subjected, did not have a much deeper effect. I suspect, for reasons that could not be explained in terms of our present knowledge of sub-conscious motivation, that the boy's own essential deprivation of his mother's affection overshadowed all the other influences, and once the symptomatic expression of that deprivation had been established, that took precedence over all other matters.

But the inevitable happened. One day Mrs Jameson descended upon the school, not with the railway guard in the sports car, but with a man whom she airily introduced as a solicitor. She announced that she was removing her son, as she was now entirely out of patience with our inefficiency. We tried very hard to influence her companion and her, but she was legally in the right. Iola was her son and she could remove him. He was in tears, and the confusion she created with the matron in rushing around demanding that all the boy's clothes be immediately collected because she did not trust us to send them on later, was a scene that we could well wish to have avoided.

Three days later a letter came from the woman, accusing us of having retained certain articles of the boy's clothing. This was consummately insolent, as during the whole of his residence at the school we had bought the boy's clothing ourselves, for Mrs Jameson had never supplied any. We had several pathetic letters from the boy imploring us to take him away from his mother and restore the tranquillity that he had found with us. Our replies had necessarily to be brief, conciliatory and friendly but without offering any possible offence to his mother. Iola understood the need for our caution, for his mother was quite likely to intercept our letters.

We were not surprised to receive a telephone call a month later from Mrs Jameson asking if her son had turned up with us, as he had run away. The conversation was very interesting. During the boy's stay with us the soiling and bed-wetting had ceased. She claimed that all the messing in the bed had resumed at home, and this was the most extraordinary accusation, that these symptoms had been caused by us and had never existed before the child came to school.

I asked her what we should do if the boy turned up at school to which she replied brusquely and cruelly, 'You can keep the little bugger if you like. I wash my hands of him.'

I said perhaps she might like to telephone to us the next day when we could discuss the matter afresh, and if she had not changed her mind then we could also discuss his possible further residence at the school. The next day she did ring, and surprisingly was far politer than she had ever been before. The boy was still absent but she said that if he did turn up she would be glad for us to keep him, and that she regretted her interference the month before.

I answered that, having had this previous experience, we would naturally not wish to waste our time if it was only to lead to a repetition of the incident, and she gave assurances that this would not happen again.

I had hardly replaced the receiver before a member of the staff told me that the boy had arrived and was sitting in the office. I went down to see him.

'What on earth can I do, Shaw? I can't bloody well stick it at home any longer. You know what she's like. You know she's a whore. Can't you keep me here and stop her getting at me again. I started all that shitting and pissing at home again, and everything's gone to hell.'

I assured him that whatever the legal difficulties we would do our best. I told him that I had heard from his mother, who had asked me to take him back, and I agreed with him that he should carry on as if nothing had happened. For nearly six weeks events were placid. But then Mrs Jameson again descended upon us with her neurotic arguments and accusations. I told her that if she did not desist, I would take legal action, for many of her remarks were actionable; and I told her companion, yet a fresh one, that should

74

these unheralded arrivals continue we would refuse to keep her son, and the responsibility would then be his. I added that they might like to consider what I had said, and we gave them a room to think it over.

Eventually they agreed to leave the boy with us and not take any action contrary to the boy's welfare or to the rules of the school. I was relieved to see them depart. The troubles continued, despite the promises, but at least they never tried again to remove the boy from school, and a trusting relationship blossomed between Iola and all the members of the school staff, which his mother's disturbing visits could not impair.

One day, after a two-month period without a visit, we received a letter from her in Canada. The letter cannot all be quoted, but it not only indicated the state of the mother's mental health, but her virulence, immorality and selfishness.

'People like you,' the letter said, 'will be bloody glad to find out I wash my hands of the little bastard. I never wanted him in the first place, and he's been nothing but a bloody nuisance since I was landed with him. It's a pity the pill or the dirty doctor didn't do their job better. However, you've got him now and you can bloody well keep him.' Surprisingly the letter concluded with, 'Please give Iola my love.'

We never heard from her again. Iola stayed with us and ultimately obtained admittance to a university. In many senses his home is still with us, particularly with one of my colleagues to whom in the latter years of his stay at the school he bore a specially close relationship. He is married, and teaching in a grammar school, and appears to be perfectly content and happy. Now that we can see his children growing up, without a blemish and without difficulty, we know that one of the most difficult cases we ever attempted repaid us in a way that fees could never equal.

CHAPTER VII

Twisted Sex

EARLY DIAGNOSIS of maladjustment can be far cheaper and more effective than later treatment. Day school teachers should be shown the significance of that puddle beneath the desk at which the new pupil sits. They should also be taught to recognize the signs of early psycho-sexual disturbance in the classroom pest who fidgets, irritates, learns nothing and quietly masturbates through a lesson. Informed teachers will secure early treatment of their problem children.

Some years ago I visited a well run state residential establishment for small boys and girls. Creature comforts were good, staff were hardworking but there was a lack of imagination and warmth which seemed to spoil the devoted work. In a playroom I was immediately surrounded by about thirty small children: they pulled at me, asked me where I had come from and where I was going. Was I going to stay there? Would I take them out for a walk?, and various other excited questions. Their behaviour to me, a complete stranger, and their obvious need to secure a stranger's attention, showed that the establishment had not provided these children with effective parent substitutes.

'Look, Mr Man,' said one child, 'I got this from home.' Other children followed with their toys. I gave admiration in as individual and pleasant terms as I could manage. One woebegone little thing, who had hitherto kept to the back of the group, shyly approached and said, 'My mummy is going to take me home. She only has to buy my bed, and she will soon do that and then I can live with her.' What a pity such a wistful thought should have to wait to be expressed to a stranger. Such longings should have been told to a member of the staff who should have given such consolation or cuddling as the child obviously needed. A little later a small eight-year old girl came up and said, as she produced a small wrist watch, 'Look what I've got. My daddy sent it to me.' I thought it odd that she should have a watch so obviously adult in type, and then I observed an elderly woman at the back of the room looking round anxiously and beckoning to the warden. It seemed she had taken off the watch to wash her hands in the bathroom, and this child had slipped in and taken it. I have no doubt that it was all sorted out and there were no recriminations, but what a tragic forcing ground existed, in this institution, for compensatory mechanisms seeking for attention, approval and love.

Surely we must not withhold help when it is most needed. We are quick to send for the ambulance when a workman falls from a building and breaks his leg. We instantly seek medical aid when our child has diphtheria. Then why delay immediate, speedy and appropriate action when a child has an accident or disease far worse than a broken leg or diptheria, the disease of moral or neurotic distress? So often we wave our hand and say, 'Ah well, he'll grow out of it.' Regrettably he often does, but grows into something far more sinister and more troublesome to cure.

We are patient with a sufferer from what we believe to be a physical ailment, but should a person express his illness in terms that render him a social inconvenience then our patience is soon exhausted. Delay in the treatment of maladjusted or delinquent children reduces the prospect of a cure, not merely because the malady worsens with neglect but because it becomes overlayed with all kinds of compensatory devices. These supernumerary characteristics constitute the sufferer's own attempts at a cure, and are therefore extremely difficult to remove.

The child subconsciously feels that the therapist is saying, 'I will help you to find greater happiness, but the first thing that will occur in such a cure is that we will discover the deeper strata of even more confusing and even more sinister ills.' Of course, such words are never used, but such thoughts can be communicated, and the child will think, 'To be cured of stealing at such a price is folly. I would rather go on pinching, and hoping in some miraculous way that the symptoms will disappear.'

A delayed treatment causes what one can only call a habit formation, in which a certain pattern of behaviour, long practised even if only with slight success, has given rise to the formation of a habit.

There has been a tendency of late to feel that the shorter the time spent in schools for maladjusted children, the better for the child. So we have the idiocy of a year or two spent in an approved school where, even with psychiatric help, no change of a fundamental character can take place within such a brief period. It must be accepted that to induce a personality change purely from environmental influences is going to take at least three and probably more than five years; and to induce a personality change by psychoanalytic or psychotherapeutic treatment is going to take nearly as long. The latter course can produce a radical and permanent result which will stand the test of time, but it is inevitably a lengthy business and no cure can be advanced by holding out the promise that if the boy behaves he will leave sooner. Rather one should say, 'The quicker we can make you happy, the quicker we shall be able to show you things that you have missed and which you will then seek to possess for yourself in a proper spirit.' The pressure on vacancies, the need to make room for others, while understandable in terms of human compassion, are not acceptable if a child needing help has to leave the school prematurely.

One difficulty is the cost of treatment. Psychologists and psychiatrists at child guidance clinics hesitate to send a child to a boarding school knowing that the cost will frequently be viewed with some regret by the Local Education Authority, and therefore send only the most serious cases for institutional care. But the younger, less disturbed child will not cure himself; rather his difficulties will be multiplied, and he will become one of the serious cases.

Evidence of this unhappily delayed treatment is abundantly clear in the case papers which come under consideration at my school. On a basis of observed and recorded behaviour at home and school reported to the clinic, treatment should have been commenced at a much earlier stage. The extent to which maladjustment can be noticed during the first decade of life is crucial and it is most desirable that those first stages of a maladjusted pattern should not be overlooked. It should not be dismissed as childish naughtiness, either through false optimism or from a reluctance to take positive action in the case of the very young. In my early years as a magistrate in the juvenile court I often encountered very young children showing most ominous manifestations of misbehaviour. Despite my knowledge of these matters, I felt great reluctance to take any step which would remove the child from its home, but through the years I have discovered this understandable human reluctance to be quite falsely motivated. The histories of these children have shown me that some severance of bad family influences in their early lives would have led to their non-appearance at quarter sessions in the third and fourth decades of their lives, and I have unfortunately seen lamentable failures from my own falsely placed sentimentality.

Some young children have a highly developed delinquent pattern. I remember a case in Texas, of a boy of nine who committed thefts and robberies almost daily, including one armed robbery. With a most consummate insolence he asserted that he was under the age of criminal responsibility, adding defiantly that as that was the legal situation nobody could interfere with him in any way. He was reported to have indoctrinated a band of other eight- to nine-year-old children. It is thus desirable that schools, particularly for younger children, should realize that they are in a position to provide the most reliable observations on what may be maladjusted behaviour. The observations of an understanding teacher, with perhaps some training in the earlier aspects and symptomatic expressions of maladjustment and delinquency, could be more than helpful in the later diagnosis of the psychiatrist. If the teacher was able to go further, either by himself, or with the assistance of a social worker and investigate the family background he would find time out of number that there had been some tragedy or some difficulty within the family that had occasioned the manifestations he has observed within the orbit of school activities.

The matter of diagnostic procedures deserves far more detailed consideration than has yet been given. It is most unlikely that a psychiatric interview or the results of a single test can be other than frequently fallible, or give more than a cursory picture of a child's total situation. The use of a satisfactory range of tests and interviews make demands on time and personnel, but it will have to be realized, if we are ever to reduce the population of our prisons and mental hospitals, that after a sound diagnosis involving an estimate of the type of maladjustment and the type of treatment required, that treatment must be as thorough and careful as time permits. It is also important to bear in mind that the practical details of residential or in-clinic treatment may vary considerably from place to place, and that the type of re-education desired will involve the co-operation of the family. Thus we should seek to encourage the principle of grouping pupils with similar demands and potentialities.

There are, of course, classifying schools within the approved school service, and there are a number of admirable institutions of all kinds which give devoted and generous service far outstripping the reasonable demands of staff comfort. But it is also a fact that selection is often haphazard and the suitability of pupils for a specific school is too often left to chance. In the smaller approved schools there have often been occasions when a fairly homogeneous and well-ordered group has been entirely disrupted by the arrival of a boy sent there quite arbitrarily by a court, and that disruption has not only been of little value to the new arrival but has gravely disturbed the therapeutic work already accomplished for the main group of the school.

Of course, even in the best possible service and with the most lavish expenditure, there will still be failures, but we should strive to limit mistakes in the early years of a child's maladjustment. It is at this time that treatment promises an easier and more lasting success than one can hope for at a later stage. Where radical psychoanalysis is employed and the child is of sufficient intelligence to benefit from it, then it can be delayed with less danger, but even in these circumstances, the treatment is far easier when the child is younger. We seek to cure physical ailments as quickly and effectively as possible; so too, should we treat the more intangible ailments of the mind and emotions.

A criminal act is invariably infantile, often babyish. It is an attempt on the part of the criminal or the delinquent to solve his problems by acting them out against society. One can see quite clearly when viewing irresponsible and irrational acts of certain kinds of delinquents that they are not always what they appear to be, and in the cases we are now describing the tragic difficulties were far deeper and of greater significance than the children themselves could ever have realized. These cases also show that the tragedies are often of their own generation and not always can they be ascribed to some selfishness or unhappy treatment shown to them by their parents or by any external body.

One such was Donald East who came to us because of his complete neglect and apathy at school. Because of his thefts from his school fellows, shops, his own home and others, and from the jackdaw nature of these thefts which had very little mercenary advantage to him, one suspected that the thefts were an attempt to reconcile warring elements within his own psyche. Among the things he stole were the well-nigh inevitable cigarettes; because they had appeared so important to him his parents had, I think wisely, allowed him to smoke. It is often better that a person does a wrong thing openly, than with concealment.

When he came to us Donald was unpopular, arrogant and demanding; he was also listless and apathetic about most things that would interest other boys at school. He seemed incapable of forming a relationship with any of the teachers or other adults at the school, either because he would soon steal something from that person and then, frightened of their possible reaction, break off the relationship, or their society only seemed to satisfy him for a few weeks before he looked for some fresh distraction. If he could find some alleged friend outside the school, usually a rather unsavoury character, he would be more satisfied; he clearly feared the demands of a more normal relationship.

For a long time we felt we were achieving nothing; at no time had our tolerant, non-repressive atmosphere and our disbelief in punishment convinced Donald that we were prepared to believe in him and to help him master his errors, and it was two years before he saw the purpose of analytic treatment. Within those two years the environmental influence had to some degree shown him better way of living, and he had copied the example set to such effect that he had received, by elective process promotion to what others would call a prefectorial position. Nevertheless the malaise was still there, and the knowledge that at any minute he might break into theft.

He was detected at last in a theft of some brassières from a female member of the staff. With quietness but utter finality, she said to him he should consult the analyst and see if he could come to some understanding of the deeper significance of a theft of that kind. The battle the boy then commenced with himself lasted nearly a fortnight. But at last he sought an interview and mentioned the theft. He spoke of many such thefts, how in the secrecy of his bedroom or the lavatory he would undress completely and put on the brassiere, adding to that a stolen pair of women's knickers, and if these garments were frilly or revealing he would be better pleased. Once, he told me, he would spend as long as possible wearing a bikini in the bathroom, imagining himself to be a girl. This transvestitism was accompanied by an orgasm. But after a while he had found that the mere wearing of these garments was insufficient. He had tied his erect penis to his thigh with cord, and with many repeated thongs almost concealed his sexual member. Once the penis was concealed he was able to achieve an orgasm without any masturbatic move on his part. His terror and misery in recounting these circumstances was immense; but without any interpretive work, and without the work that was to occupy another two years, it was only three or four weeks before the stealing came to an end. His anti-social behaviour was his attempt, the only attempt he could imagine, to keep the real concept of his sexual misbehaviour at bay and, by some magic, placate those forces that he felt were ever condemning him to a sexual existence utterly different from those around him, and of whom he showed such jealousy. This jealousy, his stealing, his criticism and malicious gossip were all because his compatriots enjoyed the secret of normal behaviour.

It appeared that his difficulties stemmed from his curiosity about his sister, three years younger than himself. He had always wondered at her lack of a penis, and as she grew older and would lock the lavatory door behind her he would try to imagine what she was doing inside the room. He told me that on one occasion he stole the key so it could no longer prevent his free vision through the keyhole, and there he would watch her urinating, but in his imagination he experienced the sensation, or what he imagined to be the sensation, himself. But why should he do this? As his analysis proceeded, he revealed his bitter envy of things he could never possess: his mother's generative and creative parts, and her breasts.

He had resented the arrival of his sister, and while this difficulty arises in many families it can usually be overcome by love and care. But in his case the steel entered him so deep that acceptance was never complete. The earlier envy of the female attributes now shared by his sister made him believe that it made his parents consider her a superior person who deserved a greater degree of love and attention than he himself merited.

By itself this would not have been dangerous, but a far more sinister process was originating at a deeper level. His desires became perverted, and produced many sadistic trends such as imagined sexual assaults and mutilations of chance girls passing by, or imagined mutilations of himself, of a kind quite obviously indicated by the obscuring of his penis while in woman's clothing. Not only was he dressing like a woman but he was also pretending that he, like a woman, had no penis but a vagina. His intense envy, not so much of the sister's parts but of his mother's parts, was the basic cause of his trouble, and it was not until he realized that his mother's creative capacities belonged to himself that he began to come to terms with what was ultimately the intense oedipal jealousy of his father. The desire to possess the mother's breasts, the desire so often shown by his brooding preoccupation with stories of torture and mutilation, had crystallized in one very dramatic interview when he burst into the study to announce his discovery of the martyrdom of St Agatha. St Agatha's torturers had torn her breasts from her body with red hot pincers.

'That, Shaw, is the basis of everything I've wanted to do in torture! I'm damned certain it's why I read things about floggings in concentration camps, and mutilations! It's why I enjoyed reading about the man thousands of years ago who was broken on a wheel for trying to kill a king. That's why I get a kick out of those things because really and truly that's what I want to do to my St Agatha.'

Of course, it was perfectly clear that his mother was St Agatha, and it was perhaps not much more than a coincidence that her Christian name happened to be Agatha. But years ago he had perchance read of the story of St Agatha's martyrdom and associated it with his anger against the bosom that was denied to him because of a sister who must be punished in the most appropriate way.

83

So he went on to describe his jealousy of these wonderful things, the breasts. He described his fantasy of sucking a penis, and his nightly fantasies of going to another boy and arranging to have his penis sucked by him. One of the most fortunate aspects of such soul-clearing within the analytic situation is that it reduces the pressure upon the boy to do in reality the things that he so desires and deplores within himself.

One day the boy asked me, pathetically but honestly, 'Oh, Shaw, when do you think I'll stop pinching knickers and brassières and mucking about like this?' My reply was, 'Well Donald, you'll stop it when you realize that your mother really does love you in a way now suitable to your age, just as she loved you by feeding you at her breast when you were a baby. You will stop it too when you realize that your sister had a right to her breast as well, and that right was not won by excluding you. The right was taken up when you no longer had need for your mother's love to be expressed in those terms. So let us try hard to see what is after all only the truth, that your mother does love you and in a metaphorical way is prepared to give you her breast, though obviously at your age you cannot expect to suck a nipple. Of course, you try to do it sometimes by pinching cigarettes. Sometimes you try to do it by nibbling your pencils, and by all the other little phallic tricks like the nightly fantasy of getting people to suck your own 'do-it-yourself' nipple.'

'What do you mean' he said. 'My "do-it-yourself" nipple?'

My answer was that surely he could see he had invented the idea of having his own breast. Having his own breast would surely mean he did not need to steal or take or manipulate anybody else's breast, and so he invented the idea that his penis was a nipple. That, incidentally, is the main basis of most of the misbehaviour of those unfortunates who seek elaborate masturbatic activity by masturbating within another's mouth, or more commonly merely asking that others should masturbate them. Their object is to show that they, perhaps they alone, have the prized object, the fount of all love, the nipple and the breast, and not until that basis of the perversion is understood can the pervert hope to be released. This boy had arrogantly usurped his mother's attributes, which through the birth of his sister and other almost accidental issues he had envied, and having once embarked upon the misadventure of wearing women's underclothes, he was clearly at the mercy of that perversion until someone came to his rescue.

After a short period of analysis his superficial anti-social behaviour disappeared, but it took him nearly two years before he and I could feel confident that his innate selfishness and envy of his mother's capacities were gone for good. He had had to clearly understand that greed itself is an attempt to take a desire past the stage of satisfaction. Greed is the desire for having more than satisfaction. Once he had come to this realization he was able to take the next step.

We had thought that the lesson had been learned and that we were within very easy distance of the boy's complete cure when suddenly a different manifestation arose: intense jealousy of his father. It was shown by constant criticism of me, belittlement of my efforts and the attribution to me of base motives which, he gossiped, existed against every boy in the school. Perhaps at this stage it is important to realize that although the earliest envy is of the mother's breasts, the next step upon the slippery slope to perversion is to envy father's possession of the mother. This discovery was made by Hamlet and King Oedipus; it is rediscovered in many families today and in most of the families of maladjusted boys. At this stage it was necessary within the confines of the analytic sessions to explain and re-explain to the extent of tedious boredom to Donald, what he was doing to me. How he could not bear that I should have possessions that he had not. How Donald envied the fact that I had a wife to whom I could go at night time, whereas he would never be able to re-possess his mother and retrieve her from the competitive father. It was many months before the boy came to terms with the unreasoning jealousy of his father's prior demands on his mother, but at last he learned to accept that he was loved by his mother as a mother would love a son while she loved her husband as a wife should love and that the two were not opposed, nor would the absence of one add to the amount given to the other.

Suddenly and dramatically Donald's schoolwork improved. Within a few weeks he was showing a difference; and in maths, starting from an utterly negligible knowledge of algebra which he had completely avoided during the whole of his school life, pleading ignorance, within one term he had got as far as geometrical progressions and was embarking upon the calculus. His improvement in other subjects was remarkable; and from being a person who was tolerated rather than liked, he turned into a boy who attracted friendship and respect. He developed a belief in his own ability to help other boys at the school, and by the time he left, curious as it might appear, he was indeed helping other boys by his example and counsel in the way he himself had been helped over so many years.

He went on to university where he read Chemistry, and is now a chemist in industrial employment. He has visited us with his fiancée, who is a pleasant young woman, and I have no doubt that the lesson he struggled so hard to learn—that he need not envy that which is his by right—has been remembered.

CHAPTER VIII

From Sex to Love

AT THE age of twelve Ernest Folkard was expelled from a large grammar school in the north country. His behaviour had been so bad that the headmaster had warned other schools not to accept him as a pupil. He was referred to the local clinic and at last came to us.

His chief symptom was exhibitionism. In the classroom he would show his penis unashamedly. He had exhibited himself in the streets on his way to and from school. Occasionally he had reclined on a chair in front of the low sitting room window at home, undone his flies and exhibited himself to passers-by. This misbehaviour was by no means solely directed at women, and on the whole he appeared to get greater satisfaction if he could attract a man. At the school from which he was expelled he had made repeated attempts to seduce older boys, sometimes with success, and because of the activities of this one twelve-year-old boy the whole atmosphere of this very large school had become sexually corrupt.

We decided to take him, if only at risk, for a probationary period, and during those first early weeks Ernest gave us every example of his complex behaviour. He had been with us only a fortnight when he came to see me with the accusation that older boys had caught him, stripped him naked and painted his testicles with black shoe polish. Knowing that this fitted with his fantasy life rather more than with the probable behaviour of our older boys, I asked him why it should be only he to whom such bullying had been shown and why it was only he in the whole history of the school who had complained about such misbehaviour. I pointed out to him, too, that his evident pleasure at telling me of the incident certainly did not accord with his ostensible grievance at being so treated.

A day or two later, he came to me with the same complaint and again I repeated the general argument that he had heard before, adding that if he really was being treated in this manner he should perhaps be careful not to associate with those he thought might treat him so. Then, with a leer, he said: 'Don't you want to prove to yourself that I'm speaking the truth? You have only to look at my balls to see they're covered with shoe polish.' I said, 'There's no need to look at them. If you say they have polish on them, either they have polish in reality or polish in fantasy. At all events that is what you are saying, and what you are saying is far more important than any fact or doubt or any particular lie associated with other boys' behaviour.'

He looked disappointed and said, 'Don't you want to look at my balls?' I said, 'No, if I want to look at balls, I can look at my own. Many years have passed since I lost interest in that kind of anatomical curiosity.'

A few more weeks passed; his next visit was to complain to me that he had been the target of all kinds of improper suggestions from older boys who had bribed him to commit mutual masturbation. There were dozens of similar accusations and an attempt to dissuade him only led to an invitation for me to witness such scenes myself. At last, taking the bull by the horns, I said, 'You talk as if you want me to seduce you. But your words are those that show me that you wish to seduce me!'

He then smiled with a dreadfully sophisticated grin as if he hoped that, at last, I would allow myself to act with him in some perverted kind of sexual embrace. I told him I desired no relationship of that kind, and invited him to tell me why such should be so desirable to him. It took months for him to fully develop the stories of no fewer than nine homosexual relationships he had had with men since the age of eight years.

My experience has shown me that adults in authority who misbehave sexually with boys are perhaps doing him a social rather than sexual harm. A boy needing an image of a father figure, a good example from the man in charge of his boy's club or his schoolteacher, has that feeling so bitterly disappointed and besmirched by the discovery that the hero figure was only there to satisfy some purely selfish sexual taste. The harm done by the unhappy pederast is likely to be the social one of bad example, rather than corrupt the boy who is already more often than not sexually disturbed, for it is only the maladjusted who lend themselves to the advance of the homosexual adult. There have been numerous cases where the girl who rushes home with a story of a man behaving improperly in the train can be shown herself to have advanced and precocious sexual tastes, and has invented the man who touched her leg or exhibited himself. In genuine incidents it is often the girl's provocation or seductive air which tempts a man into a situation for which he can be charged in the courts. We cannot excuse the seducer's behaviour but we should remember that illicit sexual encounters are frequently the result of collusion, or even instigation by the girl or the small boy.

In the case of Ernest there was no doubt whatever that any man who interfered with him sexually had done so with his encouragement. An innocent man, who has no such pederastic tastes, will not notice an invitation. So I was able to show Ernest that it was by his wish that the seductions had occurred, and after nearly a year of patient discussion, with purposeless accusations on his part against innocent parties, we were able to agree that he was seeking to satisfy a need which to him was natural and imperative, but which to others appeared to be a perversion.

The first important piece of self-discovery was when he told me about being bathed by his mother as a small child. He said in a shamefaced but, for the first time in his conversations with me, an honest way, that he liked his mother patting his bottom, and he would manoeuvre himself into such positions that the pats were prolonged. In all respects his feelings for the nightly bath routine were ones of an intense erotic relationship with his mother. When he first spoke of this he said: 'You know, I wonder if I'd have been such a fool with my penis if my mother hadn't messed me about in the bath?'

I pointed out to him that it was highly questionable that his mother had messed him about in the bath, because, from the way he had described the situation to me, it was he who had planned that the bathroom relationship should continue. Even if his mother had been over-demonstrative in fondling him, she probably only did so from the purest motives of maternal love and it was he who had turned them into something else.

He went on to tell me that he used to wonder what went on in his parents' bedroom when he was expected to be in his own bed in his own room. He had brooded on the intimacies of their privacy and their own love relationship.

The next factor that appeared to be of importance was his production in the art room of pictures illustrating the theme 'Waiting Outside the Headmaster's Study'. I asked him what he was waiting for, and he said, 'Oh, I was always being caned.' It was a fact that frequently he had been beaten on his bottom; possibly the motives of those doing it were good, perhaps they were bad. But one of the dreadful things to emerge from these fearful pictures came when I asked him to draw what was going on *inside* the headmaster's study. He drew a scene of the most filthy eroticism of which I should imagine even the most perverted artist incapable. Pieces of buttocks were flying about everywhere on the headmaster's floor; canes were flying about the room. Angry men wearing pince-nez glasses were darting about lashing at boys' bottoms, and every boy was smiling as if he were greatly enjoying the sensation.

Ernest sadly admitted that he enjoyed being beaten upon his buttocks. Indeed he had invented an expression for it. 'I like,' he said, 'having a whackyfied feeling.' To him a beating was always associated with an erect penis, and sometimes when having a beating he had experienced an orgasm. To stress the perverted nature of such experience is needless. But the point must now be made that the boy had started to talk about the dim recesses of his feelings, and that was a great advance; hitherto he had been locked up in the belief that no such perversion could ever be understood by anyone else and that the only way to dodge such perversion was to act it out with all kinds of accusations against innocent people.

As interviews continued it became clear that he wished to prove to himself, by exhibiting his penis, that the member itself was still present on his body. For his sins, particularly those against the mother when he sought to supplant the father in her bed, he feared castration, and that fear, neurotic and irrational as it was, had most sinister and forceful support from an angry denunciation from a headmaster, who said to him after a hostile speech about how he devalued morality within the school: 'The only thing to be done with you is to castrate you, and by God, if you go on as you are doing, I will see that it's done!' One can excuse the headmaster his anger, but it is a pity that it fitted only too well with the boy's own deep, unconscious fears which in fact his own behaviour was designed to exorcise and remove.

The next most important event in the history of this boy's cure was when he went to the sewage disposal plant at the school and managed to wreck a rotating arm and cause over £100 worth of damage. It was a mystery to all others who had done the damage, for he told me in the privacy of an analytic session and these confidences are always respected. He told me he did not understand why he should damage on purpose a plant of that kind; then he remarked vaguely that a plant came from a seed and the seed changed to an embryo. After a long investigation of all the erotic ideas that to him were associated with an embryo, I discovered that the feeling he called whackyfied was really a hope that the cane itself would penetrate his anus and there would be a glorious sexual feeling. In fact whenever he pretended to himself that that had occurred, an orgasm followed.

His destruction of the sewage plant was a part acting out of this fearful concept. For as a little boy, certainly well before the age of eight, he had been puzzled about where babies come from. Not wishing his own pre-eminence as an only child to be assailed, he hoped that his mother and father would give birth to no more babies. One way of effecting this end would be to take away the father's capacity to make more babies, that is, to castrate father. And having conceived that irrational, unconscious plan, the boy went further and conceived the idea that if father found out what his plan was then, tit for tat, the same thing would be done to him.

He asked himself where babies came from, and formed the theory, common to very small children, that they came out of the anus. There were only two parts of the body that produced things and one was this mysterious hole in his bottom. What is more likely than that babies emerge in this way, and if so, to equate certain aspects of birth with defecation? This boy had so equated the emergence of a baby from a bottom that he could have an erotic experience merely by imagining some anal insertion as part of a castration punishment. By breaking into a sewage disposal unit he could in effect destroy everything that had come from everybody's anus and thus remove all possibility of further births and all competitors for his mother whose embrace he so desired.

At this stage in his private sessions, in which he endlessly repeated incidents from his past, it was necessary all the time to redirect his attention to the present. I repeatedly reminded him that we need not regard analysis as a kind of confessional in which every wrong he had ever done had to be mentioned. We now had plenty of examples of his difficulties and all he was likely to add now would merely be repetition of similar cases. It was better that he should try to understand exactly what he was doing today rather than put right what he did yesterday.

At this point he tried to use me as a sexual object. First I was a mother who should pat and fondle him and he would, as if accidently, bump up against me in the passage, or come to the study door upon some quite unnecessary errand. When looking at a piece of paper together he would bump against me; when standing near to me in the school library he would drop a book so that he had to push against my legs to pick it up again.

Gradually that acting out disappeared only to be replaced by the temptation to have some improper sexual relationship. He would put it apologetically; but obeying the rule of analysis that everything in his head must be spoken, would say, 'I'm sorry, I keep on thinking I want you to bugger me.' This could easily be interpreted as his misuse of love and affection and attention, and he had continually to be shown that he would get proper attention or affection from me, but he could never have it in the debased form which he sought, for that would be to negate the goodness of the very attention for which he craved.

The next stage was the production of much written material which he would pop under the study door.

'I like cocks. I think people don't like me because I like cocks and bums. So I want to end this social dislike. I want to get a big knife. Why do I want a big knife? I want it to stop my cocking and bumming. I want to cut my cock off in a place where bums are concerned. Shit goes to the sewer. And shit comes from bums. I don't like shit as such, but I do like where it comes from. At home I don't like washing up because bums aren't allowed and washing-up water goes where shit goes. But shit comes from bums and bums aren't allowed.'

The fact that was so repetitive, like pornographic graffiti on a public lavatory wall, meant that the reductive process was not continuing quickly, nor radically, because note after note repeated the same motifs just as the same pornographic drawing is repeated *ad nauseum* on that wall. While it is a relief for a person to express such feelings, the pressure that generates such feelings is still there and will require relief until the pressure itself is dissipated by an understanding of the generative processes behind that pressure.

The next thing that troubled and perplexed the boy was his discovery that he had formed a hobby of collecting worms. Ostensibly these were for fishing in the local river, but having collected a jar full of worms, he would cut them in half, and would then re-introduce each half to the other, or the half of one worm to the half of another, trying all kinds of permutations and combinations. He talked about it in some perplexity to me and it was very easy to demonstrate to him that his game was a confusion of the faecal and the phallic functions. Faecal because he had dug for the worms in black faecal mud in the garden, and phallic because of the worm's shape. He admitted to me, 'I didn't like to tell you before, Shaw, but when I cut worms about my cock goes stiff.' The next production in writing that he put under the study door, included some telling phrases.

'I have to get worms. Worms feel like cocks, so I get worms and to get worms I have to dig. I dig to get worms. I want worms because they are like cocks. Shaw tells me not to dig but to try to understand what I am about, but I like worms because they are like cocks. And there aren't any cocks so I have to dig to get worms. Shaw tells me again not to dig, but damn it, I must have worms so I have to dig. When I find a worm I hold it up. It feels like a cock. I like them but people are watching me so I have to put it down again and pretend I am doing something else. Otherwise they will think I am cuckoo.'

But the boy gradually improved. The untruthfulness, accusations, stealing and many other bitter sources of his unpopularity that had existed when he first came, gradually disappeared; and at the end of two years of treatment he was able to, start using his real imaginative ability in the classroom. To achieve such a thing at long last is an immense encouragement for anybody, let alone a boy who feels himself to be escaping from the horror of sexual perversion. Work that hitherto was conducted with difficulty or indeed not at all, from sheer incoherence and incomprehension, could now be done with speed and efficiency. The liberated talent was of an artistic and scientific nature; he had a keen imagination and an ability to attend scrupulously to small but significant details.

These qualities were present when he first came to the school but they had showed no more than as a tendency and certainly did not represent any usefulness or potential for the future.

One does not expect maladjustment or perversion or any other form of difficult behaviour to stop short at the classroom door. But regrettably there are certain naïve teachers who, knowing a child is not working to a reasonable fulfilment of his potential, can only regard it as evidence of laziness or cheek. In Ernest's case it was evidence of something far more powerful; the boy had been trying to cope with a mental disturbance which exhausted all the energy at his command, and left nothing whatever for the classroom or social activities. His envy of his father is clear; his greed for his mother is clearer still; it would not have been sufficient to show him that he should not be envious, jealous or greedy, but it was necessary to show him that he could get what he needed legitimately without any of those three techniques. But before that, one had to find a satisfaction for him in the relationship both with a good mother object who would pat him in the bath for proper reasons, but not for the reasons he imagined, and a good father object, who would love him for himself and not as a result of a kind of moral blackmail.

Finally the boy had to discover that his parents, knowing of his social crimes, were prepared not merely to forgive, but to forget. Once the boy was convinced of those things, and that conviction could only be based upon a radical analysis, then the way was clear for a complete removal of these baffling situations that had so contorted his life.

At that point I obtained his permission to hold a meeting between him, his parents and myself, where certain private details could be told to them, though not of the degree of intimacy that had existed within the privacy of our own conversations. That interview was held and, as I knew they would, the parents showed comprehension and understanding. The boy realized his selfishness could be forgiven and he understood that his parents had a right to their own relationship.

By this time all his sexual perversion had departed, and indeed I even felt during the interview that we were talking about things which need no longer be discussed.

This case is over twenty years old, the boy is now in a respected profession, is married and has a large family of children where the behaviour difficulties which might occur to an only child are rubbed off in the ordinary cut and thrust of relationships between several children.

Frank Gold was only a few months old when his father died, and his mother's sorrow at his death caused a curious withdrawal of affection from her only son. Experiences in her own childhood must have contributed towards the situation but, whatever the reasons of an unconscious nature, the fact was that not only did the boy lose a father but he lost also his mother's love.

When Frank was about twelve years old he began to show personality disturbances which, had he been more fortunate, might have been apparent in his primary school, but unfortunately were only recognized when he started his grammar school education. The general complaint about him in his case papers was that he was a distracting influence to other children, that whenever there was trouble he somehow seemed to be about. But when one asked for additional information upon evidential grounds, such data could never be supplied. The subversive effect he was reputed to have on his fellows was unobtrusive but nevertheless all-pervasive.

A boy whose maladjustment cannot be described is one who is indeed going to be most difficult to cure. If the condition can be described, or if the tragedy can be defined, there is a least some foundation on which to base the method of approach, but if no symptomatalogy is evident, it is difficult to prove to a child in need that any disturbance exists. His academic performance in the classroom was adequate, and he was well enough behaved. He was willing and agreeable and any visitor at the school was impressed with his courtesy and charm. Nevertheless we found that he was a centre of curiously undefined storms. He was the focus of subversive activities and although these incidents never took a coherent form the ubiquitousness of his presence on these occasions gave us much of a challenge, seeking as we do always to preserve general tranquillity.

After he had been with us for six months a member of the staff, pausing by his bedside, happened to lift his mattress and found underneath an exercise book filled with many examples of sadistic pornography. Words like 'prosty' 'cunt' 'tart' and words of even greater distress were scattered over this book, embellishing pictures of a filth that in the absence of pictorial illustration must remain undescribed. Stylised pornography is an interesting subject: such pornography can be similar to, or even identical with, the motives behind the carving of the legend 'Tom loves Mary' incised with an arrowed heart, on the living bark of a tree. The writer on the tree is stating what he wants to be true, not what he knows to be true; the less laudable graffiti scribbled on walls or advertisement hoardings on the railway platform shows a similar misgiving. Something that a person feels he wants and knows he cannot accomplish, has to be expressed, and his way of expression is to destroy or decorate public announcements or his text books. It is an expression of need, just as a hesitating suicide, before he takes the bottle of poison, telephones to a relative or leaves a note knowing it will be found. All those attempts are cries for help, which, if understood, can perhaps prompt the help that is so necessary to save the sufferer. Unfortunately in the case of Frank the exercise book was hidden and had been found only by chance. For analytic treatment to be successful the initiative has to come from the analysand and not from the person who seeks to cure him. By various techniques my colleagues had tried hard to get the boy to come and see me, trying to show him that, whatever his sexual sufferings, relief could be obtained by talking it out. But to all overtures he returned a bland assurance that all was well with him and that although others perhaps needed help he could stand alone on his own two feet. So a year and a half passed with little result.

It is always dangerous for the analyst, however pressing are the needs of time in the short life of a child, to be other than cautious. A mistake made can be put right only with very great difficulty, for a child's recollection of a therapeutic error is something that seems to impede a successful analysis to a degree that can often make analysis impossible. But time causes impatience and in these situations risks have sometimes to be taken. It can be better to take a risk than to acquiese in a situation that leads only to stagnancy. One has to know one's techniques, but above all it is a matter of instinct and timing and, we must admit, luck.

I went to the boy and told him I was dissatisfied with his health, dissatisfied with his happiness, and dissatisfied with what gossip told me was underneath the mattress of his bed. We went to the bed, and when I found the book his first reaction was to say, 'But that is not mine. Why say I put it there? Anybody could have put it there.' To which I replied, 'Look, I'm trying to help you. I can't help if you are going to lie. You and I both know you did these dirty drawings. Why should we now conspire to lie about it? Especially when I know about your mother being in a mental hospital. I know about the death of your father and I know you are adopting crazy ways of compensating for these two bitter losses in your life.'

It is not easy for me to express the full dramatic emphasis, even theatricalism of a speech of that kind. The timing and emphasis are so important, and it is only through experience that one can learn to use the intangibles of those techniques to combat the frailties that are so terrified of admitting even their own existence. The boy began to trust and understand. He was able to produce little examples in themselves, of only superficial importance, about his mischief and malice. At last, within the privacy of our interviews, we agreed we had uncovered most of the obvious matter, that we had done what we could but we had not yet explained the exercise book underneath the mattress.

It surprises many people who do not understand maladjustment that most sexual perversions are private, and often remain so for the whole of the pervert's life. Most perversions are not in themselves against the law. Many are unknown to the pervert himself; they are expressed in all kinds or irrational ways such as, for example, imagining he is a sewing machine or an omelette and

97

when that stage of irrational degeneration is reached one cannot talk of the possibility of any psychoanalytic cure. But we had the concrete evidence of the exercise book, and at last Frank Gold saw that as evidence of his distress.

There had never been any suspicion of sexual impropriety before, but he said to me, 'If you knew what I thought about and what I did, you would never speak to me again.' I replied, 'Let us see if that is true. If in fact what you tell me so appals me, then you are right and I shall never speak to you again. But if on the other hand we can both seek to understand, then perhaps you can go on and tell me of even more things.'

He answered, 'That's all very well. But you don't know what a bastard I am. It's all very well for you to sit there and say that, but you're not the one who does the things I do. I'm the one who does that, and I don't know how you have the cheek to expect me to tell you what I do.' I replied that I did not want to be cheeky or insolent. I wanted to help; and I felt that whatever folly he talked of, he had exaggerated its importance and its effect upon me. I asked him to take the risk. He did.

The first thing he told me about was how he used to tattoo his chest by giving it little nips with his finger nails. About two years ago he had started tattooing his chest by inking a needle or pin and sticking it into his chest. I asked him what kind of pictures he drew and said, 'I can't tell you that. I'm not certain I know, even.' This explained another rather trifling domestic mystery. He would never have a bath in the presence of other boys. We had tolerated that situation by making a special domestic arrangement giving him the privacy of a bathroom, and we had also understood that for the same reason, whatever it might be, he would naturally not wish to go in the school swimming bath.

I asked him if there were any visible signs on his chest of the punctures he had inflicted upon himself. 'No, not unless you look closely,' he said. 'But if anybody saw it they might guess what I had been up to. In any case I'm not taking the risk.'

I asked him if there were any other things he did and he said, 'Well, the worst thing is something I can't tell you.' I replied that understanding was unlikely to come that way. That he had tried for a long time to find out why he did these things but had failed. That it was likely too, that I might fail; but then I might succeed, and if

I only partially succeeded, at least it would be an improvement. After a few more weeks he said, 'I think I can write it.' And he did start writing. There is no need to quote from the writing, but the first contribution included a picture of what he chose to tattoo upon his own chest. It was an enormous breast labelled underneath 'balloon'. To him it was quite inexplicable why he should on one side of the paper draw the balloon and on the other side a deflated balloon. But the mother's original love had turned out to be what can only be described as hatred, and the symbol of love in all children's eyes, the mother's breast, became deflated. Perhaps it was a kind of despairing optimism that left one breast full against the tragedy of the deflated spoilt breast on the other side. Associating Frank's drawing with his mother did not remove the boy's lack of a mother; nothing would ever alter the fact of his mother's utter rejection. We had gradually to build within him the capacity to withstand that rejection and to show him this was such a unique experience it was unlikely ever to recur.

As the next few months went by, he spoke even more freely of his various sexual fantasies: how his masturbatic fantasies would always involve the presence of a second party; how those fantasies were conducted in terms of love, flowers, beautiful scents and imagery of that kind. When I tried to show him that here again he was seeking to conjure a situation of love from a merely erotic act, there was more understanding acquired by Frank. Masturbation to him was the first love experience he had ever had, and in fact his only love experience available. By having these fantasies he could at least pretend he had an intimate love relationship with someone else, however degraded it might be.

The third most significant revelation he made was that his fantasies included an extraordinary ritual with younger boys, in which they would shyly come to him to ask his permission to speak and, with condescension and love, he would invite them into his house, usually a well-apportioned mansion or palace. They would then say, 'Will you please be good to us? Will you please be kind to us?' He would then take them to a bedroom, feed them with luxurious foods and let them sit on his lap and he would rub their noses with ruthless sadism against some harsh fabric he was wearing. Sometimes his dress would be a uniform, with many medals on his breast. The climax of the situation would be when he took the boy's nose and mouth and rubbed it ruthlessly against the harsh metal on his chest.

He came to understand how, in the first place, he sought to remedy his own deficiencies as a child by offering that love to the fantasy children, building to the climax when they would be given the prototype and essence of all love. At the very climax, it would be smashed into the harsh torture of what he himself had suffered. Not only did that explain many things about his behaviour to himself but, as with the fantasy tattooing it explained why he had been for three or four years collecting military medals. Now the two incidents of the bathroom and the medals could not be understood in isolation. Obviously it does not matter very much if a person's sense of modesty, whatever the basis may be, prevents him going into the school swimming bath. Clearly, it does not matter if a boy collects medals for some personal reasons. But when one discovers the basis of these two reactions, one realizes the significance of a symptom and one's own total lack of observation of much which, if understood, would have shortened the path of analysis to a cure.

By this time Frank's social misbehaviour had disappeared, and indeed, his attitude had changed to such a degree that he was reasonably certain of a welcome and, as is so often the case, approval encouraged further approving behaviour.

But we had not finished and one of the difficulties of all analytic work is to be sufficiently resolute to continue the analysis even when the symptoms have gone, because it is at that point that one's relief at having accomplished so much should not be allowed to prevent one going on to finish the job. In this case the benevolent attitude of the boy towards the school authority, and his changed social mien, marked yet another trick on his part. He had stopped collecting the rasping medals, he had stopped tattooing his chest and had now accepted the fact that he could never have a mother, accepting too the fact that the other source of love from his father was dead. But he had decided to be a do it yourself father and mother combined. But with his own cornucopious breasts he fantasied giving, giving, giving, whereas before he had been taking, taking, taking. As he had no mother he would be a mother himself, that was his intermediate solution, and he imagined himself feeding little children on his bosom. It was fortunate that his own perspicacity and the patience of those working with him was sufficient to take on and accept the task of continued analysis. He was shown that he could be creative at a male level and there was no need to usurp the creativeness that could only exist at a female level. True, in all of us there is a mixture of male and female and the creative side is more frequently female than male. But in his case he presumptuously assumed the female function because in his bed the fantasies now of feeding the little children were complete without the final sadistic medal torture.

His reply to that kind of interpretation was, 'Oh my God. Is this bloody analysis job never going to be finished?' My answer was that it was complete now if he wished it to be complete, but while he adopted any compromise which rested basically upon a fabrication he would not receive complete happiness. I explained it was not my function to give sympathy for his deprivations. Anyone could do that. My function was rather to continue with an exploration of his pretext and his evasions, leaving it to others to provide sympathy.

As the analysis proceeded it became clear that he had abandoned the idea of being a pretend mother, feeding himself vicariously by creating all kinds of non-existent fantasy children who would fasten leech-like to his capacious breast, and he realized that his true function must be as a man, whatever the liabilities of the past.

He left many years ago, and in a letter he wrote to me recently, reminded me of the conversation I had long since forgotten. The letter started, 'Dear Shaw, Now I have been married for three years, I will remind you of something you said to me! "You have been denied your rights and never are you likely to have them until you are married, Frank. Once you are, you will find that all the things you and I have been talking about, in a sense have been so much wasted time and I think you will wonder why we found it necessary to talk for so many years. You will find that real unforced love, which is based upon an adoration of the love object, contains qualities which can only be called exquisite!" ' The next letter came a few months later, when he told me with pride of the birth of a son.

This particular case illustrates not only the utter privacy of the perversion that is never observed by outsiders, but also the ease with which this particular child could have passed unnoticed into permanent mental disorder had it not been for the observation of certain teachers. These wise people recognized that behind the queer indefinable misbehaviour, some menace lurked which, given the right treatment, could be removed, enabling the boy to show his own courage, and his own high order of intelligence.

CHAPTER IX

Adoption and Illegitimacy

THOSE who have not made a study of these affairs will assume that an adoption has given an unwanted child a happy, settled home for the rest of its life, and that the child, otherwise doomed to a parentless existence or institutional life, is now saved. Unfortunately, what goes on before adoption, what occurs during an adopted child's life and what takes place after the child's adolescence has been completed, are sometimes very unsettled events. More study than has as yet been bestowed is needed and, unhappily, this is a subject which baffles study due to the very variable circumstances of the adopted child, its natural parents and its adoptive parents.

There is an obvious difference between these two sets of parents, but more differences exist which are less obvious, and in our experience adopted and illegitimate children break down more often than do children born of married parents and brought up by them. But it would be entirely fallacious to conclude that adopted children are certain to have more troubles than those born naturally to married parents. There are no reliable statistics nor is it likely that there will ever be so, for many difficulties both with ordinary and adopted children are never reported, and thus no direct comparison can be made.

For every maladjusted child who goes to a clinic, there are twelve or twenty who do not come to the notice of a clinic. It has been suggested, again without basis, but from informed workers in the field who have gathered considerable expertise and understanding, that the adopted child is far more likely to be reported to the social welfare centre and the clinic if he does show behaviour difficulties. Adoptions are rightly private, and while social workers and others associated with adoption can have opinions, their experience is likely to have been based upon those children who have broken down during adoption, rather than upon adoptions which have, and I have no doubt they are vastly in the majority, happily succeeded.

Those children who are illegitimate as well as adopted are more likely to break down during their childhood or early adolescence than children who have not that further liability of illegitimacy. But again, that is based upon opinion and not upon fact. Our experience with those cases shows we know the need for considerably more research upon adoption, differences between adoptive parents, their motives, the results of those motives upon the adopted child and a host of other factors which have received but scant attention up to the present time. Such work would have to be conducted upon a much larger scale than the number of children who pass through our hands.

As the chairman of a juvenile court and a former member of a County Adoption Agency, I have felt continual misgivings about our wisdom in agreeing to some adoptions. The enquiries of the guardian *ad litem* are exhaustive and their recommendation is usually followed by the juvenile court. Social workers attached to the adoption agency are carefully trained professionals who have acquired considerable experience of the less obvious motives of those who adopt: their reports are in the main usually accepted by the committee which forms the County Adoption Agency. But misgivings of the deeper motives of adoptive parents will continue to exist, as no mere interview could ever explore the deeper unconscious motives and emotions of those who, for one reason or another, failing to have their own children, have decided to adopt some other person's child. Motives of this kind are deeply buried in the subconscious—they rest upon biological disappointment. Later there follow various doubts of the character or intelligence or health of this child they adopt. Furthermore, the adoptive parents, believing rightly or wrongly in their own sterility, have to face an issue which fortunately few parents have to face. The disappointment of a married man who is told finally by the specialists that he is sterile is something that can only be experienced by those who have suffered it. Even more intense must be the suffering of a woman when she deeply desires children and discovers she cannot bear her own. This discovery is a blow at the very purpose of her womanhood. The pride a man experiences when his wife is pregnant, and when she gives birth, is enormous, but the really deep springs of emotion are something that only a mother can experience.

Upon such backgrounds adoptions are conceived. This is not to say that the motives in themselves are always bad, because if one decides to do something about one's disappointment instead of meekly accepting the inevitability of it, that is the counsel of courage and wisdom. But motives are not always what they seem. No matter how clever or able the guardian *ad litem* or the social worker or the adoption agency may be, human motives at this level may defy investigation.

Another complicating factor which is a surprise to many is that after adoption has taken place, it is quite frequently the case that the adoptive mother becomes pregnant. At first I was baffled that this should be so common; it had happened in a little over seventy per cent of the cases we had at the school who had suffered troubles as a result of adoption. But I think I understand it better now. It seems that a woman may believe so strongly that she cannot bear a child, or have such a deep-rooted fear of pregnancy, that it has a physical effect upon her. Perhaps it would be the result of some sexual inhibition driven into her by sex-hating parents, or perhaps she felt a complete inadequacy as a child to deal with her dolls and now felt a similar incapacity to deal with a real, live baby. One of those two feelings or a combination of both could result in a situation where she does not become pregnant and the doctor has to conclude that she will not become pregnant. But then, after adoption, she discovers that a baby is a wonderful thing, and she is perfectly capable of bringing it up. The psychological fear is removed and thus the physical barrier is removed as well. But it may well be that her initial uncertainty and imbalance is transferred, by association, to the adopted child, which is the reason why a large proportion of them need psychological help in later life.

The woman is usually the one who is most enthusiastic to adopt and initially opposition comes from her husband, or at least there is a lack of enthusiasm on his part. This frequently emerges during the first interview and in probing in greater detail one has often found, particularly by asking questions of social workers and other professionals connected with the case prior to the actual adoption, that the man caused technical obstructions by misunderstanding telephone calls, or failing to keep appointments. It is as if he has accepted his impotence uneasily, and feels that, if he acknowledges the need to adopt, it is a permanent acknowledgement of his own incapacity and incompleteness. For it is often impossible for a man to admit that his own inability to create life with his own sexual member is inadequate. The presence of an adopted child is always a reminder that such an admission has been made.

In some circumstances the father might well fear the emergence of a competitor for his wife's affections. After all, it is not difficult to imagine that a wife, frustrated in her wish to have a child, might feel the adopted child to be the apple of her eye and regard him as the centre of family attention, even to the exclusion of others whom she loves.

But whatever the reasons are, with children who subsequently become difficult the mother does appear to her husband to be adopting a competitor. She seems to need a baby, or a love, to fulfil the female desires that her husband has failed to satisfy. I do not for one minute suggest that any of these curious processes are conscious or malevolent, but in a study of adopted and illegitimate children who have been brought up by good, generous and apparently normal adoptive parents, these factors frequently emerge. They have contributed towards the child's difficulties and have sometimes just as tragically contributed to difficulties between the adoptive parents. The problems of adoption often embrace the problems of illegitimacy; of the many adopted children we have had, some three-quarters appear to have been born to unwed parents.

While the adopted child is growing up the parents are likely to experience more difficulties than with a child born naturally to them. For an adopted child growing up is beset with more problems than a child born into an ordinary home. For instance, if the family structure is secure enough the death of a true parent can often be withstood, but the death of an adoptive parent, or much worse, the divorce of adoptive parents, contains terrors for the child, rarely equalled in other children.

The parents are sometimes disappointed when they find they have adopted a dull child and their guilty pretence to prove that they do not mind does not carry conviction to the adopted child or to themselves. Strangely, the opposite can also be a problem; the adoption of a child of superior intelligence. Of the adopted children who pass through our hands, we have had some cases like this.

There was one such parent, a batman in the army who had a mentally defective wife. She was a high grade defective, but nevertheless her defect was marked. They had wanted children, but for reasons which were not defined in the case papers, she could not conceive. This is going back some time now, because I do not believe that with our present adoption laws and regulations it would be possible for two such people, who obviously could not give a child a stable home environment, to adopt today. Years ago it did happen, and the child these two adopted turned out to be a genius.

His isolation in being brought up by two such terribly dull people was marked and he treated them, not exactly with derision, but with impatience and intolerance. Fortunately the future of that child was assured and we were very successful. But it was a task which demanded extreme patience.

Difficulties take diverse forms. One, for example, is a curious embargo on conversation within the family at home about the facts of the adoption. Many adopted boys have told me how often they have come into a room to be met by a silence, or sudden hush and a realization that there was a topic of conversation going on considered improper for their ears. Of course, they guessed what the subject was, but out of partial embarrassment, and a desire not to hurt the feelings of their parents, they did not raise the question directly. Where an adopted child is told by his parents that he is adopted, he knows already, intuitively. This is not to say he acquired the information from some chance gossip of a neighbour or relation. The fact of birth, where we emerge from the most lovable and loved person in the world, is an experience which cannot be transferred to another from whose body we did not emerge. She may be a thousand times better morally, she may be more compassionate and tender than our real mother, but the biological fact cannot be contradicted. It has fallen to my lot to

107

tell many boys of the fact of their adoption, and in nearly every case the boy has said that he had guessed there was some kind of mystery in his background, but that he had never cared to voice his doubts.

I have also told many boys of their illegitimacy. They too, always appear to have known there was something different about their birth. It was a completely intuitive knowledge.

At the school we have studied most carefully the drawings and paintings of illegitimate and adopted children; before they have been told of the facts of their birth their work has shown a disorientated composition which, with the knowledge that we had, frequently has implied their own knowledge of their abnormal background. Thus one boy's picture was of a man and a woman with their children, the children being always on the far side of the paper. Another boy would draw a man and a woman and, when asked whether they were with anybody, replied, 'Ah, yes, they had a little boy with them but he fell over that cliff, that you see down at the bottom of the picture.' In the pictures such children draw which involve people there is a curious barrier in the relationship between the man and the woman and the smaller beings in the same drawing. It is so obvious that, even when necessary information is withheld from the staff, as is sometimes the case for perfectly proper reasons, the art master has been able to guess from the particular arrangement of a drawing that such and such a child has been adopted, has no parents, or that his parents are divorced.

All adopted children should know that they are adopted as soon as they are old enough to receive such information; there is no problem if it is done in the right way. One tells a child, say at the age of four or five, that he did not come out of his mummy in the way that other children came out of their mummies and although he is loved and wanted and kept warm and protected in his family, nevertheless he was not born in that particular way. The phraseology matters little; it is the tone that matters, and the relationship between the informer and informed.

Many parents have told their adopted children, either directly or by implication that they are not adopted. It is not often that there are particularly sinister or underhanded reasons for this: the argument this kind of adopted parent will suggest is that the child is happy, so why say something that might, at worst, disturb his happiness and at best could in no way improve it?

There was one case where the parents had not told the boy of his adoption, and despite our very urgent suggestion that they did so, or allowed us to do so, for a whole year they refused. One reason we wished to tell the boy the facts of his background was that he was spinning all kinds of fantasies to other boys about his real parentage. He invented the idea that a well-known duke (he identified him by name) was his father. He fabricated such stories not to make people think him more important than he was, but to try to satisfy within himself some mysterious curiosity, which he knew would be refused intellectual satisfaction. Naturally, without the adoptive parents' permission I could not act, but the boy often told me he believed that he had been adopted or was illegitimate and asked me if I could find out from his parents if this was the case. I asked him why he had not tried to do so himself. He replied that he often had, but there was some queer thing inside him, or in the attitude of his parents, that caused him to disbelieve his parents in advance, and thus to invent the mirage about the duke.

If information is not understood, and understanding does not always follow information, the imagination will take its place. In this particular case we were finally able to convince the parents of the wisdom of revealing the true facts of the boy's birth, and the boy was told. Thus we were able to start what proved to be a not very difficult cure of the boy's troublesome behaviour. An adopted boy will believe he is different from other boys, and to tell him that such is not the case does not always carry credence. If one wishes him to believe that he is the same as other boys, that belief must be conveyed by the actions of those other boys and adults. Mere verbal assurance will accomplish little or nothing.

The illegitimate too, find it most difficult to believe they are as good as others. I always remember a boy who kept on grumbling to me, 'Why the hell am I a bastard?' and mentioned cases of people who had knowledge of his illegitimacy and were prepared in some underhand manner to point an accusing finger at him. I surprised him very much when I told him that whether he was illegitimate or not mattered very little, and people could not for that reason accuse him of bad faith or bad behaviour. It was something perhaps that he might have to suffer, but it was not something he had caused.

But all my reassurance had little effect. I said to him, 'You told me you're a bastard. Am I a bastard?' He replied, 'I never troubled to find out.' I answered, 'Well, if it doesn't matter to you whether I'm illegitimate or not, and after all I am a most important person to you, how on earth can you imagine that anyone else can care a scrap whether you were born in wedlock or out of it?' He laughed, and although that exchange did not remove what he feared was a stigma, it did enable discussion on the matter to proceed far more effectively.

I have often wondered why the word bastard is used by stupid people as a perjorative term. 'You dirty bastard!' or, 'He's a silly bastard!' is nowadays often flung, jocularly, at people who are not illegitimate. Remarks like that are often casually used in ordinary social conversation, and if a bastard in the dictionary sense of the word is present, surely his feelings must be hurt. I feel this so much that I very often warn illegitimate boys that others use the term without the slightest regard for its biological significance. They are made happier when they realize that no matter what the accident of their birth, no matter how their parentage was arranged by a rather obscure providence, they are in no way to blame. All that does matter is that they give to society whatever they have to offer, content that society will accept those gifts.

Another point I occasionally make with a child who is dismayed over his illegitimacy is that we should not judge his unwed parents. Whatever they were when he was conceived, we surely have the right to believe it was an act of love, and I suggest that we have no right to criticize the result of that act. I always try to explain to boys, illegitimate, adopted and others, that sex can only be good. To besmirch a good thing is an act against all harmony, love and peace. We have not the opportunity within the confines of a discussion about adoption and illegitimacy to stress the point further, but one of the satisfactions I and my older colleagues have at the school is the knowledge that the marriages our children contract do not appear to be based upon promiscuity or sexual misadventure. They do appear to be based upon a concept of love frequently lacking in the child's own background, sometimes, more happily, abundantly present, and they are certainly based upon the example we seek to set.

The different kinds of maladjustment and difficulty shown by

110

children who have not accepted their birth or adoption are manifold. One such boy refused entirely to go to school for quite a long period. Clinic treatment had been attempted without success. The parents alternately remonstrated and encouraged the child but all the time there was this steadfast refusal. They had told him he was an adopted child and had done their very best to integrate him with other children born to them after his adoption, but all the time there was an undercurrent of envy and jealousy and a strange unexpressed hostility that they felt might signalise something far more dangerous. When he came to us he was moody, and reluctant to form any relationships; when relationships did arise he would be quick to abort them by some insult or unfair demand. He did, nevertheless, ask me to see him privately.

He told me of his adoption and I assured him that I knew of it, but he offered all kinds of doubts about the accuracy of his information. He did not doubt that he was adopted, but doubted the time of the adoption, the description of his true parents, and the information he had been given about the place of his birth. True, the information about his father and mother was somewhat scanty, but the adoptive parents had been replying to his questions with tact and honesty.

Repeatedly over the next three weeks he asked me whether I had found out any other details, and I always replied that I had not as yet completed my enquiries. Finally when these supposed enquiries were complete I sent for him, and told him facts that were really identical with those his parents had given him but put in a different form as if they were the result of much patient detective work. All that I had done was to correspond with his parents who, as always, were willing to give information of any kind they thought would help the situation. Their capacity for giving the information was different to mine, because of the environment of the school, and my capacity fortunately turned out to be more successful. So I told him the one thing I had found out from his parents that they had not told him because they feared that it might tempt him into enquiry which would be embarrassing to all concerned: that his father was a certain high-ranking naval officer.

Immediately, as his parents had feared, he said, 'I'm going to write to him.' I replied, 'Look, he has no interest in you. You have

111

been adopted. You were conceived by somebody to whom your father was not married. That is where the matter has to rest; whether you like it or not is not at issue. We know you don't like it. But you have two loving parents now and goodness knows by some of your tantrums and curious antics at home you set them so many tests that above all you must be convinced that they will put up with almost anything from you out of their love for you. So why chase after an unknown father who has never shown any wish to acknowledge you as his son?'

Some of this was obviously very difficult to say, but no person should attempt to assuage the misery of an adopted or illegitimate child unless his relationship with that child is one of compassion and charity. Repetitions of this information over the succeeding weeks brought about an end to his moodiness and anti-social behaviour. He needed no more time with me and shortly after left the school. It was one of those cases where a real understanding can be acquired very quickly for the devilry of maladjustment had not gone very deep. His difficulties were very superficial, had been mishandled, had now been correctly handled and had cleared the mists of doubt right away. There are such cases that happen from time to time, although the type of boy we usually accept at the school is invariably much more deeply disturbed.

One of the difficulties in conducting interviews with children is their impatience at the irresolution and tentative nature of our discussions. I tell them in those circumstances that I am not prepared to be more dogmatic until we have assembled much more of the jig-saw puzzle and have a coherent problem before us. I explain that if I made a mistake I would forfeit part of their belief in me. Although a mistake can be excused, and I am bound to make some mistakes, the fewer the better for the total progress of the therapeutic treatment. But the impatience often expressed by the child is acute.

A mother once told me that, after she married her husband, 'He always hated my son.' The boy was not her husband's child but was born illegitimately some years before. Her husband never expressed any interest in the boy, nor offered him any of the ordinary paternal gestures made by even a stepfather. When I saw the two parents together I faced them with this fact, saying to the father, 'Do you like the boy or do you hate him?' and he confessed to a very real loathing. He justified this by the boy's bad behaviour, truculent talk and generally uncooperative attitude.

'But surely you do not really believe that this loathing, for such is the word you have used, is merely because the boy is rude or uncouth? Surely this loathing existed long before and it is because of that the uncouthness has arisen, rather than the uncouthness arising for any reasons of its own?'

The father, an intelligent man, agreed with me, and much patient work was done between him and a colleague of mine who saw the man regularly. Gradually we reduced his antipathy to his step-son, and tried to show him that the boy's anger with him was just as much his fault as his son's. In the end, he turned out to be as good a therapist as we could ever have been, and the entire position changed.

In my interviews with the boy I had explained to him such matters as illegitimacy, adoption, why people occasionally had children when they were not married; and I answered a whole host of queries the boy continued to put to me without repeating himself over a period as long as six months. During that time his behaviour was good. Once he was convinced that others were sufficiently interested in him to take up his affairs and do something about them, his maladjustment rapidly declined. On reading his case history one felt rather surprised that his thefts, his callousness, his rudeness and his refusal to attend school could be treated so simply. His father and mother spoke to me after he had left the school, and said, 'Do you know, when we met you, that was the first occasion on which the fact that my wife had had an illegitimate boy was ever mentioned between us? We had never discussed it until that day.' 'Well, it's been discussed *ad nauseum* ever since, so we might perhaps adopt your practice now and never discuss it again!' I replied.

Another boy defined his main difficulty clearly. 'They say they want me at home, but the more they say it the more I doubt it. If only they'd shut up saying it, things would be easier.' His behaviour at home had been very difficult and included a fear of going to school; he had lately refused to go to school at all.

This was another very easy case that improved over a matter of a few months, but as well as this sort of case there are the children

113

whose adoption and illegitimacy have soured them to a terrible extent.

A case that recently occurred in a juvenile court can illustrate a deeper disturbance. A boy had been born illegitimately, and when he was a few months old his mother married another man. The three of them appeared to form a harmonious unit. All promised well. After the marriage another child was born, and then three more. As the children grew up the first-born, the step-son, got into grammar school, but all the others failed to pass the eleven-plus examination. At this point, resentment began to rise in the step-father towards this boy. He could not bear the disappointment of his own children failing when this by-product of his wife's pre-married life had succeeded. His pettiness and anger was evidenced in all kinds of trivial ways; by his handing the jam to the other children first at the tea-table, by little remarks, by deriding references to those who knew too much and swanked that they had gone to the grammar school. It is remarkable that this lad maintained his studies at all, and one assumes this was due to the guidance of one of the teachers at his school who, knowing more about the family than he admitted, was able to give the boy a kindly and firm guidance without in any way making disloyal remarks about the members of his family. At one time this man offered to take the boy abroad with him and his wife. When the step-father asked where the money was coming from, the master said the money would be provided by the school. The step-father said he was not going to have the boy pampered and, despite his wife's entreaties and the boy's pleadings, that foreign holiday was refused.

It was at this point that the first theft took place. The father accepted this as justification of his attitude to the boy. Feeling now that he was the cuckoo in the nest, the boy speedily set about justifying that label, expressing resentment of all the other children, referring to them as dullards in response to the opposite insults at his expense. Bad behaviour and stealing was not evidenced at school where his performance continued to be good.

After an appearance at the juvenile court he was asked to keep an appointment at the local clinic but one weekly appointment is not sufficient to resolve difficulties of this kind. It was better than nothing, and indeed all that a busy and overworked clinic may be able to offer, but it is a pity that appointments did not occur more frequently. The next appearance at the juvenile court was for a theft from a local shop and again the probation order was extended.

Latterly I have heard that the young fellow was successful in achieving three 'A' level passes in G.C.E. but his step-father characteristically refused to tolerate his going to university, although a place was offered on the strength of the 'A' level passes. The last I heard of this young man, quite recently, was that he had appeared again in court and was sentenced to a period in prison. It seems to me that had the results of his step-father's persecution been detected by the time he was, say, fourteen, or had the step-father's full dislike been expressed more violently at the beginning, then perhaps the boy would have had residential treatment at an earlier stage which, of course, offers a chance of success that no imprisonment ever could.

The point of this short case history is not that tragedy arose but that an apparently good situation turned into a very bad one. The step-father could not contain his anger and hatred when he saw his own children faced with the challenge of the cuckoo in the nest. It is sad and ironic that the step-father now regards his anger with his step-son having been perfectly justified because of the young man's presence in prison.

CHAPTER X

Depths of Bastardy

THE HISTORY of Oswald Prince's behaviour difficulties provided by the child guidance clinic showed that he was adopted at the age of six months, and an onset of stealing, smoking and lying had begun when he was about ten years of age. His smoking was of a pathological kind for it involved an accumulation of cigarettes, not in tens or hundreds, but in thousands; and such a hoard could only be accomplished by means of theft from tobacco shops.

There was also a pathological intensity to his untruthfulness. At home he would tell the most extraordinary stories about events that he alleged had happened at school, and at school he would tell atrocious stories about his parents' behaviour. His tone was so convincing that many people would suspend disbelief for quite a long time.

He had been told of his adoption, and his adoptive parents, living in comfortable circumstances, had done all they could for the boy; even when the difficulties emerged they continued to show the most remarkable patience. But when obscene language started they found their bounds of toleration had been exceeded. The obscenities were dreadful in their content and torrential in their flow.

Soon after his arrival at the school Oswald asked if he could have private interviews with me. For the next year I listened to his exaggerations—accusations against his parents, reflections upon teachers, and above all, vile stories about his schoolmates. One of the most repetitive stories of malignant scandal was his accusation that a headmaster of a previous school had had homosexual intercourse with him. His description of the alleged rape was given in delighted and analytic detail.

He spoke of his absolute conviction that sooner or later I would cane him, and refused to believe I had no cane in the study.

'Of course you've got a cane,' he said.

I suggested that if he was so certain I had a cane we should search for it. His search was very thorough, and it took a long time to rearrange the furniture and put things to rights after he had left the room; but needless to say the search was unsuccessful. At the next session, when I suggested that perhaps now he believed I had no such cane, he contradicted me again.

'No, it merely means you've hidden it too cleverly. Perhaps it's under the carpet.'

'You could feel all over that,' I replied, 'as the presence of a cane could easily be detected without ripping the carpet up.'

The next significant discussion we had was about his adoption, and this occupied months of interviews. He told me he was the son of a well-known politician, mentioning the man's name. I asked him who his mother was, and brusquely he said she was a public lavatory attendant, and at that point he broke wind very rudely.

'Why do you make that noise?' I asked. 'Is it to show me what little respect you have for me because I am, in a sense, the father you regard as having disowned you, and in another sense such a lowly parent that all I am fit for is to look after a public lavatory?'

Oswald giggled, and broke wind again. Then followed in his interviews all the unpleasant references to my character that he could imagine, and above all his complete conviction that any analytic session he had with me was merely the prelude to a homosexual attack, as it was to hit him on his bottom. He imagined the cane would be a part of a homosexual attack. In a conventional school his behaviour would certainly have called for severe punishment, and perhaps the punishment chosen would have been that of a thrashing. But would the man giving the thrashing have realized that what he thought he did in the interests of discipline was in fact being distorted by the boy into a homosexual attack in which the cane gave him sexual satisfaction at each impact? I frequently tried to show him his self-contradictions and to lessen his contempt of myself, as removing what was perhaps the only key to his misunderstandings, but the allegations against my character only shifted to the other male staff.

Oswald was almost parasitic with members of the staff; he would demand their time unceasingly and if they indicated that they had some other duty to perform he would criticize them bitterly for their neglect of him. He would come to me and complain that such a staff member had tired of his company. He would go to another teacher, retail to him boastfully some interpretation of mine within the analytic situation, and go yet to a third man to deliver some monstrous sexual anecdote involving all of us. He sought to draw every person of any authority or importance into the maelstrom of his distorted emotional life.

Light came one day when I was taking a visitor round the school. Oswald happened to be seated alone as I entered the school library. As a matter of courtesy I introduced the boy to him by his name of Oswald and there as far as I was concerned the incident was forgotten. But in his private sessions with me Oswald referred to it many times.

'Something very queer happened,' he said. 'When you brought that man into the room I looked up in curiosity. Then you introduced me. I've forgotten his name now, but in bed last night I dreamed that man was my true father.'

This was the first positive thing the boy had ever said to me for over a year. The lying, stealing and obscenities had continued unabated for the past year, but now he slowly began to recognize his mental difficulties. After he had stolen some cigarettes from a staff member he greatly respected, I was able to show him that the theft was really one which showed his great desire to associate himself with that man, to possess understanding, and the quiet confidence that he so wonderfully displayed.

Soon afterwards Oswald asked me to find out more about his real parents, and to discover more about the motives of his adopted parents. Incidentally when a deep analysis is being conducted, it is an error to become involved in any reality situation of this kind, and it is far better to arrange that the boy goes to a colleague to undertake the reality functions. In this case however, it was unlikely that the boy would have spoken the truth with any colleague. And even if the man had heard the truth and undertaken to make the necessary enquiries, little would have been achieved except to provide the boy with a fresh target for abuse, doubt and denigration. Unfortunately, living within the confines of a school and having to accept all its systems, traditions and codes, one becomes involved with these boys' reality situations far more than should be permissible if the analysis were being conducted in a more orthodox way.

The enquiries were completed, and the parents replied to me with customary charm and co-operation. I asked them to write to the boy themselves, telling him I had suggested they do this, so that he could have answers to his questions from people more important to him than I could hope to be. My importance was of analytic and curative significance but it did not equal the importance of the parental influence. The adoptive parents told him his mother's name was La Plata, a woman of Latin American extraction. They explained to him that there had been no trace of her since his adoption at six months old, she was twenty at the time of his birth, and had been a nurse. Since the adoption she had emigrated, they thought, to Canada. Oswald seemed glad to have this information and expressed more than ordinary gratitude that his parents had been so open and honest about it. That evening, however, I had a telephone call from the staff member on duty; Oswald has smashed a hundred plates in the school kitchen. He had taken advantage of the kitchen being unattended after supper, and piled up the plates so that by pulling the bottom one away he caused the whole tower to collapse.

The next day he came to me considerably disturbed to say he had not been aware of what he was doing until the pile of plates was in front of him in the large kitchen. Then he suddenly realized the connection between the surname 'La Plata' and the common noun 'plate', and had smashed the tower. In his disturbed state it was not surprising that his hatred for the biological mother who, to use his own words, had thrown him 'into the gutter', and then departed to look after her public lavatory, should cause him to act out his hatred in such a malicious, destructive way.

Within the school disciplinary system a special committee has charge of the kitchen and Oswald Prince was made to pay for the bulk of that damage out of some money he was required to earn and from his pocket money. Although the lesson thus learned could not alter his attitude to adoption and illegitimacy, we hope it was justifiable to make him pay for the privilege of indulging his neurosis instead of letting others pay for it.

After this incident, although the thefts largely ceased at the school, they continued whenever he spent a week-end or holiday at home. They were mainly money thefts now and I was quick to point out to him the association between the search for the perfect 'mummy' and 'money'. He felt that the maternal springs within his home environment lacked perfection, particularly in view of his disappointment about the La Plata lavatory attendant mummy, and his thefts were carried out in order to acquire a perfect mother instead of the imperfection his rage and misery assured him continued to exist. The biggest theft of all was from a local catholic church, where he broke open two offertory boxes and spent the money on cigarettes. He returned to the scene a week or two later but on that occasion was caught by an angry priest. He was handed over to the police, but when they realized he was under treatment they decided, with the approval of the priest, not to prosecute.

It is not usual for such toleration to be shown to a disturbed boy and I am quite certain that in those circumstances the understanding and charity shown by police and priest far exceeded what any young criminal is entitled to expect. In this situation his anxiety and concern were apparent in a way that none of his previous crimes had ever occasioned. He talked to me miserably about the theft from the church and I was able to show him and he was able to accept that he had been robbing Mother Church.

In his envy for something that had been lost when, again to use his extravagant language, he had been 'flung into the gutter', he now looked for a new mummy, to take him into her arms, sit him on her lap, being his and his alone, and the only invasion of that complete possessiveness was to be expected from the adopted father, in the guise of the angry priest. One can go so far as to say that the theft from the church was planned as a rape of Mother Church, as a way of possessing the mother completely. The boy's utterly purposeless use of the money, and his return to the scene of the crime inviting discovery, shows how far removed from reality his behaviour was.

In his day to day life at the school, he did not form genuine attachments to others at all readily, but was able to assume a friendly, pleasant manner. In a careful analysis of his daily behaviour it was very difficult to distinguish clearly between occasions where the motive was a genuine desire to please, and where it was more calculated. His sexual references continued to be startling and offensive, but not quite as bad as at first, and certainly we did not hear them so often.

Gradually he became more truthful and began also to understand the real purpose of his private analytic sessions. Then one day I received a letter from him.

'*Dear Shaw*. As a result of great mental stress I feel I ought to write to you about a few facts that I cannot bring myself yet to tell you verbally. You may know of my thoughts about associating sexually with boys. So far this is not active and as far as I know no other boy knows of my ideas, but one boy in particular attracts me to such an extent that I can go to any lengths, and have gone to any lengths, to trap him into conversation and delay him about things he is doing so I can spend longer in his company. His name, as I expect you can guess, is Jones. To be quite frank, the strain on me since Jones changed his dormitory to another room has been unbearable. I have wanted so much to go to bed with him. I cannot masturbate with the thought of girls in my head. I used to be able to, but now I can only masturbate if I think of Jones and he occupies all my thoughts when I am in bed. In my thoughts I have been to bed with him and it is to me one of the most thrilling and exciting things in my dream life and I literally long to repeat it. I hope every night I will dream of him and I hope every night that what my imagination tells me I could do, will be done again and again. I know I can't do these things but if some solution is not found soon, I don't know what I shall do.' He then signed himself with his Christian name and added a postscript, 'For goodness sake be careful not to tell Jones of this. He knows nothing and if he did I don't know what I should do to myself or how I could continue to handle the temptation.'

His subsequent interviews with me were concerned with the matter described so urgently and pathetically in his letter. If ever there was a cry from the heart of a person who wished to be relieved of a dreadful burden, it was in this letter, and I was determined to restore this boy to a reasonably full and complete life without this monotonous, masturbatic, homosexual preoccupation.

Disparagingly, the boy had referred to his natural mother as a lavatory attendant. While a description of that kind is intended by the unconscious mind to relieve the thinker of any lasting love for the disparaged object, in fact it accomplishes none of that design, and merely reinforces the feeling of abandonment. This theme was constantly present in our discussions, but his idea that a pseudo love contact with a boy would provide a solution had to be disproved. I urged him to understand that such a relationship could give no ultimate satisfaction any more than all the other tricks he had used to comfort what he considered to be his unloved and unwanted situation.

At present it is not against the law of this land for consenting adults to have homosexual relationships with each other, but while that reduces the possibility of blackmail against the two parties, it is quite ridiculous to expect it to reduce their guilt. A homosexual act is an act that is uncreative and must always be so. It may be that companionship exists between two male adults and it may also be satisfying in the sense that they give to each other an attention and respect that either feels would be denied them if they sought a more normal relationship with a woman, but the fact remains that the two partners in a homosexual embrace cannot continue their relationship without continuing guilt. This is not necessarily a moral issue. Their relationship is a denial of the whole purpose of sexual activity. The consequences of this guilt are not limited to a mere uneasiness but can often be expressed psychically. Psychic punishment often follows the perpetration of unnatural and destructive actions, expressing itself in the form of headaches, psychosomatic disease and other unpleasant symptoms.

At a certain point in our sessions Oswald remarked, 'When I think of all the time I wasted in telling lies all because I thought I could dodge my punishment! What a pity I did not realise that a lie is foolish, for although it may deceive other people it can never deceive the liar.'

So at last the boy had learned, as was indicated in his long letter to me, the advantage of the truth, and that to acknowledge the worst carries the hope that the worst can be understood and improved.

122

With the frankness he now began to develop, his relationships with other people became much less parasitic; although he was searching for his mother he could not understand that the search need not be prosecuted in the school.

He then began to reveal jealousy for his adoptive mother. At times he would express himself with a surprising virulence against, for instance, his mother and father having a holiday together while he was at school. Not only did he resent their holiday together, but he experienced pain at his exclusion from the family activity. It even put into his head the idea of running away from the school to break into his home to discover the exact address of his parents' hotel so that he might join them there. He criticized his parents for enjoying themselves in his absence, and he felt that his mother was conspiring with his father against his interests. He told me of attempts he had made as a much smaller boy to monopolise his mother at home, and how he would join avidly in any slight, petty criticism of his adoptive father. The plans and plots this boy contrived to monopolise his mother's love because in some way he had exaggerated the unfairness of his own rejection by his natural mother, were inexhaustible and imaginative.

At the time he wrote to me he had decided to surrender all demands upon his mother and father. He had been thrown into the gutter, he would accept that; he had been rejected by the adoptive mother, he would accept that. Then when in his fevered imagination people were sympathetic he would say, 'Me, rejected? What a fool you are to think that! I don't want the mother! Look, I've got two breasts of my own,' and then surrender himself to the love of a male.

That situation is woefully common amongst homosexuals, where the 'feminine' partner will say to himself that he has all the attributes of a mother, attributes which he lacked as a child and now envies. It is usually the 'feminine' partner of any homosexual relationship who makes the initial approach, and in this case Oswald made his fantasy approaches to Jones, who for the whole of his school life remained in complete ignorance of it. It is quite likely that, had Oswald not had the opportunity of analytic treatment, he would have been forced to an active expression of his fantasy, but because he was allowed to discuss these matters with somebody he could trust he was able to contain himself.

Oswald showed many problems in the intermediate stage of acting out his parental relationships with members of the staff. When he felt angry with his true mother he would abuse me and break wind at me. He would also attribute base motives to me; but when he realized that, despite all, I was prepared to understand even if it did not command his respect, he ceased to treat me as an object of derision, or as a kind of public lavatory in which he could put all his muck.

Before we came to the end of Oswald's analytic treatment, the homosexual Jones fantasy took one further twist; the desire for Jones and substitute Jones to suck his penis. It was as if he was saying he would never admit to wanting the basic maternal love at the breast, but the need was there; if he himself could be proved to have the nipple then all would be well. Consequently someone had to be found to use his penis as a nipple and if that person existed even in fantasy, then there was temporary satisfaction. Of course, such gratification can never really satisfy, as any perverted act has to be continually repeated. It is the creative act that needs not a repetitive compulsion but a creative re-introduction. Ultimately, Oswald realized the shallowness of his conceit and the continued folly of pretending that he did not want something that all his life he had longed for very much. Towards the end of his sessions with me he made an interesting comment.

'Of course, Shaw, you might have put it much more simply. You could have said: "Fancy thinking, Oswald, you lacked a mother, faking you were one all the time. That's the foolish thing you were thinking." ' I reminded him that whatever my ability was, the speed of an analysis depends upon co-operation and the degree of comprehension shown. Finally he understood the nature of his attempts to come to terms with his own insecurity. The feelings concerning the politician, the lavatory attendant, the cigarettes, his manipulations of all love relationships, the persecution of staff members, the imagined seduction of men, his attempts to seduce me, the curiously significant fantasies about another boy—all led to his realization in the end that the fundamental lack originated in his self-torturing relationship with his absent mother.

I advised him to start writing a diary, and over the next year he wrote a daily journal which was shown to me at weekly intervals. The morbid content gradually diminished and latterly became

124

entirely absent. His aspirations, as expressed in his diary, were those of a normal boy now between sixteen and seventeen years old, and he revealed a lively interest in intellectual matters.

By the time he left us his relationship with his adoptive parents, while not intensely intimate, was one of trust, and as their attitude to him had never been one of denial the relationship became good. His next three of four years were spent away from home at university and as now he is working several hundred miles away from home any difficulties of propinquity to his adoptive parents does not arise.

This story illustrates that despite good will on the part of adoptive parents and high order of intelligence in the adopted baby, some intangible and indefinable quality can give the child the idea that he is unwanted, and the misery of that rejection can turn a boy towards homosexuality. This process need not occur, but it ought to be checked wherever it does. For, whatever the state of the law might be, the Oswalds of this world are condemned to an uncreative, unproductive and miserable life.

CHAPTER XI

Bend Sinister Unbent

PETER QUINBY was a very difficult adopted boy who had smashed glass in automatic machines so that he could steal cigarettes, and this had led to his appearance in the juvenile court. When mal-adjusted children commit such offences as breaking into cigarette machines or any box or container of objects they consider to be of value, it is a reasonable assumption that they are subconsciously breaking into some female part they regard as locked against them.

On one occasion I was involved with a boy who would break into a house only if he could find a very small window through which he could crawl, and before doing so he would remove all his clothing and fold it neatly in a pile. He would then steal an assort-ment of objects which had no practical value for him, but which were highly significant in the psychological sense. The stealing was little more than a secondary symptom to the basic subconscious wish to be back within his mother's womb again, naked, warm, safe and free from all competition for her love.

There is no doubt that housebreaking of this kind, particularly when done by boys or young men, contains a very clear infantile or sexual element. Many years ago I heard of a young housebreaker, lately released from a Borstal institution, who would break into houses only when he knew there was a child's perambulator inside. Having done some damage inside the house, usually by cutting up settees so that the springs shot out, or smashing some objects of furniture, he would then assiduously defecate into the perambulator. This young man seemingly could not understand that he was not a housebreaker or burglar but a messer of prams. It was an obvious case of extreme jealousy of a baby's privileged position in a household, and I would imagine that all could see it except the sufferer himself. It is just another illustration of the great basic desire in all of us, the desire for a mother's love for which we realize there is no substitute.

All these attacks upon closed places, machines, boxes, settees, despoilation of prams and ugly snatchings at an object which, until it was snatched, represented no prize whatsoever, are generally associated with conflict with parents. Such conflict is more common with adoptive parents, because they are not felt by the child to have that deep bond of affection which he demands as his right.

A baby or infant demands not only to be held by its mother at frequent intervals, but to be with her as much as possible. If a child believes his mother has found some superior attraction, even if it is only a game of golf or the entertainment of friends at certain times of the day, he may use it as some justification for the foundation of an infantile feeling of insecurity.

Not only did Peter break into all the automatic machines he could find but he smoked continually, was extremely presumptuous and offensive in his relations with adults, made no progress whatever at school, and in general was uncouth, uncooperative and extremely demanding. Once when I was talking about this boy and his trick of breaking into automatic machines I was a little put out at the innocence of one of my critics who suggested that the best way of stopping him from stealing was to thrash him. I expect that to make a delinquent's act call down upon him the refinements of medieval torture would have the effect of changing his behaviour; after all, the ducking stool did sometimes work with scolds if it did not drown them. But the people who believe so much in punishment can never have lived with a maladjusted delinquent or have had the task of restoring his respect for people and society.

At the first private interview with Peter I became sadly aware of

127

his deep feelings of hostility and resentment, and I felt at times that it would be dangerous to encourage him to express these in any analytic or cathartic form. Ordinarily one can expect aggression and resentment to be expressed and, with suitable understanding on the part of the person attacked, it can be contained. But this time I felt the dangerous strength of his hostility might create a situation in which there could only be psychotic chaos. First he had to be taught how to express his feelings of turbulence and anxiety. There are many instruments by which a child can express these feelings: the aggression of a game of rugby and the shouting at a game of soccer are certainly far greater reactive opportunities than games of tennis or chess. In Peter's case we found he would spend many hours in the music room in what appeared to be a constructive manner, but nevertheless the sounds that to others appeared to be of a musical nature were to him sounds of hostility. As Charlie Chaplin has remarked, there is sometimes little difference between a criminal and an artist. They are, he has said, psychologically akin, as both have a burning flame of impulse, a vision and a deep sense of lawlessness.

I was extremely fortunate that this boy was a creative genius, and in my private sessions with him I harnessed his poetry, music and literature to help him express his dreadful thoughts and see that volcanically eruptive feelings can be understood and brought under control. Through the medium of his art he was able to appreciate the reality of situations that existed at home: concern for his parents' health, for instance. Despite my early fears his aggression and disturbance were brought partly under his own control more easily than anyone had expected.

With great reluctance, and much blushing and stammering, he told me of a dream which had concerned his adoptive mother.

'It is difficult to tell you, Shaw,' he said, 'because I have never dreamed anything like this before, and I think it has something to do with you telling me how difficult it is for me to accept my adoption and illegitimacy. Anyhow, in the dream I was in bed with my mother and I pulled down her nightdress and looked at her breasts. At first she refused to let me pull off her clothes, but in the end she didn't mind.'

I asked him how far he had undressed his mother, and he said: 'Only down to the waist, all I wanted was her breasts.'

128

'Surely you realize,' I said, 'that those cigarettes you hoard and smoke are associated very closely with your dream, and are near to something you think you have forfeited for ever. Do you not see that the cigarette is your mother's nipple, thought by you to be forfeit, and thus you condemn yourself to a theft of the orally-needed object, an object which you feel is forbidden to you?

Over the next few weeks we discussed in detail his feelings on smashing the glass of a machine, and compared them with the dream feeling of exposing his mother's breasts. He told me he felt that retaliation would somehow occur if he continued his snatching and raping of the automatic machines. Over the past few weeks he had felt an almost overpowering compulsion to smash crockery in the kitchen, desks in the classrooms and other people's property, the only exceptions being the piano and various possessions of his connected with English and poetry lessons. He had managed to control this desire to smash, but he could feel hysteria inside him.

'I realize this hysteria has been building up, waiting to get out,' he wrote. 'It seems to be telling me that somehow I've taken too much in the past and now I am going to be punished for what I've thieved. The situation is ludicrous. Is there anything I can do about it, please?' The note ended: 'Love from Peter.'

But we reached a complete conversational impasse in his next session; it was impossible to get him to talk or to listen to me. After that session he wrote another note to me.

'Dear Shaw, Last term I sent you a chit asking if I could write to you if there was anything I did not care to say. You said I could: here is the note. During all this talk about automatic machines and hysteria and everything else there is a secret I have held back all the time, and even now I can only tell it to you on condition that you never mention it to me in the study. Ever since I can remember, I have had a compulsion to feel inside women's pockets, and once I took a razor blade with me on to a bus so that I could sit beside a woman and, if her pocket was on the outside of her clothes, I could quietly cut away the stitching and so take away the outside of the pocket. A woman did sit next to me and I got my blade started, but she began to fidget so I couldn't complete what I had set out to do. The next time I tried it I went on top of the bus and that time I had a kind of pointed penknife which made the cutting of the stitches easier and I was able to cut off the pocket of the

129

young woman sitting next to me. She never felt a thing, and I took the pocket home and hid it beneath the floorboards of my bedroom. You may not be able to believe it, Shaw, but now I have nearly fifty pockets I have pinched that way. Sometimes I get them from cloakrooms, and at my last school I went into the staff cloakrooms to cut off women teachers' pockets. There they all are at home, and what I do when I am feeling fed up or when some of these horrible thoughts get me is to take them from their hiding place and masturbate over them. That's the thing I can't tell you. What can I do about it? Somebody's got to stop me thinking about and doing such things. Will you?' Again the letter was signed 'Love from Peter'.

Despite his stated wish that we should not discuss the contents of this letter, nevertheless he began to do so. A few weeks later he wrote to me again.

'Lately I am worried and unsettled by numerous things: smoking, cancer, death, funny dreams, girls, my future, and a fanatical desire to be famous, but what I have to say will shock you more than all that. When masturbating sometimes, I think that I must have sexual intercourse with my mother. It doesn't seem to connect with anything to do with her pockets or with other women's pockets, but I'm sure the idea of having intercourse with her is something to do with the same thing. I didn't want to tell you this at all but it might help me a lot if I get it off my chest. It's not a hard luck story, I'm past that stage.'

It must be remembered that this boy had been rejected by his biological parents, and now feared or believed the rejection was about to be repeated by his adoptive parents. This dual sense of rejection seems to be inseparable from what children consider to be the stain of adoption. During all the discussion and correspondence set out above, Peter made constant references to his illegitimacy, wondering what others would think of such a thing if they discovered it. As I have said before, reassurance has only a minor part to play in such fears.

We discussed further his strange theft of a large number of women's coat pockets. The fact that the thefts were sexually motivated were clearly shown by his sexual activity with them at certain intervals. I asked him what might have appeared a very naive question to one of his sexual awareness, if he knew where

130

babies came from. He replied affirmatively. I then said it was surprising that he had to go about stealing, as it were, kangaroos' pouches or, in other words, ladies' vaginas, to investigate more closely this mystery of birth. His reaction to that was electric. He jumped from his chair, rushed out of the room, rushed back again and said excitedly, and with a curious theatrical finality, 'My God, you've hit it!'

Hit it perhaps we had. It was only an intermediate target, but it was sufficient to stop the compulsive obsession of stealing women's pockets, because he now knew what he really sought.

'Where did I come from? Why was I abandoned? Why, out of all the boys I know, am I the only one to have been abandoned?'

Although the dangerous trickery on buses now ceased it was followed by curious reading of newspaper items about abandoned or unwanted children, and as a member of the school library committee he was very active in enlisting support for a lecture by the local Children's Officer. Through his sessions with me he understood that these social activities were motivated by personal feelings masquerading under a socio-political label, and this helped him to overcome the shock of his discovery about the pockets. Because of his masturbation with the stolen objects it was clear that, in some way, he imagined himself to be his father, or at least imagined himself to be in the position of potency and power that a father represented. His adoptive father was so frequently in hospital that the poor man was virtually incapable of filling any active heroic role in the mind of the boy who so keenly desired a father-hero figure. So Peter became his own father, and possessed his mother himself. In his dreams he had looked at her breasts, and had had intercourse with her. The masturbatic feeling with regard to the stolen objects was an expression of the same perverted impulse carried out in solitude so that any social disapproval could be expressed only by himself, the sufferer, and never by an avenging social agency such as that which existed when, for example, he would break into the automatic machine to gain possession of his mother's breasts.

His confession in the letter that he was fearful of cancer was also illuminating. He had read much of the correspondence on the relation between cigarette-smoking and lung cancer but, unlike most boys at the school, continued to smoke. He no longer took

131

his cigarettes by theft, but his smoking was as guilt-ridden as his masturbation and his behaviour with pockets on buses. It was not surprising, therefore, that smoking, a symbolic feeding at the breast, had now become something that symbolized his entire regressive pattern which had to be given up if ever he was to achieve real maturity.

I usually see children for three-quarters of an hour at the same time daily. The regularity of an analytic appointment is something that must be maintained so that attempts on the analysand's part to evade the appointments can be correctly assessed, and so that they can be more easily integrated with the school timetable. But, from the very beginning, Peter's sessions were characterized by the fact that he was constantly seeking more than his share, though sometimes he was moved to evade the appointments altogether. But I now felt it necessary to see Peter daily, even at week-ends, not because of any urgency, but because of the almost terrifying variety of his fears and fantasies. If ever it was impracticable to see him one day I would see him twice, early and late, on the previous day. During these particularly active weeks a total fusion of all the various factors that had been emerging was sought, and by discussing the peculiar sexual relationship with his mother, and all the other manifold factors that have been revealed above, it was possible to fit the jig-saw of the entire analysis together. It is not often we are able to take the thousand and one pieces of the jig-saw and correlate them so successfully, but in this case there was a surprisingly complete synthesis. After several sessions of this accomplishment Peter suddenly burst into tears, and his sobbing was audible and unrestrained.

Wonderfully clear it was, that for the first time Peter Quinby had seen in himself the small, pathetic, babyish, deprived child. The full realization, with all its therapeutic significance, cemented the jig-saw into a permanent pattern which is likely to be kept by the boy for the rest of his life.

With the conclusion of the successful analysis the boy had achieved a growth to maturity which enabled him to do things that he could not previously have contemplated. Needless to say his terrors departed. His honesty, which had been there all the time, now became uppermost; and his creativity, instead of being perverted, was allowed its full expression. To some extent his interest in piano-playing waned; it had always been a rather erratic entertainment for him, and its place was taken by the more introverted, contemplative pleasure of listening to classical records and attending symphony concerts. His main imaginative work was the production of fertile stories and dazzling literary compositions. It was not a surprise, therefore, when he elected to read English at university, and quite recently he obtained a first class honours degree in that subject. He is now working in a managerial capacity for a commercial firm.

Quite recently he has introduced us to his fiancée, and even more recently has sent us a list from which we may choose our wedding present at their marriage.

Having been discovered lying wrapped in several layers of old newspaper, Ralph Smith was taken into an orphanage; his parents were never traced. So far as the records can tell us, and from conversation with members of the staff, we believe he was happy at the orphanage. At the age of three he was adopted.

An adoption at three years old, of a child who is sooner or later going to discover his unusual background, cannot always be a good thing. A very complex set of symptoms began to appear when Ralph was twelve. Symptoms do not suddenly develop, the seeds were germinating from the time he left the orphanage to join his adoptive parents. But it seems likely that if he had been left alone in the orphanage his future would have been less confusing. In a well conducted residential home as his was, he would have been no different to many of his fellows. After he left the home, and later discovered that his father and mother were not his true parents, he became different. If only that difference could have been noticed when he was the three-year-old, grasping his own little bundle of goods to get into his new parents' car to travel to what was to be for the first time in his life a domestic background.

When Ralph first came to us he was thirteen years old and showing many tempestuous difficulties. He was continually stealing, in a pointless and purposeless way. He was utterly incapable of obeying simple and commonsense rules: for example, when fined in the school court by which the internal school discipline is maintained he demonstrated his complete rejection of all discipline within the school by climbing up a very high drainpipe and

133

refusing to come down from the roof until he had guarantees that he would never again be criticized. It was impossible to prevent his delinquencies, both within and without the school, and it was his complete refusal to accept any responsibility for his actions that gave rise to his social difficulties.

Unknown to the adoption society or the orphanage, Ralph's adoptive father had been divorced from a previous wife. Although he was in good financial circumstances, he was an insecure and unconfident man who did not enjoy an easy relationship with his second wife. The woman showed a subtle but violent ambivalence to her husband, and after the first two years of her marriage she expressed intense hostility against the divorced wife. When we discovered the full truth of the marital difficulties it seemed almost impossible to imagine any worse disharmony.

Mrs Smith displayed a tearful self-sympathy for her early struggles before she was married. All employers she said, were cruel, all managers unreasonable and all workmates likely to gain some advantage over her unless she was constantly alert. In her frequent rages she had attacked her husband by hitting him with chairs, and on one occasion a vacuum cleaner; to avoid these physical attacks he would barricade himself in a room. Once he had fled to the attic and, piling the usual oddments one finds in an attic upon the trap door, sat on it himself to prevent his wife's access.

At other times this frightened husband would show a different attitude and try to preserve peace within the house by an icy silence. He refused to show the slightest affection for any of those now dependant upon him, with the exception of the son of his previous marriage. This boy was five years older than Ralph, and in a position of privilege of an almost unprecedented kind.

Ralph's thefts started at home and, through the advice of a well meaning neighbour aware of the family tensions, the boy was sent to stay with an aunt so that he might have some escape from the disharmonies within the household. If this had been envisaged as a permanent arrangement the considerable understanding and skill shown by the aunt might have remedied Ralph's difficulties, but those planning the change thought a stay of four or five weeks long enough to effect a cure of Ralph's troubles. Not long after his return home, Ralph was referred to us.

Nail-biting, stealing and lying were familiar enough to us, but we were exasperated to discover that at night he crept to the school garages and, by skilfully picking locks, took cars belonging to staff members. Fortunately they were returned without harm; but such a symptom is indeed ominous for it almost invariably escalates to serious smash-and-grab type raids. As a symptom, bicycle-stealing in the past used to be one of the most difficult conditions to treat; that difficulty has now been replaced by those adolescents who interfere with other people's cars and motor-cycles.

Life with Ralph was never without incident, but he did begin to quieten down: partly because he saw we were not going to be tricked into any violent reaction against him, partly because he knew we were seeking to understand the nature of his own lack of trust and faith in others, and also because, imperceptibly, a patient and good moral attitude on the part of an adult must score results even if such results lack speedy response. But an innate pessimism prevented him from believing any good could come from trust in other people, and in fact he never did trust me. All the time he was at the school he was the central source of criticism of my actions, and if there was any opportunity to be against authority, Ralph seized that opportunity. It was only towards the end of his stay at the school that his attitude changed and he made a contribution to the self-governing system within the school instead of seeking to destroy all that others could create. Despite his failure to trust me he did trust a valued colleague, and would discuss his difficulties with him.

The first revelation he made was that by theft he had amassed a collection of forty-three rings. Most had been stolen from jeweller's shops. As with so many collectors there appeared to be a compulsive desire to add to an accumulation of similar objects. He once told my colleague that, having stolen a ring, he would admire it for only two or three moments before adding it to a list. Having once listed it, it then joined the other things, hidden in a box lined with cotton wool. Having once put the ring into the box, his interest was then exhausted.

Whenever Ralph discussed these rings with his analyst, images of marriage arose very quickly. The rings were all symbolic of a marriage that had not occurred, and when the promise of marriage offered by adoption had also failed it led to the unconsciously dictated thefts of the visible signs of marriage and a man's love for his wife. In this persistent and compulsive manner, the boy collected the tangible evidence of love and marriage which, in his family, was clearly to be seen did not exist.

It was nearly two years before the boy one day asked his analyst if he might be able to return the rings. A year after that he managed to return some of them anonymously. In the case of the shops he could remember, he made the restitution accompanied by a member of staff. The source of some of his thefts was not known, and so the reparation the boy wished to make at this later stage was partly prevented. It was decided to send the residue anonymously to the orphanage in which he had lived. Whilst this was not an entirely adequate solution, it was an extreme step towards this boy's moral regeneration. An act of that kind is useless if it comes as a response to persuasion on the part of a well meaning adult, but if worked out by the boy it can have great therapeutic value.

Some time later he became troubled by nightmares. He would awake in the early hours of the morning, screaming and shrieking. One of the difficulties of understanding these nightmares was that he could not describe the nature of the horror, nor could he draw pictures of it. All he knew was that the unnamed dread, if allowed to run uncontrolled, would lead to his total annihilation. It was as if he believed he was going to hell.

As the analysis progressed it became possible for the boy to say there was some idea of symmetry in the nightmare dream, and the full horror was experienced when that sense of symmetry was broken. If everything in the dream could be maintained in an orderly arrangement, then the horror would not emerge, but once the symmetry was disturbed, he felt the horrible danger of his personality being destroyed.

The boy came to understand his terrified quest for an orderly, unflustered situation within a normal family relationship. In every relationship he had experienced since his adoption there had been a marked lack of symmetry and order, and his fear now expressed itself in this terrifying nightmare.

In confidential therapeutic conversation, very rapid, indeed sensational, relief of symptoms can be achieved, but the mere absence of a symptom does not mean its basic cause also has disappeared. The need to act out the symptom in an anti-social manner no longer exists as it is being acted out within the therapeutic interview instead, but a faulty optimism has to be guarded against unceasingly. Despite the cessation of Ralph's nightmares, it was evident that certain other difficulties continued.

For example, Ralph never felt secure about his attitude to cars or motorcycles. A curious drawing was executed in one of his art lessons which pictured several objects: books, chairs, tables and all the usual furnishings of a sitting room. Somewhere on every article were the initials 'HSO'. His teacher pointed this out to him, but he had no solution to offer. In the night, the teacher was awakened from his sleep by Ralph anxiously shaking his shoulder.

'I know what that 'HSO' means that we were talking about this morning', he said. 'It's terribly important. Can I see you?'

Rallying his senses, the teacher agreed and Ralph started a long account of his car and motorcycle thefts.

'I know what it all is. A long time ago my aunt committed suicide. It wasn't the aunt I lived with when all the rows were going on at home but another aunt who was staying in our house. One day when I got up and came down to breakfast, I realized that something very terrible had happened and the next day they told me that my aunt had died in the night and there had been an awful rumpus. At first they wouldn't tell me how she'd died and they tried to make me think her death was quite natural, but I soon found out that she had committed suicide. It was only when I read the papers that I found out she'd drunk some concentrated sulphuric acid. The formula for sulphuric acid is H_2SO_4 and there's the 'HSO' on all the furniture in the picture I did in class yesterday.'

He went back to bed and the conversation was continued the next morning. Dramatically the session that took place the morning after the interrupted night speedily established that H_2SO_4 was also contained in the accumulators of motorcars. The boy's grief (not so much for the fact of an aunt's death, for he had no particular regard for her, but grief for her decease as a mother) was too much for him to accept. It was therefore repressed, and later emerged in anti-social behaviour. Why Ralph should repress the suicide, and later try to express it unconsciously in terms of interference with sulphuric acid and motorcars, are questions that cannot fully be answered. We decided that his folly with cars was in some way connected with the suicide of his aunt, and since the compulsive car thieving soon ceased after that point, we can only assume the logic of our explanation had some quality of corrrectness which alternatives did not offer. In dealing with infantile impulses it is not possible to assume that words used are understood by the hearer in the way intended.

Ralph's mental condition continued to improve, but he doubted the possibility of rapprochement at his home.

'I can never go back to my adoptive parents,' he said. 'I go through the performance of writing to them from time to time, and they send me birthday and Christmas presents, but there is nothing between us of any value. Is there no way I can admit this to them without hurting their feelings any more than they have already been hurt?'

With some nervousness, and considerable caution, we approached the parents to establish what real interest they had in Ralph. We were relieved when our approach elicited the fact that their interest was very slight: they were prepared to go through the conventional gestures, but we agreed it would be stupid for the boy to make his permanent home in their residence.

A recent letter from Ralph, who is working happily in Australia as an accountant, included an interesting remark.

'You will be interested to hear my hoarding instincts continue. I have saved several hundred pounds and suitably invested this as the basis for the purchase of a house for my future marriage. I hesitated a long time over the decision to propose to my girl because my own path in these respects has been a pretty thorny one, but I think that those experiences are all now so completely in the past, that my own marriage can be a good one. At all events I am aware of many mistakes of greed and selfishness that I shall never repeat now.'

He ended his letter by a very appreciative remark concerning the colleague who had been closest to him. The type of letter he sent to us during the first few years after he had left school indicated quite clearly that the school constituted his family; and I suspect the orphanage could have been a good family if he had never been adopted at all.

When adopted children become maladjusted, it is my experience that the basic motives of the adopters have been suspect. The type of child we are likely to see is not the one brought up by harmonious sensible adoptive parents, but the child who through no fault of his own has broken down into anti-social manifestations of insecurity. However well-intentioned the adoptive parents, they cannot escape all blame when this occurs. The adopted child is far more vulnerable to doubts and disappointments than are more fortunate children, and extra care is called for. A further complexity arises from the distortion or refusal by the child of the facts of his origin, often avoided when the home atmosphere is honest and open, and the child is therefore more willing to trust his adopted parents. Evasion of the subject of upbringing in a relationship already disturbed will result in total suspicion, after which any attempt to rationalize the parents' omission will become increasingly difficult.

Adopters have very different motives, ideas and social backgrounds and much will depend upon their own upbringing as children. These factors play a part, not only in their decision to adopt, but in the type of child they seek to adopt, and perhaps more important than any other factor is the type of reaction they unconsciously seek from the child. We have had adoptive parents who are angry that the naughty child has not shown more appreciation at their own sacrifice. Although these are vastly outnumbered by adoptive parents who have shown goodness and care for the adopted child despite some anti-social breakdown, nevertheless the gratitude-seekers do exist and, in our experience, they should be told of the immorality of their attitude.

We are most fortunate today that adoption is conducted upon a scientific and humane basis that was not always the case at the time of adoptions I have spoken of. Two children we have had were adopted by spinsters, and their sufferings were intense: it is virtually impossible now for a spinster to satisfy her own searching for connubial love by adopting a boy. They were both used by the adoptive spinsters as substitute husbands. Today, wide enquiries are made to ensure that concern is shown not only for the welfare of the child but for the adopting parents also. The system is administered by trained professionals and controlled by far-seeking Children's Committees, and it is unlikely that a child will be given to unsuitable parents. If these judgments are combined with a genuine charity and compassion, with respect for the feelings of adopter and adoptee alike, then failures should be rare indeed.

CHAPTER XII

The Symbols of a Thief

WILLIAM EVANS' mother was angry when she discovered she was pregnant and unsuccessfully tried to procure an abortion. Her dislike of pregnancy was something more than selfishness for she developed a serious depressive illness after the baby's birth and cruelly neglected him for the first two years of his life. At the end of that period the poor woman became a patient in a mental hospital, and when William was four years of age she committed suicide.

His father then went to live with another woman, taking the boy with him, but he soon started drinking and this led him to neglect the child. The woman died within a year, and at that point the father abandoned the boy and disappeared. William was then five, and he was looked after by an aunt and uncle until he came to us.

The aunt described him to us as a little animal who dirtied his trousers, wet the bed and even wet the walls of the bedroom rather than use a chamber pot or the lavatory. She described his violence when thwarted, the temper tantrums when he bit and fought. The aunt could not be blamed for this; she was an excellent woman who had handled William with care and wisdom.

At the age of ten William became seriously ill and was admitted to hospital; there he contracted pneumonia and lay helpless for many weeks. When he returned to his aunt's home he was much more subdued and manageable. (We later asked many questions of

141

the hospital and doctors involved, but it was never possible to obtain a definition of the original vague but apparently significant ailment.)

The improved behaviour did not last long, however, and he was found to be pilfering from shops. At school he had become a leader and a bully who invariably chose as his companions older boys of bad behaviour. Soon the stealing became more serious; he made frequent journeys to Woolworths and Marks and Spencers, helping himself from the counters and, when detected, invariably giving the excuse that he had been about to pay for the article.

When he arrived at the school at the age of nearly eleven years, he had a record of many years of stealing and pilfering. He showed much anxiety and guilt feeling, but in a strangely unrelated way—he could give a truthful and accurate account of his delinquency but without displaying any real feeling, almost as if he were talking about another person. He was impassive, and when addressed at any length he showed an almost complete inability to pay attention. Whenever direct verbal reference was made to his delinquencies, he dismissed the matter and always referred to it as something that had happened in the past and would never recur. He was not lacking in moral feeling but that feeling was entirely separated from his conscious personality. Such a split personality is extremely serious, for it is difficult to treat delinquency when there is such total denial of responsibility.

When his psycho-therapeutic sessions had been fairly launched, the first fact that emerged was his dislike of his uncle. The aunt, a good woman, had not cared to speak of her true feelings about her husband. He was an irritable, violent man, whose impatience was exacerbated by arthritis which finally rendered him completely bed-ridden. The boy spoke of his uncle's anger, saying, 'I like my aunt because she stops my uncle thrashing me,' and, 'The police once told him not to thrash me.'

He was very concerned over his mother's suicide. When speaking of it his tears flowed and his conversation was hysterical. It was an event that he could not have witnessed, but nevertheless he imagined it with such a clarity that it was almost as if he had seen it happen. His confusion and incoherence over this seemed to be related to stealing bicycles. He repeated to me about twenty times, 'I stole bicycles to get money for them.' But when I asked him

142

what he did with the money his replies were always vague.

He then told me that his own father had also thrashed him before he joined his uncle and aunt; on one occasion he had run out of the house screaming for help and on his return had been kept on bread and water for the week-end. I did not know whether or not to believe these stories. He then mentioned his incontinence, and said it was surprising that since he and I had been talking together his bed-wetting and other soiling had ceased.

However he continued to steal. Bicycles attracted him fatally, but having stolen one he was frightened to bring it back to the school for fear of admitting to himself and others that he had again committed a delinquent act. It was never safe to leave him in the staff room for immediately, when the adult left the room, his eyes would roam, looking for something to steal. His thefts were innumerable; frequently they were of small objects, but more often money which was invariably spent on cigarettes. We explained to him that the cigarettes was something he sucked, and the two round wheels of the bicycles he stole represented the breasts he so dearly wished to have.

We never allowed ourselves to forget that not only was this child unwanted during the first five years of his life, but that he had been unwanted even when he was within his mother's body. The woman's guilt, later expressed by her suicide, must have been sufficiently strong for her to neglect this little baby atrociously. It left permanent scars on William, for he went on stealing things he could suck, or contemplate as breasts. But he had no conscious knowledge why those things exercised such an overwhelming attraction for him.

He talked at great length of his experiences before he joined his aunt and uncle. On one occasion when his father was beating him his penis had gone stiff, prompting him to hold it for protection during the beating. With seeming irrelevance he then remarked that his mother once said to him, 'If I catch you playing with your starling (which was evidently her word for penis) it will be cut off and then you will have to wee out of your bottom.'

Such threats, which the boy told me he half believed, go far to explain the trials the aunt had to undergo when William first went to her. In the strange way the unconscious mind has, he was working out both the father's action and the mother's threat when he soiled

143

in the manner which so distressed his aunt. It also caused her to have to rebuke him which further emphasized the boy's feeling that he was forlorn and alone.

As time went on the thefts decreased as the boy's fundamental needs were satisfied by us as far as possible. No person on earth could make up to that boy for what he had lost, but everybody who understood could do something to lessen the sense of loss. After two years he went home to his aunt for a holiday, and she was delighted with the different William she now saw. She had made plans for William's holiday, and his response was such that he added to her pleasure. The fact that his response and gratitude had given her such delight was one of the most significant discoveries he made in those thwarted years of his life.

Unfortunately there was still difficulty in the family. Her husband's health had continued to deteriorate, and being confined to his bed had made the man even more irritable and over-sensitive. He was disagreeable and unreasonable with his wife, and he now believed his illness had been partly caused by worrying over William and that if the boy had never come to live with them his illness would not now be so severe. Quite naturally William began to react against these unjust accusations and his aunt wondered if it was altogether wise that his holidays should continue. William, his aunt and I met to discuss the problem. I emphasized we could understand the point of view of both William and his aunt but we were not entitled to neglect her husband's view even if we had little sympathy with it.

William understood and said he thought he could stand provocation at his uncle's home now, and if on subsequent holidays he found his temper rising, he would write to us and ask that the holiday be curtailed. Such an attitude, so divorced from the split we have described, showed how deep and reasonable was the boy's change of attitude.

This case illustrates the negative aspects of punishment and the positive aspects, not only of giving love, but of acknowledging that it is the quest for love that so often causes theft. The stolen objects symbolized the love William had been denied; when love was assured his symbolic theft of love could be abandoned.

Albert Bishop's stealing started when he was ten and a half years old and he came to the school six month's later. For most of his life he had lived with extremely quarrelsome parents. When we first interviewed his mother she seemed a pleasant and truthful woman, deeply interested in Albert's welfare and the rest of her family. But she soon began to speak bitterly of her husband's accusations that she was a prostitute, accusations, she told me, that were flung at her in front of the children. She mentioned her innocent friendships with men and her husband's persecutory suspicion of such friendships. She claimed he had told Albert that it was her fault that he had to be sent away from home.

Albert's schoolteacher, a man of exceptional insight and kindness, had remarked: 'If all who deal with Albert had the kindly influence he meets at school, he would never have been involved in the trouble which arises when he goes home after school. But having found ways of getting things for nothing he eventually became a menace to the other boys at school. If only the influences at home were removed, this boy could do exceedingly well with his quick brain.'

Indeed something had gone wrong at home, but the boy had withstood the influences for many years before beginning to steal as a way of externalizing those difficulties.

When he first came to us, he was superficially calm and self-contained, but his lack of spontaneity and boyishness indicated that he was only prepared to make contact with us through a limited part of his total personality. Whenever the conversation approached certain personal matters, he became tense and anxious, and it was clear that under the composed facade he was a dreadfully worried child.

He was genuinely perplexed both about the origins and circumstances of the stealing. At a very early interview he told me he was greatly puzzled when he threw away three shillings he had stolen. There was obviously some very deep-seated emotional need which motivated his behaviour. With his gradual acceptance of the stability and calm of the school environment his attitude improved, although the stealing persisted.

The main difficulty after the first few months was from the damnable kind of letter he was receiving from his mother. Although our first impression of Mrs Bishop had been pleasant we had since

145

had cause to review that impression. In one such letter, she complained bitterly about the rancour shown by her husband. The two were now separated, but appeared to create unnecessary opportunities for meeting each other, mainly, it seemed, in order to say unkind and wounding things. Mrs Bishop would then write to William with details of the encounters, treating him not as a son but as somebody to whom she could pour out the most intimate confidences.

'I do wish you were home again,' she wrote. 'It is terrible not having you here and feeling that when I am asleep at night there is nobody in the house to look after me. It is no good expecting anything from your father. I met him in the street the other day and all I got was abuse. I wish something could be done about it; if only you were bigger and older I'm certain you would stand up for your dear mother.'

Such a letter, treating Albert as an adult rather than a boy, was sinister both in its expression and unconscious intent. It was difficult to criticize Mrs Bishop directly because Albert had shown us the letters under the seal of secrecy, and had we told her of our knowledge she would have protested to her son in a wounding manner with further unfortunate effects upon him. The next letter contained angry abuse of her husband and enclosed a note that she herself had received from him. The note said: 'I called but you were out. If you'd been in I don't expect you would have let me in to spoil your nice clean house by my dirty person, which in any case, I expect would have been full of your boy-friends so I wouldn't have been wanted.'

Mrs Bishops' general misuse of Albert, her intimate letters to him and her continual involvement of him in her marital strife and bitterness hindered his progress. In as kind a manner as possible we explained that a boy should never become involved in the disputes or difficulties of adults. She agreed immediately with this idea, and expressed herself horrified that anybody could ever hold a contrary view, but it was clear to us that she could not relate such a protestation of belief to her own behaviour.

Albert's intention in his schoolwork was to give the minimum of compliance necessary, but certainly to give that much and convincingly. It amounted to joining in with games, athletics and other pursuits, and producing a bright smile at the right time. This was his defence against self-realization; he showed a general nervousness of what he would have termed dangerous involvements. He tended to feel his way delicately around them, never plunging boldly in, and he was vulnerable to emotional challenge.

Although his mother's unwise letters continued, we never found any real sexual component to aggravate his evident distress. This was especially surprising in view of the patent fact that his mother was using him as a love object of an age equivalent to her own. It was clear at times that his own sexual role puzzled and disconcerted him but this enigma yielded quickly to ordinary intellectual pursuits. His self-discipline and repression of emotion could, we felt, be overcome; he greatly needed affection and support, and had replaced these with persistent stealing, which he found puzzling.

How stupid it would have been to punish Albert Bishop! Action of a repressive kind by adults whose respect he sought would have inhibited him even more. Punishment would have merely produced a low-spirited boy who might have pleased silly people who equate good behaviour with a child who gives no trouble. But the underground persistence of dishonesty and compromise, showing only an external adjustment, would eventually have produced a hardened delinquent. We avoided all forms of retaliatory punishment, though, needless to say, this was sometimes difficult; it is easy to believe that a thief is benefitting from his thefts even if he never has anything of a tangible nature to show for all the trouble he had in perpetrating them.

'You are not stealing the thing that you think you steal,' I told Albert. 'It's all a useless business and you and I had better find out why it is useless and why you do it. Every time you pinch something I will give you a shilling, and as you usually manage to steal things without being caught I will double the amount when you escape detection.'

The boy's astonishment was considerable. For the first time in his life, there was tolerance for something which hitherto had caused unanimous disapproval. Quickly he put me to the test, and stole repeatedly. Many shillings had to be given to him to keep my promise, but one day he came to me.

'I don't know what you've done,' he said. 'But I haven't stolen now for over two months.'

I replied that it was what he himself had done that mattered. He understood, but more important than the technique treatment was

147

the fact that he could feel he was within distance of obtaining what he sought, without stealing.

Cowardice causes those who fear action to cavil over the actions of others. Many have criticized us and our techniques, especially the one in the case of Albert Bishop. Those who criticize are probably incapable of turning an unhappy, dishonest boy into an honest, happy one, and their fearfulness can be safely ignored as not coming from those whose opinions are worthy of respect. Sometimes therapy can fail, I admit; but in this case it was entirely successful. The boy's stealing ceased completely, despite the very real commercial advantage to him of the shilling reward every time he stole. It revealed that Albert was searching for something that the theft symbolized much more than the generally useless objects he stole.

No longer did Albert look to the skies to see what the clouds threatened, instead he would search the horizon for the rising sun. His games were now played with zest that completely belied his erstwhile listless obedience, and he tackled his lessons with an excited enthusiasm. His attitude to his schoolmates was one of carefree spontaneity, and to adults he showed not only respect but an ease which showed that trust had taken the place of doubt.

Albert Bishop read psychology at University and is now working in that field. He is married and his wife is expecting their first child soon.

CHAPTER XIII

Theft from Vampirism

WHEN Bernard Chard came to us he was a compulsive thief and school truant, and demonstrated an extraordinary hostility to his father. This poor man had suffered from all kinds of psychosomatic diseases for all his life, and was a very weak character. While interested in his four children he had little or no contact with them. He seemed quite unable to withstand his wife's temper tantrums, or retain a job at the salary sufficient to support his family. Over the preceding six years he had had twenty-five different jobs, and although he was not dishonest or lazy such a record did not recommend him to any potential employer.

Bernard's mother had been brought up in an orphanage. During the six years prior to the boy's arrival with us, her capacity to cope with the large family had deteriorated enormously and, perhaps with some justification, she had developed a hostile attitude towards her husband. When Bernard was nine she had had an attack of religious mania. She had neglected the house completely but at the same time had over-protected the children, never allowing them out of her room at night and seldom allowing them even to leave the house to attend school. She had inculcated in the children a hostile attitude towards their father.

Various social workers had tried to persuade her to accept some form of treatment. On one occasion she had been interviewed by a psychiatrist, but that interview led to the involvement of the

psychiatrist in her antagonistic attacks and she made many slander-
ous remarks about him in the neighbourhood.

The children were by then running wild. They smashed windows,
fought in the streets, insulted adult neighbours. When their father
punished them it strengthened the hostility in them. Shortly afterwards the father was tragically killed in a road accident. Soon afterwards the children were taken out of their mother's care as she was
now certifiable, and because of his very difficult behaviour Bernard
came to our school.

For the first four weeks of his residence with us Bernard suffered
from an acute anxiety about the separation from his mother, and
broke down into weeping whenever he thought of her. His hostility
for his father, now dead, transferred to all male adults within the
school's environs. It was difficult to make him understand that his
mother's illness was the reason for his separation from her, and
that the staff of the school wished only to help him.

His acute reaction to the double crisis in his family made it
difficult for us to estimate his fundamental stability. For the time
being all we could do was to hope that no further deterioration
occurred while Bernard learned to believe that our motives were
good. But as his tears dried, so his stealing started. He stole foreign
stamps, brought them back to the school, and was then surprised
when other boys criticized his action. He came to me protesting
against criticism of his theft and I pointed out to him that if stamps
were the only things he wanted it was quite possible for me to
supply them as I kept a stock of foreign stamps for philatelists at
the school. He had been anticipating punishment but I told him
I was more interested in him than in the abstract ethics of punishment. What was more important to me was that his stamp collection
should prosper in a way that could not be the case if he pinched the
stamps.

This type of conversation between us continued for some weeks
and gradually his behaviour improved. For nearly three months he
did not steal. I asked him why this was, and he answered:

'I don't get into trouble now because I have so many things to do.'

He then burst into tears and started talking distractedly about
his disordered family. It was apparent that any reference to his
difficult behaviour would remind him of the even greater derange-
ments that existed at home. He was in the process of building an

impenetrable mental wall against recognizing his bewilderment. He spoke of his father striking his mother hard between her eyes on several occasions, and pleaded to see his brothers and sisters again. A marked conflict of emotions had developed in which, on the one hand, he wanted to be close to his brothers and sisters and see his mother again at her hospital, and on the other feared that seeing his family again would remind him of unhappy things which he now hoped were far in the past. But this time his belief in our good will was sufficiently strong enough for him to accept our advice that when in doubt over matters of this kind it was better to postpone action.

Bernard's behaviour improved still further but he still found it almost impossible to talk at any depth about his family affairs. But I knew that until he had talked about his family no permanent difference in him was to be expected, so at some risk I forced the situation. Fortunately he began to come out of his shell.

'There are many things you know about my family, but you don't know how hard up we were. My father was not able to bring enough money in, and my mother went shop-lifting for food. She would take all of us with her, and we would be told to watch the shopkeeper while she pinched different things. By talking to us at the same time as she was doing the pinching, or making us talk to the shop assistant, she managed to get away with it without being caught.'

I interrupted to say that whatever we said about his mother, we should not judge her in any way, just as we were not allowed to judge each other within the confines of the interview. That assurance was necessary for Bernard's twisted concepts of loyalty would have soon dried up the springs of his information. He explained that had his mother not stolen in this way there would not have been enough food at home, and while I could not quite believe this, it was possible to believe in the total involvement of the mother and her children in the thefts. When Bernard got older his mother would send him out to do the shopping, advising him how to do the stealing and giving him enough money to pretend, if caught, that he was about to pay when the impatience of the shop assistant caused him to make an unfair accusation. Her teaching was tragically foolish; the poor woman, driven by what she considered

151

to be an answer to the family poverty, had now successfully corrupted her son.

During one of these intimate, and tearful, sessions, he told me of a dream he had had in which he and his mother were in a bare, unfurnished room. There had been terrible quarrels and his mother was now sobbing, and sending out S.O.S. messages for help. It was difficult for him to realize that it was his sub-conscious mind that had made up these dreams, that had put his mother in this position of isolation, and he was now blaming himself for her present difficulties. On the one hand he felt he was the person who caused the trouble, and on the other hand dreamed that he could save her from isolation. I tried to emphasize that he was not to blame and he should not seek out disapproval and self-pity. It would not help him to overcome the neglect from which he had suffered. We discussed the fact that while it was clearly wrong for his mother to react to her personal distress by involving her children in theft, it was a human situation and many kinds of frailties could be forgiven.

By now the boy's own thefts had ceased; it was clear that they no longer satisfied any need in him. His classwork and his relations with other boys improved. But he was still very tearful and anxious at any discussion of his disordered home life.

After he had been with us for a little over two years his mother left hospital and she and I met. She started the conversation by stating that for the whole period of separation from her children they had never written to her or told her anything about themselves. The same criticism was levelled against me, against the social workers involved with her case history, and against anyone who had had anything to do with her. These allegations were quite untrue, as we had written frequently to give her news of Bernard, but I did not contradict for she was still far from being a fit woman.

She told me she had recently left a job because she had been accused by a co-worker of theft, and was now working as a shop assistant. Within a few days she hoped to start work as an assistant nurse in a hospital. She mentioned her friendship with the matron of this hospital, but as she elaborated on this theme it became quite clear she was talking about something she desired to happen, not about anything that was actually going to occur. Then for twenty-five minutes she spoke of the previous trouble at home and went on to make all sorts of extraordinary claims: how

152

she had befriended a poor boy living in the neighbourhood; given her assistance to an elderly asthmatic patient; cared for many other people in her neighbourhood at times of need. Obviously this whole account was a fantasy, expressive of something she would like to be true.

At the end of all this I was able to talk to her myself, and it appeared that she was satisfied with our care of Bernard. I mentioned we had written to her from time to time, and she now agreed with this and expressed her gratitude for our having done so. The overall impression was of a tragically unstable woman, and we decided it would be unwise to allow Bernard to spend holidays with her.

A year later we had to break the news to Bernard that his mother, again in hospital, had committed suicide. In a pathetic sort of will she had left all her possessions to the boy, and in a curiously incoherent post script to the document requested that I should look after him. This we were glad to do; I told Bernard that his home was with us, that despite any of its imperfections it would be a place where he would be wanted, respected, loved and appreciated and looked after with as much warmth as we could give, and for as long as he wanted.

His remaining years at the school passed happily enough and any compulsion to theft was quite alien to his sunny, spontaneous character. His life with us ended when he went up to university to read French. He was successful in achieving a second class degree, and is now engaged in teaching.

Soon after Charles Drew came to us, he attempted to commit suicide on three different occasions. After the second we reported the matter with some urgency to his parents, but his mother and stepfather said, with great casualness: 'We knew he did that kind of thing, but we didn't tell you because if you had known you might not have taken him at all.'

Among aspects of Charles' maladjusted behaviour were theft, truancy from school, and fantasies of wealth and grandeur. In the execution of such fantasies, he might happen to meet with elderly folk at a railway station or on the sea front and would tell them how his father was a bishop or his mother a titled lady. By describing his rejection by his parents who, despite their prominence and wealth, would give him none of their attention or money, he would seek to draw the sympathy of his listeners and entice them into giving him some tangible expression of their kindness. These fancies would quickly become known to his mother and step-father, for at the time they were living in a seaside town where such gossip quickly made the rounds.

Charles' paternal grandmother was an active, energetic woman, who possessed all that she surveyed and surveyed all that she possessed. Those living with her had little chance of independent thought or action. When her son died while flight-testing an aeroplane, she characteristically tried to take over complete control of her dead son's wife and family. Naturally her daughter-in-law resisted such dominance but, because of the old woman's wealth, she maintained an uneasy link with her. She tried hard to dissimulate her feelings of dislike, to ensure there would be no alteration to the old lady's will. After two years, however, she met her second husband and became Mrs Drew.

This remarriage was much against the will of her domineering mother-in-law, and was only accomplished in the teeth of violent opposition. She stated her determination to cut Mrs Drew out of her will, and did all that she could to maintain control of Charles; she argued that she would now leave all her money in trust to the boy, and at times accused Charles' mother of obstructing his best interests. Mr Drew had adopted Charles through the usual procedure but he was a cipher in these arguments and, perhaps wisely, did his best to insulate himself.

The turmoil of these acrimonious, argumentative two years, starting with the tragic death of his father whom he had regarded as a hero, led to the emergence of all the difficult symptoms which showed themselves first when Charles was nine. Little was done about them in the beginning because it was felt, quite reasonably, that they were reactive to the various family pressures that had developed, but as time went on it was realized that time would not perhaps deal kindly with his difficulties, and might even make him worse.

The first ominous symptom we immediately noticed when he first came to us was a complete refusal to respond to the name of Drew. He insisted on being called by his father's name, and refused to give any response if his adoptive name was used. He told us that when he came of age he would change his name by deed poll to the surname with which he started life.

The step-father was a good man who did all he could to keep a good relationship with the boy, but apparently had not succeeded in establishing a contact with Charles. They shared interests of an athletic nature such as fishing or boating, but there was no real contact or level at which the boy could talk to Mr Drew in the manner in which any child should feel able to address his father. This distance became greater when his half-brother was born, and as he grew up so the doubts of Charles' parents became urgent. His jealousy of the younger boy was so obvious that at times they wondered if it were possible that he might do his younger brother a mischief. It was clear that Charles' sense of isolation and almost complete despair was caused by his desire for his mother's attention. Here there was indeed real competition, both from his new father who naturally loved his mother, and who was loved by her in return, and the half-brother who was loved by both parents at the same time. Where on earth, imagined Charles, could he find a safe niche in which to live with love and harmony?

Later he privately acknowledged to me how he had plotted to do away with his young half-brother by elaborating some accident which could not cause blame to be directed to Charles himself. Whenever he saw his half-brother doing something academic or athletic he feared that the younger boy would achieve a higher standard of competence than he could attain. Although he knew the comparison to be incorrect, nevertheless it tormented him.

Soon after his tenth birthday the idea of suicide first occurred to him. He had read of a pathetic case which bore some slight resemblance to his own confused family background, and that had also involved the concept of suicide. He tied a rope with a noose at the end of it to the edge of a high door, put his head in the noose and kicked away the chair on which he was standing. Fortunately the postman was passing at the time and no harm was done. But when other attempts followed it became clear that they should have been tackled far more seriously than was the case. But Mrs Drew had always shrunk from it; it was as if the realization of the depth of his disturbance was far too much for her to accept.

Whatever the reasons, the attempts continued, but as with most

155

would-be suicides every attempt was preceded by a cry for help. Sometimes the attempt was heralded by a few days of moodiness and misery which advertised itself to everyone, as if the boy was asking others to help him. At other times, he would make a very odd telephone call to a friend, saying he was going on a long journey, implying that it was a holiday and that he would not see the friend for a few weeks. At these times his fanciful, pity-seeking stories to acquaintances in the town would increase.

Amid all the maladjustments and difficulties of behaviour the symptom of stealing seemed to be very unimportant, purely compensatory for lack of satisfaction at a real and much deeper level. His truancy from school and general expressions of despair were at attempt to bolster up his very weak ego in the face of his own intense belief in his utter unworthiness.

When Charles arrived, we made it clear that we were going to shield him from his own family difficulties, even if it meant for some quite considerable time that holidays would be spent at the school. We explained that this was being done in his interests but if he felt our attitude added to the weight of his burden then he must tell us. Gradually he settled in, but it was clear that although he had very high intelligence he was, like many others, unable to use this capacity. Once human consideration arose and a personal or emotional response was called for, he was gripped by the immediate needs of the situation and set out to make what custom and convention informed him to be the appropriate reply according to his complex system of rules. This controlled personal manner was far more a matter of neurotic repression than of any true self control, for his suicidal attempts showed that whatever the expression 'self-control' means, it was insufficient to control those attempts.

After he had been with us for about six months he trusted us sufficiently to talk more openly about his suicide ventures. It quickly emerged that all at home would be better pleased at his absence, but that one person who would be pleased by his presence would be his dead father! By death there would be a reunion with the one person who would love him to an extent that had never been known from anyone else. These reflections were a solution of a problem which sometimes seemed so oppressive to him as to make the idea of death something far more welcome, especially as it meant that he would thus rejoin the person who had become the most important in his life.

Gradually his disturbed attitude decreased. He had been wary and cautious of relationships at first, but quite quickly now he learned to open up and maintain quite good relationships with other boys. His fantasy-spinning disappeared, and we did not feel there was any need to continue the surveillance that had been necessary in view of his previous suicide attempts. His stealing also ceased; in general he discovered he could believe in the goodwill of others and believe that even with his constricted environment, he could expect love, affection and security.

We have described children who stole, and emphasized that the stealing arose not from a need for the article stolen but from the need for love. In these cases, although it is sometimes a lengthy process, a cure is a matter of comparative ease when compared to a situation where a strong sexual element has contributed towards the maladjustment. Obviously matrimonial disputes and love confusions must inevitably be associated to some extent with erotic concept. Drew's main problem was his rigid conscience. Had he not had a conscience of such implacable rigidity, he would not have found his rules to be necessary. To add to this by punishment or veto would have been unscientific, and at no time during his stay with us was it necessary to punish him, even for his thefts.

He is now an officer in one of Her Majesty's Services and is obviously a contented and well-balanced man. It may be significant that for his life work he chose a disciplined service, and to this extent he is complying with a pattern of living which, although modified by us, we did not completely remove. Perhaps he still requires a framed existence that a person with less rigidity in his boyhood would not need. Be that as it may, his happiness and contentment with his wife is very evident.

His grandmother died and left part of her money in trust to Charles. He used it wisely to set up trust funds for his own two children and there has been no tendency to dissipate the money. This well-balanced and competent man, so free from the tensions and sufferings of the past, is a living proof of the need not to punish a boy who appears to be doing something wrong, in the way that Charles did.

157

All these boys with their bad backgrounds seek in a wrong way for a satisfaction that should be theirs by right. With us their compromises and vain attempts received understanding instead of condemnation, and we may wonder how many of the criminals in our courts throughout the country every day suffered the same tortures in their home backgrounds, thus producing the same maladjustments as these boys. With these adult criminals real reformative work has been left too late, but it does not mean that we should regard their punishment as being more important than their re-education. Their chances of accepting help are slight because quite obviously their rejection has been total, and one of the most difficult tasks we have always had at the school has been to maintain our patience with boys whose anti-social behaviour is reaching intolerable lengths.

When left too long without suitable treatment, adults are not very likely prospects for either a cure or an improved condition of their unhappy state. Occasionally some hypocritical sublimation is achieved, but we aim at something that is far more durable than a sublimation. All short cuts within the psyche have to be paid for, and there is no way of avoiding the result of psychological error. The penalties we pay differ, but the pain we experience exists always. One has only to glance at the paraphernalia and spectacle of the courtroom to see a situation of intense suffering with little comprehension. Where we have been able to be discerning of suffering we have always found a cure possible. Sometimes, I confess comprehension has been woefully unimaginative and insufficient, but we must continue to persevere until such time as our understanding is sufficient to deal with all the complexities of boys' backgrounds and behaviour.

CHAPTER XIV

The Nature of a Thief

ANY DEFINITION given as to the nature of a thief by one who does not work with him will fall far short of the depths of human misery the thief is seeking to plumb within himself. Theft is hardly ever anything but the end product of a complex attempt of the unconscious mind to solve its own confusions. On the one hand is the spectacle of the thief's jealousy, envy and greed and, on the other, there is his belief that the love he needs will never be attainable. The last feeling leads him to the assumption that some tangible object such as money or a possession will remedy the gap between the love he really needs and the incomplete love he thinks he can obtain. As far as the thief is concerned this gap is limitless. The only act that contains promise is a panic-stricken theft of some article or money.

A legal attitude to his act ignores the circumstances that are behind it. A merciful treatment creates what keen justice will destroy, but a constructive therapeutic attitude does not excuse the selfish disentanglement of the boy's own problems at another's expense. Rather it shows the boy that what he needs cannot be obtained by such short cuts, which lead only to temporary satisfaction and a morass of lies to cover his detection by the injured party or society.

'Ah yes, you may be right, but I'm too clever for you,' the delinquent thinks. 'I shall never be caught, and if I am then I will wriggle and turn with all the twists of legal cunning until everybody else becomes so bewildered that they will be only too glad to drop the matter and wish they'd never brought it up in the first place.' It is curious to the honest spectator that the thief can so easily justify his theft, but this justification flows simply from the intensity of his anger that another possesses something he feels he lacks or has forfeited. This anger and envy is a brief madness, and to vindicate himself he now has to invent some hostile act, committed by himself, towards the possessor he envies. Such a lurking envy forms a platform from which all thefts are launched and unfortunately the first object of a theft is frequently displaced to seemingly innocent targets. Later we will describe the real and fundamental basis of all thefts, but for the moment one must understand that the younger the child, the quicker a cure can be accomplished. However, if one has left the position so long that infancy and childhood have grown to adolescence, the chances are that the thieved object has now changed its purpose and has shifted from one target to another. Sometimes in a most complex fashion this new target is accepted by society as being socially agreeable in a way that naked theft could never be.

We can take the case of the scholar and literary forger, Thomas James Wise. He was a thief, as the depredations (from the British Museum) discovered after his death prove, but less well known is the fact that as a younger man he would steal sugar from cafés which he hoarded at home in jam jars. Had the deprivation suggested by his sugar thefts in adulthood been understood, the British Museum might not have suffered its serious losses and unhappy mutilations to books at the hands of T. J. Wise so that he could make up his own imperfect copies. I choose the example of a collector because so often a collector is following a symbolic theft and is seeking something no other process or selection can satisfy. I am not thinking of the person who collects a few examples of one genre but of the person who obsessionally goes on filling his house with articles of one kind, filling every room so that ultimately almost all domestic comfort is excluded. That person is in fact acting out his burning need to accumulate possessions, which a less fortunate or less wealthy individual has to accomplish in ways such as theft. The rich collector may be satisfying exactly the same unconscious motives which also need satisfying in the thief, but because he is socially acceptable and appears to be contributing to trade and other kinds of worthwhile objects, the real depths of his insecurity are not seen until, for example, one studies the case of a collector such as Sir Thomas Phillipps.

The life style of Sir Thomas, the biggest collector of manuscripts the world has ever known, shows an attempt to remedy gaps in this vast collection that has taken many decades since his death to be sorted. So vast in fact was his collection that he never had time even to unpack the boxes of more recent acquisitions to his library. The demon in him inspired his world-wide hunt to procure the manuscripts he wanted so badly. His violently paranoiac attacks upon his son-in-law Halliwell and his own daughter, after the former was shown to have stolen certain books from a university library, shows clearly and tragically how near he was to theft himself. He attacked and persecuted his son-in-law and daughter in ways that are scarcely credible for their virulence and hatred, but all the time when one studies his life closely, one sees him attacking the thief in himself and not really the thief in his Aunt Sally son-in-law. Only upon such a basis of deprivation can one understand the whole of Sir Thomas's life. In some of his letters to his daughter, he shows clearly how much he hates her for giving her love to her children, when he himself was born illegitimately. He went further. After the death of his first wife he tried to contract marriages with others, and his correspondence with the father of one would-be spouse was characterized by unnatural considerations, domestic arguments and a cold, unloving financial negotiation. Gaps of affection in his childhood were to be filled by books and manuscripts in his enormous house and if he could so fill the gaps then all the unconscious loneliness could somehow be allayed.

Stealing is a subject that gives rise to emotional response as much as the subject of sex does. Many shop-lifters, expressing their inner conflict through thefts, find that the thefts in turn introduce fresh trouble and worry: a Court, unfortunately, deals only with the theft. Often a woman shop-lifter truthfully says in Court that her husband knows nothing of her misbehaviour and that her worst fear is that he will now have to know. Amid the sophistry and subterfuge it is nearly always impossible within Court to unfold the real cause of the shop-lifter's misbehaviour; and when so many cases are swayed by the obvious mercenary value of the stolen goods, the difficulties become even greater. In general terms the real motive is

F

to relieve some of the inner mental conflict by trickery such as theft, in the vain hope that on such lines a solution to the deeper problems will emerge, or, as a result of the act, the deeper problems will be lighter to bear. The sin, however, increases the burden and the sinner ends in believing, as do his or her critics, that the theft was the origin of the sin and constitutes the matter which all are primarily considering. The thief therefore becomes the booby in his own trap.

I would be an innocent and stupid magistrate if I did not remember that there are sinister and dangerous major thefts too—of old masters, smash-and-grab raids increasingly involving violence on the part of the criminal, robbing of bank messengers, protection rackets which parasitically feed upon others' honesty, thieving of gold bars and other major acquisitive crimes. But in conversation both with the criminals and with the police, under a general atmosphere of frankness and candour on both sides, various factors immediately emerge as common to nearly all such criminals. They are mostly children of divorced parents, illegitimate or adopted children or children who in some way have lacked an early relationship with a mother. Perhaps their father's crimes have so influenced and affected the marriage that the children too have become drawn into the whirlpool of suspicion and horror such crime has caused within a family. They have almost invariably experienced a lack of affection in childhood and sometimes this has been coupled with ill-treatment. One should first understand the effects of these bad upbringings, if one is to understand the gravity of their criminal nature.

In serious situations it is necessary to segregate the criminal, in some cases for a period of many years, in order to protect society from his malevolence; but at the same time as society is being protected very often during his lengthy stay in prison, the criminal himself is being rendered more vulnerable to a repetition of such criminal behaviour. Although his segregation is inevitable, proper and unavoidable, very often the need for it has arisen because the diagnosis of his condition was made too late in his life, and in turn this leads to the need for a continuation of such segregative measures.

It is admirable to recognize the mischief and misery within ordinary class-room activities in a day school and then to seek some therapeutically advantageous steps for the child by approaching the

162

Child Guidance Clinic: but one would be both a fool and a stupid optimist to pretend that all such cases even if detected, would yield to treatment. The average intelligence of criminals is significantly below the average intelligence of the population and, the less intelligent the subject, the less likely he is to understand the approaches that we at the school so successfully use. There seems to be nothing unfair and improper in choosing only gifted children for our treatment; we should be adding to general folly if we chose children who could not be cured, and attempted to cure them.

One difficulty, and it can be a major one, is the incredulity on the part of the criminal himself as to the real likelihood of a fundamental cure. As a result of his childhood experiences he has managed to form relationships only with bad companions of similar character to his own, and within that very small group there is a diffused loyalty directed towards the ends of crime. It is untrue that there is honour among thieves, because so many detections by police have been successful because thieves have informed upon each other. Indeed when one considers the whole structure of criminality, one has to be very naive to believe that there could be any permanent concept of honour in the ranks of criminals, because criminal behaviour is quite often alien to a concept of honour, loyalty, trust and the fundamental element within a relationship, which is love.

The unstable child has many illustrations outside his family of dishonesty. He reads advertisements which cannot possibly be true in the praise they give to their products. He reads of deceptions in newspaper reports which are more often reported than the honesty and goodness of most people and in that way unconsciously adds to a pattern he has already formed of indifferent and unhappy behaviour. So, as a first exercise in helping a young thief, one has to present to him a standard that he has for some years chosen to believe does not exist. That is not done by chasing him to a religious service on a Sunday or by forcing outward attendance at morning prayers. Neither is it to be done by urging him to 'pull up his socks' or similar advice. Moralising of this kind has ceased to have any purpose, if indeed it ever did have a purpose: instead a far more difficult task has to be attempted, and this is the task of presenting a consistent and equable example which in itself could never accept the lower and more selfish examples which at this time are shown by the delinquent boy. Confectioners and tobacconists seem to have become used to occasional thefts and appear to accept the losses arising from the activities of child pilferers as part of their overheads. They no longer inform the police in a way that used to be the custom and, when discussing the matter, resignedly shrug their shoulders and accept the lower standard of behaviour that quite clearly is part of our social lot today. The do-gooder, living in the locality of a children's home who seeks to help the children by occasional invitations to take tea or go on an outing with them to the local cinema, would be terribly affronted if one of the girls she is generously entertaining steals a pair of nylons. She will utterly fail to realize that the theft of the nylons was intended more as a compliment to her than an insult. I remember when the school was co-educational, how I came into the kitchen at my home and discovered a girl stealing toffees from a box. I was most embarrassed and wished I had not come into the kitchen to see her doing such a thing.

I said to her, 'Look, if you really want those toffees you can have them as a gift.' I made it clear by subsequent remarks and by my tone that I was not offering this advice in any patronizing or forgiving form, but that I was stating it as an absolute fact, showing her that I valued her personality sufficiently to give her some toffees and that I did not see her as a beggar or a supplicant who had to cadge the sweets.

The next day she saw me alone, and pathetically she said, 'Oh Shaw, when I see you sitting with your wife, with your feet up, gossiping or listening to the wireless or doing things about your house, I feel envious and hope that one day my marriage will be exactly the same.'

I accepted the compliment, but in my reply I asked her how toffees fitted into this.

'Surely you can see that when I go back to the school after leaving your house I want some souvenir.' she said. 'If only I can keep that souvenir it's a kind of sign that I, too, will have the happiness I want. You know what happened in my family that stopped me having any happiness.'

Those personal thefts are really most heart-breaking and frequently they are nothing more than a means to gain some memento of a pleasant evening or a pleasant relationship, which the thief wishes to perpetuate by this magical act. Often within my house I have missed small objects which I know very well have been taken, usually by younger children. If I can identify the child, which is usually easy, I always give him some positive gift within a day or two of the theft and just as frequently the missing article is surreptitiously replaced within a week. The whole point is that he did not want to hurt me any more than I wanted to hurt him; but he did want a little bit of me to keep because there are parts of me that indicate something which he has hitherto lacked in his life and realizing this, even if but dimly at the moment, wishes no longer to lack.

While we must sadly admit defeat in the case of those criminals who do really dreadful things in society at large and, having regard to their many previous convictions, are sentenced to what amounts in many cases to a life-long incarceration, this does not mean we should mildly acquiesce in a negative impotence to deny help to younger thieves. The origin of their theft, not dissimilar to that which generated the thieving of the sophisticated adult criminal, can be understood if the understanding is started early enough in the thief's life. Each thief is different from another thief. The multiplicity of types of stealing and the similar variation in motives for robbery make one believe that there are a million delinquent acts, all different, although the delinquent himself thinks that all kinds of stealing are closely similar and one theft resembles another. The truth is that even within one thief himself there are different kinds of theft or pilfering which add to the difficulty of relieving the thief from his swindling habit.

A commonplace event, when looking at the variety of articles stolen, is that very few of these stolen articles have a life that lasts more than a few days. The thief appears to have been motivated by the act of theft itself rather than by the gain of the article he stole. The fact that it was wrong could not deter him as the compulsion to thieve was sufficiently strong to obliterate any deterrent thought, be it of a better morality or derived from a threat of detection with consequent punishment. These stolen articles are always broken or lost very quickly. The pen that has been stolen usually breaks its nib, or else happens to be lost in some way. The larger article stolen is frequently broken or indeed sometimes quite purposely thrown into a hedge or outside the school grounds. The act of thieving is important and the stolen object, as often as not, is an embarrassment to the predator. The illusion must now be destroyed and the logical act of disposing of the evidence reveals the underlying disappointment. When I point this out to children they are invariably surprised but the same lack of variation is shown in their complete agreement to my thesis; they always then give me a whole list of articles they have stolen over recent years, and as quickly as they have stolen them so they have been either destroyed or lost, always, they emphasize, by what appeared at the time to be pure accident.

With children who steal the reality of their theft should never be forgotten. This does not mean to say that a spoken reiteration of the wrongness of their act is going to alter their behaviour; there are many such cases that have been put on probation and indeed many Probation Officers who will quickly witness to that fact, and within the scope of one's own neighbourly knowledge one has come across children upon whom no amount of coercion or punishment has effected any reasonable change in behaviour which the punisher genuinely and sometimes generously wished to secure. There is every good however, in pointing out to a young thief that the shop keeper from whom he has stolen is a man who often has to make his income by very hard work and that his income is of quite a modest nature. One boy who had stolen from a local newsagent-cum-sweet shop, was astonished when I told him what in my opinion was the real amount of that newsagent's income, and he felt how unfairly he had treated an inoffensive man. I do not argue that such a remonstrance effects a cure, but little harm has ever been done by making a fool face the facts of his folly or making a delinquent fact the facts of his delinquency. Reality does occur in these matters and any action which hurts the feelings of another contains an element which should never be obscured when talking to the wrongdoer.

Similarly one can sympathize with a child who, never receiving a parcel or letter through the post himself, is so jealous of others receiving parcels that he steals them. In such instances it is clear that eating the contents of the parcel is done in a gluttonous, voracious manner so that the thief never really savours the taste of what he is eating, but instead has to swallow it down in greed, because the article he has stolen is not really what it purports to be, but a contact with parents who love him enough to send him a parcel. That contact, denied to the thief in reality, makes him do what he does to the exclusion and total disregard of the other child's feelings and wishes. At the school we have a socio-legal process whereby the offended child is able to secure restitution from the thief and to some extent that does modify his outraged feelings, but the punishment, while utterly proper in reality as far as the thief is concerned, is not an action which taken alone is going to cure the thief. While such reasonable sanctions keep the matter alive in the delinquent's mind, and perhaps emphasize to him the very real nature of his problem and the even greater urgency of an effective solution to it, in fact they effect very little reduction in the problem itself apart from that mild contribution. Similarly should a boy steal from a member of the staff an article which more normally is used for the entertainment of a group of boys such as a gramophone record, or tape recorder, then the detection of the thief is fairly easy. The simplicity of detection should not obscure the complexity of the theft, and although under those circumstances more often than not the stolen article can be recovered undamaged, the thief is effectively rebuked and punished for the act of selfishness through the school court. This never reduces the selfishness, but it does make the thief more co-operative in his private sessions with the analyst or whoever is seeing him under the seal of professional secrecy to give him appropriate psychological and moral guidance. Although one can pardon and be compassionate, one should never give a child the idea that one is colluding, for should a child form that idea he will quickly change it into a concept that the staff involved are actually conspiring with him to give him some mercenary advantage over his fellows; and once such a slack and lazy definition arises little can be done to help a child who is hankering for such an opinion.

I have often said to a boy, 'You seem bent upon making me lose my temper. You could succeed or perhaps you will not succeed but you are not going to trick me into doing something that will harm you further than you have been harmed already. If I felt that it would do you good to knock you backwards down the main stairs, I would do so, but believing as I do that it would intensify your fear and increase your tendency to do all kinds of things people don't like you doing, I will not treat you in such a manner.

Thus the efforts you now expend in trying to make me lose my temper would be far better spent in trying to find your own temper because all your naughtiness and nastiness to other people is clearly not a sign of having a good temper yourself.'

The tone is of crucial importance in remarks of this kind. If the tone is not correct, or if the relationship is bad, or the smile and throw-away jokes are not present in the sentences, then such speech-making is entirely wasted and may even make a difficult position more complicated. Avoiding as we do the false promise of punishment we have all the multiplicities of theft to consider. We have to discover whether the basis was mercenary and selfish or, going through all the imperceptible graduations from that stage to the type of thief who steals because of a miserable home background, select the right definition from which we can all proceed; but basically and fundamentally, however unlovable the thief might be, we have to realize the real need is for love, and unless that need is satisfied, then any other work we do will be so much wasted effort. To satisfy a need is not to satiate it. To qualify a need is not to give the one who has the need a glut of what he seeks; the measure has to be estimated so that sufficient charity is available, but there must not be a sentimentalized identification with the crook, so that he gains in a secondary way from others' toleration. No thief should be permitted for one instant to gain from his theft or feel that he has outwitted others or even worse, attract an exhibition of sympathy which fundamentally his behaviour does not merit.

Despite all such qualifications in terms of caution against seeming to condone a bad action, one must remember all the time that the primary need of a thief is affection, and, even in the case of the smash-and-grab raiders and the wage snatchers, affection was the need that was never satisfied when it could have been satisfied, and therefore these raiders have perpetually to seek satisfaction at the expense of society until they are too old and senile to continue their felonies.

CHAPTER XV

Withdrawn and Depressed

IN SPITE of the perhaps alarming stories I have told, not all cases at our school are wildly or even mildly exciting. Some boys were distinguished by their seeming dullness combined with an apparent inability to give any other impression than that they were vegetables. At any one time at Red Hill School, rather more than a tenth of our pupils are in the genius class, and all others have intelligence quotients above 130; but they are not all sparkling with wit and energy. A few are lazy, such idleness being inherent in their personal problems. Others dislike lessons and seek non-intellectual spheres of activity. Some are so weighed down with family troubles that most of their energy is dissipated in brooding and vain attempts to sort them out, the remaining energy being insufficient for what would otherwise be the rapid advancement in the classroom that could be expected from their high level of intelligence.

Isolation is an experience that befalls all of us, at some time, but even a brief period of it is a curse that most of us seek to avoid. Is the loneliness suffered by a mental defective so difficult to evaluate? What do his grins and chattering mean and how far does his smile and laughter show delight? Do his tears show as much sadness as we think? Charity bids us assume he is as sensitive to others' affection for him as is a person of normal intelligence. It is good that the nature of his condition is obvious to us all, and we therefore defend him against his adversaries or critics and protect him from

169

situations his inadequate ability charges with the probability of failure or danger.

Recognition of an isolated genius is so much less frequent, but his loneliness can be equally as numbing as that of the feeble-minded boy. It drives him to aggravate his condition by withdrawing to a state of isolation which he imagines will protect him from the need to explain his discoveries and thoughts to his fellows who, experience has shown him, are unable to exhibit a quick and ready comprehension. It also protects him from the irritating contact of those who are, by comparison with his own intelligence and rapid fluidity of thought, almost moronic. And isolation can also be a front against society for fear it will deride him for the mistakes he fears he will make.

It is difficult for a genius to compare his successes or errors with others, because he is working with an intellectual momentum far in excess of the norm. That very fact exacerbates his tendency to retreat into his shell, and to assume also that others wish him to stay there. The view may be correct that despite the heights and depths of a dullard's feelings, those of the brilliant boy vary between much greater extremes; but it is also true that consolation is more eagerly perceived and deeply accepted by the dull boy—he is more simply, and more quickly helped to return to good humour after disappointment. The genius can be assumed to have areas of sensitivity unknown to the mentally retarded.

Some gifted boys show their maladjustment in actively aggressive ways, and their brash arrogance obscures, even if it does not deny, their own sensitivity. The quiet genius however, nervously avoids fun and gaiety, and thus being no trouble to anyone at the school he can so easily escape notice, and without notice he cannot be helped. Such a boy is happy in a library, digging mustily for his thesis, but although the desire for extreme solitude must be tolerated, we should not let it continue any more than we would be satisfied to allow an aggressive child to continue his violence. The angry boy knows his behaviour can be vetoed and rebuked, and will eventually respond to the opinions of others; but the quiet withdrawn boy can plaintively argue that he is doing others no harm and therefore should not be molested.

This passive, withdrawn child might do well academically and gain his place at university, and perhaps grind on to win a first class honours degree. But experience has shown that soon afterwards he may break down into a negative state of absolute withdrawal and a retreat from that condition is rarely possible in adult life. Our duty is to recognize the ominous signs of such withdrawal and to regard the condition as urgent as that of the most aggressive and excitable boy we have ever had.

Derek Edwards was a dreamy little boy, small in size for his eleven years. His smallness was emphasized by his unobtrusiveness, and his way of making mouselike excursions around a room as if he was frightened of anybody seeing his movements before he scuttled to safety. He often wore an expression between pain and puzzlement, and gave in to quite simple problems with extraordinary alacrity. He revealed no direct signs of emotional instability but his mother gave some of a curiously indefinable variety. She said he burst into tears on very slight provocation, but she could make no attempt to define the type of provocation that upset the little boy. When faced with a direct question, she would withdraw her original statement and imply that we had misunderstood her. He was frightened of looking one in the face, and consequently at his school had earned himself a reputation for being shifty. He suffered an acute school phobia which prompted his refusal to attend school at all.

The general family picture was that his father was frequently out of work, and when he was employed, had only a very low income. When I tried to discuss with Mrs Edwards her relationship with her husband, she assured me that all was well between the two, but the nature of her reply, and the curious evasiveness of it, suggested that beneath the surface there was much disharmony.

For four months after Derek's arrival at Red Hill we took extra trouble to be sympathetic and encouraging. We expressed friendliness at every opportunity but he always managed to parry or dodge our advances. I suspected that behind this withdrawal there was some traumatic experience, presumably inside the family, from which the boy had recoiled with a decision that such shocks and dangers must be avoided in the future. Although in our experience at the school, traumata are not very often the cause of a child's maladjustment, a shock can precipitate a symptomatic exhibition of a maladjustment. Derek's complete withdrawal made us wonder whether our case history of his family background was complete.

171

Our question was never answered and this was one of those cases in which we could not discover all the details we suspected existed.

Derek continued to defend himself against any approach with courteous insistence. Except in the most trivial issues, such as passing the condiments at the meal, we were unable to encourage any affirmative response. This guardedness did not disguise from us that there could well be unexpected possibilities with this boy; common interests, common habits or ways of action which would tempt him back to the sociable world. But Derek's obstinate defences against such inclinations showed how terrified he was for anyone to gain some knowledge of him.

We had never met a child with such a heavily armoured introversion. He had areas of sensitivity which were unassailable. He suffered from troubled and anxious moods concerning inter-personal relations of which we were never able to discover the facts. In the absence of information from the boy or from his home we could only guess at his reasons for withdrawal.

We decided that this child could never accept any deep analytic treatment and we would have to find some other approach. We finally decided to find for him a task in which he could succeed but which, so far as he was aware, no one else in the school had ever attempted. This technique might be called trick psychology, and we much prefer a more disciplined approach; then our roads can be carefully defined and, after failure or success, they can be properly evaluated. But however disciplined one's attitude to analytic psychology might be in theory, when such techniques do not promise the usual response the welfare of the child must be put before any theorizing. Had our choice of Derek's task been unwisely made then this boy might have remained a failure for life. But our unorthodox approach permitted a plan which maintained its promise and ultimately gave us and the boy a solution.

Working very carefully, but with seeming casualness, sometimes by arranging for Derek to 'overhear' things, we persuaded him that the member of the staff who dealt with boys' pocket money required an assistant who would be prepared to check his financial accounts every day and balance his ledger at the end of the week. This is not a simple job for, as well as the boys' weekly pocket money, this man deals with all the other financial considerations of the boys: he arranges the collection of fines from boys who are fined in the school court; he looks after the boys' savings accounts, banking them with the post office or, in the rare cases where the amounts involved exceed that suitably kept in a post office account, invests them in a building society. The scheme was introduced very gradually to Derek Edwards, beginning with the simple checking of the daily deposits, the weekly disbursements of Friday pocket money and all the more obvious calculations. But then he started his own records which were a more effective system of accountancy and book-keeping than the adult himself employed. For the first time since Derek came to us, and probably for many years before, he was doing something in contact with another, in such a way that there had to be inter-communication about sums of money, ledgers, and investments. Starting from a simple system, Derek progressed to a complete surveillance of the whole pocket money and boys' savings arrangements at the school. It was clear that, with caution, Derek's social contacts could be expanded to better and more elaborate relationships with other people.

Later Derek was introduced to the idea of checking kitchen accounts and ordering. He extended his ledger system to include a careful costing and statistical analysis of the whole of this monthly kitchen accountancy. Naturally we encouraged him to turn what was really a simple office job into a sophisticated use of his own high order of intelligence. It would have been far easier to leave matters as they were, so far as kitchen costing accountancy was concerned. The system worked quite simply through our office before Derek's involvement, though naturally it required a great expansion of office activity to satisfy the boy's ambitious schemes, more appropriate to a school of a thousand than the fifty-five for whom we cater. Inevitably he was brought into contact with office staff and kitchen staff and eventually with boys who were members of our Food and Hygiene Committee. These relationships contained little form or real spontaneity, but the fact that they accepted Derek in a casual manner was a great advance from a defensive withdrawn attitude which characterized his person to other boys until this particular activity developed.

With a continued expansion of his business interests in mind, we encouraged him to attend local auction sales to bid occasionally for articles of furniture for school use. In any school the consumption of furniture is great, and sometimes with maladjusted children it is even greater: an economical source of supply is from local sales. At first we arranged with the friendly auctioneer that Derek's bidding be scrutinized with care, and the man collaborated. Thus Derek would buy articles for school use, having himself the sole power, so far as he was aware, of determining the actual price he paid for the goods. This activity was a useful therapy to the boy and also assisted the school on a purely realistic basis. We discovered it led Derek to make an inventory of all the school furniture, attempting costing, and finally to demonstrate to us that a certain type of cheap chair was a far more expensive commodity than a more costly chair because the need for repairs arose so frequently.

Our praise was not only of therapeutic encouragement but also of pure commercial appreciation. The other boys soon noticed Derek's activities and he naturally came in for some mild teasing, but his purpose was soon understood by the other boys and their realization gave Derek another sense of appreciation which had hitherto been so miserably lacking in his life.

We began to worry about Derek's future activities for he was beginning to exhaust the possibilities of kitchen economy. After all, a boy of twelve or thirteen years of age can scarcely be expected to run the whole school. We needed to plan further expansion of the interests which had now captured a very special part of Derek's attention. But we need not have worried for by this time his activities had become so intriguing to him that he was capable of developing them of his own accord. His communication with us and with other boys was now much better and easier although it was still severely limited. We soon became aware of his curiosity in the field of stocks and shares. He had very quickly graduated from ordinary arithmetic and algebra books to books of greater detail and information from the County Library. He learned the functions of the *Financial Times,* Stock Exchanges, and international monetary systems.

As his liberation from social withdrawal had progressed so far, we felt we should now do something within the classroom sphere to increase his general knowledge and educational prospects. We tried many devices, including the techniques which had been so successful in uncovering his business interests, but despite all our dodges, we could only obtain from him a courteous acknowledgement of the desirablity of his doing lessons but no co-operation of any depth or perception whatever. Immediately a classroom subject seemed to

174

have some bearing upon his interest in ledgers, costing, accountancy, stocks and shares there would be an enthusiastic response, but until that trigger was pulled, he might just as well have not been occupying his seat at the desk. We held many anxious staff meetings, and the general view was that, while his sense of social importance and integration was so demonstrably improving, we should not do anything that might harm that trend even if it cost further backwardness in lessons.

Then with a suddenness that had never characterized even his accountancy interests before, he showed a desire to learn about internal combustion engines, motor cycles and motor cars. He had a natural flair in this direction, and although it was impossible to test his abilities it appeared to us that his practical knowledge was of a high order, even above that of his very high pure intelligence. We began to notice that he was not concerned with the applied science or engineering aspect but rather with organisation of techniques of repair of engines. This did not require any specific engineering knowledge so much as an understanding of business efficiency, organization and methods. His reading was mainly on business efficiency, and avoiding all the how to get rich quick variety of book he was concentrating upon the real techniques of organization.

We were still concerned at his failure to attend to his classroom lessons. Much of his time at school was used purposefully and, we believed, to his psychological advantage; it was nevertheless disturbing that we could not capture his attention in the classroom in a way which would allow him to exercise his brilliant potential. We learned many years afterwards that it was most fortunate we did not press him too hard. We acquiesced uneasily in Derek's disinterest. He did enough English to pass English Literature and Grammar at 'O' level, a simple task for one of his ability, and he also passed Maths at 'O' level; but at that point all his academic energy had been consumed.

He left us when he was seventeen years of age and joined a large ironmongery store as a counter hand. We were not surprised to hear that he had been transferred to an executive position three months later. Shortly afterwards he left to join a firm of timber merchants. Here again, very quickly, his organizational ability was put to use. After four years he had saved sufficient money to start a small

175

shop of his own in which he sold paints, wallpaper and similar household decoration materials. He was one of the pioneers of the 'Do It Yourself' shops, for he quickly learned that the sale of partly prepared pieces of furniture and other products was commercially attractive.

During this time it was pleasant to have frequent visits from him. As we had enjoyed only a partial success with him, we often wondered if, in the face of a business difficulty or financial crisis, he might not return to the previous conditions of withdrawal, apathy and social indifference. But in all his visits he appeared to be interested in people and things. On one visit he told us he was going to sell his shop and move to a Midlands town where he had already bought a deserted factory building on some waste land. He had sufficient capital to equip the building with the machinery he needed, and buy material.

For five years intermittent letters came to tell us of his progress in expanding his factory, manufacturing fluorescent paints. As would be expected from one of his character, his costing was precise, and he had had the idea of marketing the paint in rectangular tins. Soon after discovering this economy he had found that by buying his own tinplate he could make his own tins at less cost and he also made his own lettering stencils. His integration of these three activities was perfect, and by careful choice of subordinates he had collected a loyal group of workers with whom he was on easy terms, thus happily avoiding all labour troubles.

Recently he paid us the compliment of staying with us with his wife and son and during that weekend he told me a story which is now characteristic of him. During a recent dock strike, when it was virtually impossible for manufacturers to keep their export promises, Derek had been obstructed from keeping his delivery date for a consignment he had planned to send to Ostend. He had promptly hired a boat at a little frequented eastern coastal town, and after making proper customs arrangements, he loaded his economically packaged paints and sailed to the Belgian port.

I asked him if he had any knowledge of navigation.

'No, but it's soon learned for a short trip like that,' he answered. 'Anyhow, once I'd hit the continental coast north of Belgium I could just sail south until I found Ostend.'

We gossiped about school days and I asked him if he ever

176

regretted his avoidance of the many-sided curriculum. He did not, though he would not like his own son to take the same risk. He was grateful that we had not forced him to a mould in which he would never have been able to fit. Two days after he and his family had left, we received a most interesting letter in which he expressed his gratitude in terms which displayed a very deep sincerity. The letter contained a cheque for two hundred and fifty pounds towards the school building fund.

CHAPTER XVI

Suspicion and Trust

WE HAD heard much about Edward Fitch before we met with that sad twelve-year old, so full of rancour that he fled from every approach and evaded every gesture of friendship. The clinic told us that although his school work had been good before he went to the grammar school, later apprehension and depression had set in. His response to even the most trivial difficulty was to deny its existence or fly from it in panic, and any attempt to help him face a trouble might lead only to a fearful resentment.

Edward's mother was an anxious, worrying type in poor health, overburdened with her housework and her work every evening to earn more money for the family. When we first met her we asked about her own life, and were not surprised to learn that in her childhood she had had a problem almost identical with Edward's. She had not noticed the same difficulties with the other four, older children, and Edward's symptoms did not emerge until he was about nine years old. They were easily handled at first, but when he transferred to the grammar school he reacted with a complete refusal to attend it. Each morning he pleaded a headache or some other illness; if he was ever persuaded to set out on the short journey to school, he would fail to arrive. Finally he refused completely to leave the house, and at this point he had been referred to us.

We had never before encountered such an excessively timid or anxiety-ridden child. There was a complete absence of any of the normal aggressive or spontaneous attitudes expected from a boy of his age: not only was there this inhibition but his anxiety was expressed in abdominal pains, stomach disorders and similar physical symptoms which, despite many investigations by the doctor, could never be diagnosed as anything other than nervous in origin.

As the weeks passed we began to realize that there was a deep relationship of an odd kind between this youngest son and his mother. Her letters to us were full of doubt of our competence to look after her son, and she expressed similar anxieties in her letters to Edward. In certain phrases she would even put into his head the idea of running away from the school. One such letter started: 'Dear Ted, I hope you are happy at school. I always remember I was never happy at school. If you find you can't settle down, do tell me and I will soon take you away. After all, you do belong to me and not to the school.'

As Mrs Fitch was unaware we had seen this letter we could do little about it, although naturally we wanted to protest. It was obvious that she wished, perhaps even consciously, to prevent the boy settling down, and it indicated that the boy's refusal to go to school was associated with her reluctance to lose her youngest child. Edward unknowingly basked in that over-protectiveness, and when home circumstances became so grave that his mother was forced to send him to a boarding school, their relationship continued uninterrupted. Her letters invited him to discover that Red Hill School was so unsuitable that he was justified in running back to her at home. One could imagine her letters ending: 'If only we could be together for ever and ever.'

We could not tell Mrs Fitch directly, because she would only more vehemently deny our accusations and probably insist that the boy left our care. We had rather to show by our attitude to young Edward that if he agreed with his mother's views, he would be denying himself the pleasure and fun of school life and committing himself to an over-protecting and mollycoddling mother. But he seemed to sympathize with his mother's anxieties, and it became clear as time went on that he was deeply concerned for his mother and wished her to be dependent upon him.

It was no surprise to discover that his relationship with a rather timid and inadequate father had been poor. Mr Fitch was frequently

179

tired and irritable, and Edward had quickly used the excuse of such bad temper to cling deeper within his mother's arms, and sit ever more firmly in her lap.

After Edward had been with us for five months, I felt it was time to seek a better understanding with his mother. She accepted many appointments, only to cancel them at the last minute; this happened six times within the space of three weeks, always with a ready excuse. But at last we met.

She had a curious way of belittling her son and laughing at him in front of me, but as soon as her denigration was complete, she would praise and belaud him to me using much the same phraseology as for belittling him. I tried to show her how her own early difficulties were now being visited by her upon her son; despite her subconscious rejection of her early difficulties, she was consciously seeking a defence to the tragedies which had never been overcome in her own childhood.

I repeated this over and over again, trying to convince her that Edward's withdrawn panicked state was his attempt to monopolize her and to ensure that she made all decisions for him and ordered his life. She found it difficult to realize how much she was still scheming on the lines which I had explained; she could see many little illustrations of my criticisms but to understand that it was now part of her general style to the youngest son was past her ability. I had to content myself with extracting a promise from her not to write to Edward in terms which might unsettle him, but to write in a neutral way, merely giving family news. Although she undertook to do this, she failed often, but as the months passed Edward's capacity to stand on his own feet increased and her attempts to prevent him from doing this lost much of their power.

His general behaviour at the school continued to be completely withdrawn and submissive; he would never contradict or disobey. But he experienced little pleasure from his passivity, and certainly never any sense of achievement or accomplishment. In this way more than a year of his school life passed; other boys ignored him and he appeared to be convinced of his own incompetence. If asked to do any task a little outside ordinary routine he would claim inability and flee both physically and emotionally from the situation. Sometimes one would find him tearfully standing in some corner of the room or corridor, and he was in fact a simpering,

180

whimpering child who was completely bothered and bewildered by almost any situation that presented itself.

I had persuaded his mother to see us at more frequent intervals and explained to her that her evasion of the interviews was fundamentally a desire on her part to shun facing the fact that she must cease to regard her son as a little baby. Although she could understand this at an intellectual level, it was difficult for her to understand emotionally. But she accepted our goodwill in the matter and, within the limits of her neurosis, did whatever she could to put our advice into practice with regard to Edward, and make him happy.

Despite the emphasis we had placed upon his mother's possessive and vampiristic mollycoddling, an almost equal factor was Edward's lack of a stable father figure. We realized this fully when he began to form relationships with certain men workers at the school. He started with those who helped us in the garden, and with our maintenance men. Later he transferred his interest from them to certain of the teaching staff.

After six months of this it was apparent that he had solved some of his problems without the aid of any practical analysis. He was now able to make decisions of some importance; to execute tasks which, although simple, were far more complex than he had previously thought himself capable of tackling. His severe submissiveness and meekness had begun to crack, and he would occasionally show a superficial irritation or readiness to enter into conflict. He began to develop a good imagination and, what was even more encouraging, reflective insight. It was clear from his conversation that he perceived thoughts and subtleties in himself rather than calls to action. The gloominess and weeping disappeared. He came to accept himself as he was and adjust to living, not an active, exciting life but a more perceptive and friendly one than he had ever managed before. Gradually the rigidity of his character relaxed. When he failed now, rather than relapse into apathy and pessimism he was able to go back over the details to see if he could do better. He still had the idea he might not earn sympathy from others, and was therefore sometimes suspicious of advances.

Although we were developing his potential we were in no way helping him to avoid the mental rigours of life at home. After his return from a holiday there would be a temporary emergence of all

181

his discouraging symptoms. It was never possible to discuss his private matters with him because the lack of response prevented any real participation in the analytic process which demands active co-operation.

But we continued to look for other ways of getting through to him and one day we noticed him hanging around the music room. He was nervous of entering, and when he did so he would merely sit and listen to the playing of others. So we arranged for him to be given a record player and were pleased to see that his choice of records was not at all representative of pop culture, but was of a reflective, symphonic nature. We contrived that our music master asked his assistance in matters which, in fact, did not really require help, and finding such aid was within his capacity, and that it reflected a newly found interest, Edward gave his whole-hearted support. A strong bond grew between him and the music master.

The rapidity with which this fifteen-year old learned to play the piano and violin was remarkable, and later he learned to play the flute and trombone. Thus he discovered an unexpected ability which seemed to him nothing short of the miraculous. Intellectually he could have taken up almost any subject with distinction; but he chose only music. I once said to him: 'It is very odd to me that music is now so important to you. Indeed I envy you your brilliance on the piano.'

I shall never forget his reply: 'Music is better than words. When you are playing the piano you feel you are doing things for yourself. When you read you are only doing what other people have done already.'

His ability with so many instruments made him an important member of the school orchestra, and thus for the first time he achieved social acceptance and respect. He was much in demand as a pianist at school plays and occasional parties. He also composed music, and when he was able to play his own compositions he was, for perhaps the first time in his life, a happy boy.

Music was the key that unlocked the door to his salvation. He had always been indifferent to classroom achievement, but he undertook classroom activities with enthusiasm and revealed his true intelligence and ability. He passed the appropriate 'A' level examinations and went on to study at a well-known school of music. He is now a professional teacher of music.

Sudden deafness and dumbness had descended upon Felix Grant when he was nine. The results of medical examination showed that these afflictions were psychological in origin. When we first heard of him, he would spend all day standing about at the bottom of the garden in between the bean poles or by the privet hedge, seemingly watching the leaves. His withdrawal was complete.

Until he was about seven years old Felix had apparently been a normal boy in every respect, but during the next two years he showed signs of uneasiness and apprehension if a male teacher came near him, and finally refused to approach any man for any reason whatever. Then he was stricken by the deafness and dumbness. The suddenness of its onset was remarkable; according to information from his mother and school, he had been speaking quite normally during the morning, but during lunch at home he had stopped speaking and, apparently through lack of comprehension, had stopped hearing also. He went back to school in the afternoon but it was quite clear to the teachers that something extraordinary had happened.

Felix's mother was a disappointed, angry and unhappy woman who would nag and decry the neighbours, the school and members of her own family. To Felix himself she was a constant critic and we wondered if, unable to withstand the pressure of the continual nagging, he sought protection in withdrawal. But there was a secret in the Grant family and Felix had been with us for six months before we learned where his father was. I tackled Mrs Grant very bluntly and directly on the matter, saying that I could not believe her story that her husband was away in employment abroad. At last, and in a mixture of weeping and abuse, she admitted that her husband was in prison. The news had been kept from the neighbours by a change of residence, and by telling Felix lies the information had been kept from him too.

His father had been sentenced to a long term of imprisonment for grave sexual offences against girls, and this fact was so shocking to his wife that she would not hesitate at any dissimulation to avoid others learning the truth. I suggested that the boy's sudden avoidance of men at the school might indicate that he had some intuitive awareness of his father's misbehaviour, the mystery being emphasized by the lies that had been told to him which no intelligent child could have believed for very long. I suggested to Mrs Grant that perhaps unwittingly, and without for one minute wishing to do so, she had betrayed her husband to her son. Even if that betrayal had not occurred, and we could never know for certain, her own feelings towards her husband would almost inevitably have been conveyed to the unfortunate boy.

Despite her nagging and bad temper I was very sorry for this woman. Most people in an equivalent position would have complained far more than she had done and the feared or imagined judgment of others upon her, involving her guilt for her husband and a complete breakdown of her marriage must have been a terrible burden.

Our path was going to be very difficult. We suspected the boy knew intuitively there was a grave mystery concerning his father and that he must have made guesses about the mystery. If only because of the absence of letters, he must know that his father was not abroad earning his living. As I had explained to Mrs Grant, Felix must suspect the goodwill of men if he avoided them, and a sudden overpowering realization of these confusions must have struck him when he was seven years old and triggered the sudden onset of the deaf mute condition.

Felix communicated with us by means of letters and scribbled notes. He would sit in the classroom reading alone, as he could not follow what the teacher was doing. Despite his limitations however, his progress is class was good and he used his energies at his lessons rather than in discussing or thinking over his condition. The library occupied most of his spare time. Occasionally he would communicate with other boys when they had the patience to write notes to him. He was no difficulty to teachers or other members of the staff, because once their wishes were made known by a note, he would carry them out without hesitation.

I dared not broach the subject of his father in writing, for I felt that Felix had chosen his situation deliberately to avoid any chance of hearing unwelcome news about his father. Dumbness prevented him saying anything that might precipitate an unfortunate and shocking discovery about his father. In any verbal relationship communication depends upon subtleties of expression, and it might have been fatal to the boy's future welfare to attempt any communication by the clumsy technique of writing. We gave him special tuitional periods to help him maintain his excellent progress, and

184

this attention obviously gave him great pleasure. It was part of our plan to offer the maximum encouragement and communication.

I collect books, and Felix was a very active reader. Often he would visit my library and wordlessly, but with a smile and suitable gesture, I would take a book from the shelf and offer it to him. I remember his pleasure when I showed him one of Repton's books on landscape gardening, with the overlays to the plates showing how Repton would change the landscape. He asked, through gestures, if I had more books of a similar kind, and I showed him all Repton's four volumes. I also showed him some very early Paris printing, indicating the differences between the various printers' devices of the late fifteenth and early sixteenth centuries. He understood a little Latin and read old French very well, and spent many hours, which for him were most happy times, at my library table.

After two or three months of this, he wrote a note asking if I had any old books on Mathematics. I showed him one of 1504 on arithmetic which gave an inductive proof of Pythagorus' theorem in Latin, and this excited him tremendously. He then came across *Calculus Made Easy* by Sylvanus P. Thompson, which starts with the facetious remark, 'What one fool can do, another can.' He spent three hours with this book, covering numerous pieces of paper with notes. I lent it to him and ten days later, sitting together over the book, I discovered that not only did he know how to differentiate but could also use the integral calculus as well, at least as far as the elementary standards to which Thompson took the study.

I took him to London where, in the shop of Messrs. Maggs Bros. in Berkeley Square, he saw Caxton's book, *The Game and Playe of the Chesse*. Filled with wonderment and admiration at this example of printing, he started spending money on chess books. During the fifteen months he had been with us he had not spent a penny of his money, hoarding it like a fearful miser, but now something had released that fear and he began to spend. His study of chess occupied many hours, and entering into the school chess tournaments he emerged as the champion.

It was remarkable to us how the boy's genius could flourish while he persisted with the deaf and dumb handicap. Chess to him was not a slow game but one to be played quickly, and about six weeks after his discovery of chess, in extreme excitement over a game, he had uttered some words which clearly indicated he had heard words said by his opponent.

His chess interest continued unabated, but he next started buying books by Culbertson on contract bridge. Occasionally he and I and two others would play a game, but it was an unexciting prospect for the three of us, for very soon, no matter what chance had befallen the players in the deal, it was certain that Felix would win. From the bidding and the fall of the cards in the first two tricks, he had an extraordinary flair for divining where all the other forty-four cards lay, and predicting exactly how every trick would be taken. While he never lacked partners or players, it was agreed that he would voluntarily handicap himself so that others stood at least some chance of winning an occasional rubber. The games continued and increasingly, in an exciting moment, he would express himself with a chance word. Progress was obviously being made. It was not being made because of his chance brilliance at chess and bridge, but because we had at last discovered a medium of communication.

He continued to visit my library and by now, instead of writing him little notes about the books, I could often utter a brief and distinct remark to which, by a gesture or nod, he would show that he had heard. Once or twice he would make a short remark which indicated some degree of feeling about the book. His maths progressed with amazing speed beyond elementary calculus to Matrices and Determinants, and having accomplished that he went on to the Hamiltonian theory and the Lorentz transformation.

After three years had passed it was possible to talk to him quite often about books, chess, bridge, mathematics and a host of ancillary subjects related to those four basic interests. I now decided to discuss with him the nature of some of his blockages, to which he raised no objection. We started to discuss family affairs and quickly we dealt with his nagging, anxious mother who had encouraged the psychological symptoms of deafness. Next we spoke of his father who by this time had been released from prison. Whilst those at his home still clung to the fantasy that he had been working abroad, Felix and I were able to discuss the matter on a truthful level. I explained to him that some of us were very fortunate in that we knew how to manage our love life and sexual relationships, but his father, through an accident in his upbringing, or some other

186

cause which was not our concern, had broken down in such a way that he misbehaved sexually. While I seriously question the wisdom of society in punishing sexual offenders and perverts, I did not discuss that particular aspect of sociology with Felix, but my own views upon his father's misfortune compelled me to put the matter to the boy in such a way that judgment of his father was minimal.

By the time the boy had been with us for four years he could both hear and speak normally. There had been no dramatic transformation as at the onset of the deaf muteness, but rather a gradual acceptance of others had developed a need and ability to communicate with them.

Work in the classroom continued at enormous speed in every subject, and it was not surprising that he passed five 'A' levels simultaneously and very easily obtained a place to read mathematics in the university. After completing his first class honours degree, he was far from being a narrow mathematics specialist, for he was interested in politics and sociology and at the university had been an active member of a political party. When he left university he joined a local branch of the same party and cultivated his various social interests. He stayed with us one weekend, and inevitably, like so many other old boys, enquired as to the welfare of some of his fellows. That led us to talk of him and his mathematics. A remark he made to me had great interest.

'Mathematics,' he said, 'is only one part of my life. The world is far too full of things, and only a fool would specialize and thus be blind to those other things. You know very well, Shaw, how I cut myself off from people for several years of my life. I am not going to do that again, because not only do I need people, some of them need me.'

CHAPTER XVII

Bruised and Bereft

WHEN Gerald Harlet came to the school, he would never allow himself to be in a room unless the door was open. Once when I asked him to come to the study, he entered only after carefully propping the door open with a chair. I pointed out to him that he must be very doubtful of my intentions to so carefully leave open an avenue of escape, and he replied that he was too frightened to be alone in a room with any one person.

A few days later I happened to be opening the garage door in a wind and asked Gerald to hold open the door whilst I got my car from the garage. But as I was about to get into the car, a sudden gust tore the large door from his grasp and he immediately ran off, screaming with fear. Two or three hours later I found him in the school dining room.

'What on earth was the matter?' I asked. 'Why did you run off when the garage door slammed?'

'I thought you were going to hit me,' he replied. 'You told me to hold the door and then I let it go and I thought you'd be furious.'

The terrors this twelve-year old showed on his arrival at school inhibited any reasonable social action. If asked to do a certain job, he would be too frightened of the consequences to refuse but, certain he was bound to fail, he would inevitably do the job badly. His solution to the problem was to avoid people and situations, and

188

he was solitary, unresponsive, tearful and frightened to a fundamental degree.

Such an inhibition of social contact caused the same disabilities to appear in the classroom and in other situations. When bedtime came he had to be carefully looked after by the staff member on duty so that some casual remark from another boy in a small dormitory would not cause him misery. On the whole, boys are very co-operative in such circumstances but they do not have the thoughtfulness that may be expected from an adult, and so poor Gerald needed constant protection.

As his first months at the school passed, his withdrawal became more and more chronic. He was like a drowning man who cannot swim and therefore does not try. He lacked any capacity to see the possibility of his own salvation or to encourage other boys or staff to give him the support he so needed.

His father and mother had married hastily and enjoyed a sensational saloon bar life. When the early erotic experiences resulting in the birth of the boy and his sister were over the affection, if affection it was, flagged. Soon there was a legal separation, and the failure of the husband to pay his wife any maintenance allowance. Mrs Harlet's bitterness was visited on her son and daughter. Soon she became a housekeeper to a 'gentleman friend' and although Gerald and his sister did not understand what the precise relationship meant, they knew it involved their mother and her friend going out together almost every evening to the public house.

Despite the association with this man his mother's bitterness increased. She was always shrieking at the children, demanding that they should do things that no children of that age should be expected to do in terms of responsibility. After sending them to do the shopping she would angrily criticize them for forgetting something or making mistakes with the change.

They were so unhappy that they ran away. I shall always remember the boy's account to me of the night that he and his sister spent in a disused railway shelter. They had gone to the main line station and, evading any porter, had walked along the line until they found one of the permanent-way men's sheds, where they slept that night. The next morning when they came out a kindly baker realizing they were hungry and had no money, gave them a loaf of bread. They hid for the whole of that day, but at night, venturing

189

from their railwaymen's refuge, they were found by a policeman. At the station they had their first meal for thirty hours and thus their tragedy came to the notice of a benevolent authority. The boy's fear and general malaise were quite obvious to those who interviewed him in the first place, and his mother's choleric maledictions, both when the police called and later when the social worker called, completed the picture that the welfare worker had already drawn of these children's unhappy background.

So the harm done to Gerald was already very severe. Not only had his father failed him but his mother had demonstrated her apathy for him, and the man with whom his mother formed an immoral relationship had also been uninterested so that wherever he and his sister turned there was no hope of love or attention. Their wandering away was demonstrative of a search for something they could not define, but which they felt they must have. The sister went to one residential school and the boy came to us, and almost every minute of the day was occupied by his fears. The difficulties of giving this child encouragement were manifold. From his past experiences he assumed that any remarks an adult made would be bound to have some unpleasant result.

When feelings such as this have sunk as deeply into a child as with Gerald, they can only be removed by patient and lengthy work. We had to be most careful to avoid situations such as the garage door episode, and to spare any implied criticism of the boy's fears. Thus, for over a year he was protected from quite ordinary reality experiences, as we hoped that a long holiday from reality might enable him to develop some defence which would help him to bear some of the stresses of ordinary life.

It was fortunate that his mother did not seek his company for when the first holiday approached he asked me in great apprehension where he could go for Christmas. I asked him if he wanted to go home, and he cried his refusal. I suggested that, if he would be calmer and listen to what I had to say, perhaps we might be able to reduce his fear of his mother. But once the idea of staying with her again was raised, his terror was such that no remonstrating or reasoning could prevail.

Eventually he received an invitation from the wife of one of my colleagues and spent a very pleasant three weeks in a domestic household without strife, perhaps the first such experience in the

190

whole of his life. These three weeks taught him more than we had succeeded in showing him since he had been in the school. One of the happiest developments of that Christmas holiday was that he was encouraged to return as frequently as he wished and, without attracting any unpopular attention or accusation of favouritism, Gerald continued to accept their hospitality. It taught him many lessons which could only have been learned by such an experience, and never from mere explanation. Pathetically, from time to time, he would ask this man why his own family had not prospered and found happiness, and his questions were answered with wisdom and truth.

Unfortunately the benevolent aspects of this relationship were not being carried into his relationships with other members of the staff and the boys. The terror of them still remained. At a meeting of the staff members we considered the fact that although to some extent we had breached this boy's defences, the relationship between him and this one staff member's family was still very fragile. It was necessary to see if we could relate what he had already learned within this one family to the concept of the wider family of the school, and we decided on a plan.

One evening Gerald was sent to my house with a pre-arranged message, and thus for the first time Gerald dared to call on me. He came to the back door and delivered the message, which was of a kind that enabled me to delay him, and seemingly without plan, but I could not get him to venture past the kitchen. He was given a cup of tea, but left most of it undrunk, and it soon became clear that I could not extend the visit further.

We tried again and again, and gradually with succeeding trials the boy ventured into my house, as if he were testing my goodwill. More than my goodwill was being tested, however; we were testing his acceptance of my wife and children in his presence. As each visit passed, with a slight extension of his advance into the house, so his conviction gradually grew that my menage, just as that of his first host, was prepared to accept people as they were without trial.

One day Gerald was in a teacher's car when they called at an antique shop and he walked quite naturally into the shop as well. There was no one else there, and the man and the boy were able to spend a pleasant hour without strain looking at the various exhibits. When Gerald returned to school he went to the library to look for

191

books on china and antiques, and as a result of this new interest he received an invitation to the house of another of my colleagues who had a large collection of books on china, earthenware and pottery.

Soon after reading the books, Gerald asked if I could advance him money to make some expensive repairs to his bicycle. He then cycled round the district looking at antique, junk and bric-a-brac shops. He bought nothing but would come back with little scribblings and seek to verify a potter's mark or other identifying material he had noted. One day he came to me excitedly and said, 'You know how rare Nantgawr china is?' In response to my affirmative reply he announced triumphantly, 'I've found a plate!' He described the Nantgawr mark accurately, and told me that the plate was marked at sixpence and was in a pile of old junk outside a shop in a nearby village. He was able to buy a Nantgawr plate, in perfect condition, along with a lot of rubbish for sixpence.

This interest in china led him to the wider interests of art and very speedily his whole attitude to the art lessons changed from apathy to one of restrained but excited concentration. We did all we could to encourage his new-found interests; he accompanied me to two auction sales at Christies and we went to some of the more beautiful shops in Bond Street selling antiques and ceramics. The antique dealers showed their usual commendable patience in discussing with this boy the elementary type of interest he showed, and his fascination continued to increase. He became a frequent visitor to the County Library and, so utterly different to the boy who would not even put his nose outside the school gates, he cadged rides in staff cars to save the fare money so that he could put it towards the next purchase of an antique.

Another exciting day came. It was a Saturday evening and my bell rang clamorously. Coming inside, without even waiting for an invitation, he unwrapped the parcel carefully on the kitchen table.

'I think I've found a piece of Meissen at the jumble sale.' It was a little porcelain box with the Meissen crossed swords underneath. I had a copy of 'Chaffers' and together we looked for the Meissen mark. He was right!

Gerald began to make quite distant journeys to museums, and remembering a good friend of mine who lives in the Potteries, I asked the boy if he would like to accept a fortnight's hospitality in

192

that region. He did, and had the excitement and pleasure of touring the Wedgwood works and viewing the collection of early Wedgwood at that factory.

He still had little interest in the classroom; but went through the motions of doing his lessons and achieved a mediocre standard in all except English and Art. In view of the boy's almost complete social integration we did not feel too disappointed at his academic weakness. As his mother had no interest in him at all now, we realized that his fortunes would probably be with us for some time to come. We decided to follow our intuitive judgment and avoid a conventional educational line. By the time he was seventeen, having passed Art and the two English examinations at 'O' level, he asked if it would be possible for him to be apprenticed in some way at a West End antique dealer's shop.

Gerald joined a dealer in china, and after three years had acquired considerable expertise. He then went to a large provincial shop for the next two years, and following that experience he spent another two years with a well known furniture dealer. In all these places he was not only acquiring a knowledge of the history of furniture and ceramics but was also developing a very marked artistic talent himself. Through considerable economy he was able occasionally to buy small pieces for his own collection, to accompany the Nantgawr and Meissen he had collected when he was a boy at school.

Difficulties often arise when a member of the staff of any antique dealer seeks to acquire stock for himself to set up his own establishment, but I am glad to say that Gerald did so with the complete knowledge of his employers, and was very careful to collect only those things that did not conflict with his employer's specialities. He now has his own shop, one of the best of the country's smaller shops. Like all antique dealers he has to work hard, but through his devotion and interest he earns sufficient to support his wife and three children adequately. Occasionally we meet and when we do he speaks, not with bitterness, but with regret about his mother's shallowness, and shows his appreciation of the generosity and patience shown to him at our school. It is good to hear the way he talks, because it is so different from the withdrawn, frightened child we first met, so completely denied the influence of a good mother and father.

193

G

Henry Hamble's father was a professional man of some eminence and culture, who had married a woman of similar intellectual calibre, but he died when Henry was only two years old. Soon afterwards, Mrs Hamble married the local manager of a chain of boot and shoe stores. Mrs Hamble was a good mother and all would have gone well, but tragically when the boy was only seven, she too died, leaving him alone with Mr Brown, her second husband. He was a good man, and had accepted certain responsibilities with respect to Henry which he sought to discharge in the best way he could manage. Not unreasonably he soon re-married and thus the boy had not only a step-father but now a step-mother.

Henry soon began to show symptoms of withdrawal, which gradually increased as the difficulty of adjusting to such a changing parental situation became more and more evident. Such emotional difficulties could not be borne by a boy aged nine. For a year before coming to us, he had played truant repeatedly from school, and his work had correspondingly fallen to an almost negligible level. He was solitary, with few friends, and found it impossible to discuss with any teacher the reasons for his lonely withdrawal.

When Mr and Mrs Brown brought Henry to us we realized we had to make full allowance for their feeling of guilt that they had not been more successful in bringing him up, and at the same time their feeling that this was a misfortune that they had neither deserved nor invited. In her conversation Mrs Brown demonstrated clearly her partial rejection of the boy, mainly because of his disgraceful school record. She was embittered by Henry's inability to use his intellectual capacity, and at the same time she suffered from some nervousness about her own rather humble social origin, compared to that of the boy's real parents. But despite her seeming rejection of the boy she was co-operative and showed a willingness to help as far as it lay within her power. Unlike some parents, she was prepared to accept the advice we had to offer, even to the extent of greatly inconveniencing herself and her own comfort.

During his first few weeks at the school, Henry refused to go to class or join in games, and showed a baffling negativism and a complete apathy to all approaches. Vaguely he indicated to me that he was frightened of Mr and Mrs Brown, not from their attitude to him, but from the intense disappointment he knew his behaviour had caused them. Six months had passed before Henry agreed to

194

attend the classroom, but once he had taken this step his relations with other boys visibly improved. Over the next two months his conversations with me were mainly concerned with the re-marriages within his family, and he showed a fundamental resentment of all these remarriages as if they had been contracted only to hurt him. I felt that he was using his first opportunity to talk about the tragic death, first of his father and then of his mother. While a mere reiteration of a difficulty does not necessarily remove it, at least the boy had a confidant who was prepared to listen to his problems. and if only by such attention show a willingness to lessen his burden. Voluminous tears flowed when he spoke of the deaths of his parents and he would often criticize some aspect of his step-parents, but this invariably caused him a terrible feeling of guilt. It was as if his parents might hear the criticism and, condemning his lack of gratitude, take some retaliatory action against him as a punishment. There seemed to be no doubt that Henry strongly felt that the present Mrs Brown rejected him and that he reciprocated her dislike.

He discussed the matter of his persistent truancy before he came to Red Hill School, and understood that the reasons for truancy had nothing whatever to do with the school, but had everything to do with his home. He found it difficult to speak of his perplexities about the family, and indeed it would have been a dangerous pursuit, for he always feared some dreadful worsening of his situation involving him in an even more desolate and annihilating isolation.

Slow improvement arose from this diffuse type of discussion with me and his rapprochement with adults and other boys was maintained. But Christmas approached, and he departed to his home with apprehension and doubt of the outcome of the holiday which was certainly shared by us. When he returned he expressed a great antagonism to some of Mrs Brown's attitudes and complained that she sought to extract a sentimental response from him.

This negative reaction might have been a reasonable one, but from my knowledge of Mrs Brown it seemed that his assumptions about her arose solely from his own doubts and worries. She came to see me when she brought the boy back from the holiday, and it was apparent in her attitude that she had a growing and genuine regard for Henry and would still be prepared to ignore her own

195

convenience to satisfy his. It seemed to me that Henry's antagonism to her was something that sprang from within himself, rather than something justified by her attitude to him. With considerable caution I explained this to Henry, and tried to assure him, not that Mrs Brown was a bad or good woman, but that because she had supplanted his real mother she was being turned in his own mind into a bad woman by his subconscious resentment.

Despite the difficulty of making a long return journey to the school, Henry's parents came to see me at fairly frequent intervals. Our conversations became franker, and they were able to accept frankness without feeling they were being criticized or were in any way subject to reproof. They acknowledged their interest in Henry was slight in the sense that, had he been an ordinary boy who did not demonstrate so many tiresome symptoms, an easier relationship could have developed.

No child can be prevented from intuitively understanding what we feel about him or his behaviour, no matter how much we try to hide it. Because, however, all the complexities of Mr and Mrs Brown's affairs with Henry were more at a conscious intellectual level, as far as the Browns were concerned, one could proceed with much greater certainty. While I did not consider it appropriate for his parents to discuss these deeply important personal and emotional matters in front of him, it was nevertheless possible for me to tell Henry of my discussions with his parents in such a way that more constructive understanding as to their position arose, and he was encouraged to think of their difficulties instead of brooding upon his own.

Henry continued to show greater interest in the social pursuits of the school and much of his nervousness and withdrawal had disappeared. His cure was far from complete, however, and our confidence for the future was mixed with reservations; with the highly advanced state of withdrawal he had suffered in the past, one is never entitled to assume too much optimism for an improvement in a new environment far removed from the environment of the primary breakdown.

After three-and-a-half years at the school, Henry was showing signs of his very high order of intelligence which was obviously a genetic inheritance. As he discovered the abilities that had lain dormant for so long he was encouraged to try harder and develop them further.

At odd times he could be found helping the gardener in the care of our twenty acres of ground. He showed no interest in ordinary gardening, but was keenly interested in cropping, differential weed killers, fertilizers, soil chemistry and matters of that kind. He began to buy books on agriculture and horticulture and it was quite clear that he had discovered a real interest in these subjects. The assistance he gave to the gardener was not only useful for his own social rehabilitation, but for the exercise of his academic talents. His interest was supported within the school by his work in chemistry and biology. Eventually he told me he would like to be, not a practical farmer, nor an agriculturist, but somebody who made a study of agriculture as a science. To this end he passed appropriate 'O' and 'A' level subjects, and gained admission to a university to read for a science degree in Agriculture.

He achieved an honours degree, and his exuberent delight was a joy to see. Meanwhile, with his academic prowess so well demonstrated to the Browns, they had become not only more tolerant, but aware that by following our instructions they, too, had made their contribution.

When Henry first graduated he joined a large local authority as a professional worker in their estates department, but as time went on he accepted a lectureship in a university, was successful in reading for a post-graduate degree, and is now employed at one of our universities as a senior lecturer.

The treatment of the passive, introverted, anxious type of boy is, because he is usually well behaved and amiable, more difficult than the treatment of more aggressive boys. On the whole we have met with good fortune and success in helping these introverted personalities although we have failed, and failed demonstrably, in three such cases where the diagnoses, unlike those described above, was primarily that of schizophrenic breakdown, and it would certainly appear that the techniques we employ are not those likely to help any schizoid child. In their cases, analytic techniques appear to offer little, when compared to the almost miraculous success yielded in most other types of boyish maladjustment. In the case of the depressed child, we seek to show an unspoken understanding instead of encouraging the child to attend for any analytic procedure in which the fount of his miseries is displayed. Proceeding from one quiet discovery to another about himself the boy can understand that his insecurity is an experience that need not, except in the tortures of his fantasies and nightmares, be repeated. On reaching maturity such children have been enabled to discover goodness and talent within themselves that they had never suspected. What we must strongly guard against is to mould any boy to a pattern which, however enlightened it may be theoretically, nevertheless might not be his true personality.

We try to encourage a boy to see that we, not only he himself, can use his ideas and, when he produces a worthy piece of work, instead of merely praising him, we ask that we might be allowed to share that experience. The fact that we then use his productions appears to be an enormous comfort and encouragement. We have to ignore demands of the General Certificate of Education examination; where these have a relevance they are used, but in a society which is riddled with the idea that examination success is a key to all life's riches, it is a distinction which should be made more often.

Family relationships behind the emotionally introverted and fearful child are always very complex, but not necessarily evil. They are fully aware of the severity of their tangled relationships, they know the full impact of the tragedies that have undoubtedly occurred within the family structure; but they sense too, in a way no outsider can understand, that a solution can never be provided by themselves alone. If adults cannot always satisfactorily solve their relationship problems, how much less likely is it that a young boy, unaided, can solve the problems that exist in the families of the depressed child.

Another fact that seems to emerge quite clearly from our knowledge with such boys is that their relationships both within and without their families are often asexual. It would seem that the capacity to show emotion to another has become atrophied. Within the fantastically complex orbits of aggressive human misbehaviour, one finds a sexual thread ubiquitous: but in the cases of depressed children sexuality does not seem to apply in either their inner behaviour or their overt actions.

It is important for the withdrawn boy to be unaware of our professional attitude towards him. Once he is cured, it is perfectly proper for the rationale of that cure to be discussed with him, and for him to appreciate that others thought sufficiently of his welfare

198

to treat him with understanding; to be aware of the process while it is actually happening, would further increase his inferiority and convince him he could never survive in life or achieve anything worth accomplishment without others holding his hand or over-steadying the ladder on which he had an emergent ambition to climb to his life's goal.

Withdrawn children who have usually lost all concept of the permanence and security of a family structure have to be convinced that even for them such a structure can be brought into existence. Within the school, therefore, as the withdrawn child makes approaches to other children and adults, we have to develop a concept of a family. As the years pass, we see the child selecting, from the men and women at the school, those who can act as foster parents. This does not mean to say that the boy has chosen artifici-ally, as an actor might take on a role. It is a subconscious choice on the part of both the boy and the adult involved. So long as the choice evolves from an easy, tolerant, but purposive atmosphere, then for both the boy and the adults the work is more of a pleasure than a therapy. Should a note of artificiality or condescension be suspected by the boy, then the work can fade into failure.

CHAPTER XVIII

Aggression

IRRITABILITY, bad temper, sulks, violent verbal attacks on others and assaults that can cause death or can even culminate in an involuntary or planned murder: consideration of the vast field of aggression with difficult children shows that there is one group where the aggression appears to be something recently generated, and a maladjustment that the child, without any deep or radical analysis, can be taught to bring under his own normal control. Sometimes failure to control that infantile temper and aggression leads to the more violent aspects of assault and, when untreated, can lead to a world of fantasies and distorted thoughts which may even culminate in murder.

While the basic factors of family difficulties present in the cases of children who are mildly or actively aggressive are similar to those exhibited by such children who in adolescence or adulthood actually commit a murder, we are not yet fully aware of what factor is present in some that allows them to go to the dreadful extreme of actually taking life. We hope such knowledge will come to us, but as the similarity between the two extremes of aggression is marked, it is difficult to imagine that such knowledge will come easily, and even when discovered will be used in a way that will result in the cure of all unhappy patients.

One mild case was the son of Mr Kitchen who first took his son to court to complain of the trouble he was having with John. He

200

had been to various voluntary agencies and social workers, but they all appeared to feel the boy constituted too great a problem for any help they could offer. He had been suffering from temper tantrums, threatening violence towards other members of his family, and had been stealing from anyone who was careless enough to leave some valuable object about, but it was apparent that these symptoms had only emerged with the main tragedy that occurred in this boy's life. His mother died eighteen months before the onset of the really severe symptoms, and unfortunately the boy had been witness to her death. He was standing about twenty yards away from her while she was waiting alone, near a lamp post, for the oncoming bus. At that moment a car, driven by a drunkard, came skidding across the road, knocked into the lamp post, ricochetted from that and, knocking John's mother against a wall, crushed her to death. Despite the shock and the dreadful emotions that must have overwhelmed John at that moment, he immediately ran for the police and ambulance.

The mother's funeral over, the first difficulty was his absence from school and the discovery that he was hanging around in the graveyard. This then evolved into stealing the flowers left on other graves and putting them on the grave of his mother. A third change was actually stealing the flowers and taking them home, as if to retain a keepsake of his mother and the love he had for her. This hardened to a virtual refusal to go to school and his determination to hang around the cemetery.

One could easily question what it was in the relationship between the boy and his mother that occasioned such a remarkable reaction to her death. Many boys do suffer the death of one parent, but few react in such a demonstrative manner. The majority, of course, have the common sorrow to share with the parent who remains. That common sorrow appears to give a support, which perhaps in this case was denied, and the tragedy was made even more complicated by the fact that the father himself was an undertaker.

The boy came to us with all these difficulties, but quite clearly before one could deal with his mutinous aggression and refusal to co-operate in any ordinary pursuit, one had to show him that whatever had gone wrong in the past was unlikely to be repeated in the future. As we pursued our conversations with him we discovered all kinds of arrogance and irritability directed towards his father.

201

On one occasion the boy had flung at him the cruel remark: 'It's all your fault my mum died. If you'd had a motor car she wouldn't have been waiting for the bus. So it's your damned fault!'

The accusation, unfair and irrational as it was, indicated the extent to which John's mental condition had broken down.

After Mr Kitchen had taken the boy to court and charged him with being beyond his control, there was a temporary improvement in John's behaviour, but such sudden changes could not be permanent and it was unfortunate that the school holidays had started, thus giving the boy an opportunity to help his father in the undertaking business. This was an unhappy situation for the child and it was not surprising that he started running about the streets and staying away from home until all hours of the night. He did not associate with bad boys but wandered around in a solitary manner, without making any companions.

When he came to us, it was obvious that he could not co-operate in analytic sessions and therefore our therapy became somewhat simpler. At all times, despite the provocation he gave, we expressed sympathy without condescension. We were adept at finding situations which emphasized his dignity; we found situations that placed him in positions of responsibility which he could accept and gradually his aggression diminished. Ultimately we were able to regard him, like so many other children who have passed through our hands, as having had his experiences of misery, but who come to believe that that experience can be limited.

Having obtained a reasonable standard of education, which fell far short of university standard, he left to enter clerical employment, and we have always been pleased to hear that he has progressed to a position of managerial status. Eight years ago he introduced us to his wife. She seemed a homely, companionable person, fourteen years older than himself. The marriage continues happily, but they have not had children, although recently they are considering adoption.

Another case of mild aggression was that shown by Kenneth Lomax. He had come home from school one day and, pausing at the back door, heard voices in the kitchen. As he entered he saw two detectives speaking to his father. Naturally, the police waited for Mrs Lomax to take the boy into another room before continuing their conversation with Mr Lomax, but unfortunately the boy's father had to go to the police station and, being a man with previous convictions, he was ultimately imprisoned for larceny. Within a few weeks Kenneth's behaviour had deteriorated to such an extent that his teachers recommended expulsion.

When he came to us he was as full of prickly reaction as a hedgehog. He insulted adults; he refused to execute even the most normal requests. The reply he would give to a courteous suggestion or friendly gesture was, 'Shut your f—— mug!'

Shortly after his arrival at the school he began to steal. It was difficult to form a relationship with him as every approach was regarded as a trick which would later be turned to his disadvantage. In such situations one can only go on with patience for condemnation only increases the ill temper of the child. However justified a rebuke would be for his unspeakable insults to all workers within the school, such a rebuke would only reinforce his unfounded idea that others were there to persecute him.

Gradually he was able to reduce his bad behaviour to a fear of others' knowledge of his father's disgrace and the belief that no matter how cunning he was in covering his traces, in the end everybody would know of his father's imprisonment. Even when pleasant things were said to him, he felt there was an unspoken jeer behind the words; and when offered a sweet or present, he assumed this was only a trick to reduce his defences so that the shaft of accusation could be planted even more deeply. After he had expressed these doubts to me I tried to give what reassurance I could without playing down the reality of his father's disgrace, for reassurance is only given with difficulty when the tragedy exists. Nevertheless Kenneth did appreciate patience and came to understand that our failure to respond to his jeer of hatred was something that could perhaps be turned to deeper advantage. A mild response to his insults was therapeutic, but a vigorous retort with anger would have resulted in an even greater stream of abuse. Finally he accepted the thesis that whatever his father had done was no reflection upon him and he, Kenneth, could forgive without conceit or shame on his own part.

At last he realized that whatever the situation was at home there was no reason for him to imitate it and when, quite by chance,

I pointed out to him the folly of those who thought they would imitate what their father or mother had done, he jumped out of his chair in excitement and shouted, 'Do you mean to say I won't be a thief?' I replied that there was no need for him to be one any more than anybody else, and whatever his parents or uncles or aunts or any other of his relatives did, it bore little relationship to what he would do. 'Yes,' he said. 'But what about that business that you've got to support your father through thick and thin?' I said that I thought I knew what he was talking about and reminded him that indeed he had to honour his parents when they did honourable things, but nobody would expect him to give honour to a dishonourable act. Equally, nobody should feel bound to dwell upon a dishonourable act in such a way that the feelings of the person who had committed the act would be further hurt.

Kenneth met his father privately at my house soon after Mr Lomax left prison and they both agreed the past was something that could be erased; the boy stayed with us and, taking advantage of a relief from his difficulties, he persevered in his classwork so that he could go on to university.

We would like to say that his father resisted further temptation, but that would be untrue. Kenneth, however, was able to withstand the next difficulty the father had with the law and, in subsequent troubles that his father's behaviour caused, Kenneth remained uninvolved.

No deep analytic therapy was attempted with Kenneth. Because of his belief in others, even while he fought them, the nature of his father's behaviour was borne by him in such a way that the marked reactions occurring before and for some time after his arrival at the school ceased because they had no longer any basis. Very recently he called upon me to ask what he should do. His mother had left his father some years before and his father was now writing to the boy, pleading for assistance, and saying how much the boy owed to him and how his dear old dad would appreciate anything the boy could do for him. It was difficult to counsel this young man now in possession of a Science degree and married, but nevertheless I repeated that we could still only honour those who did honourable things, and that his responsibility lay to his wife and children first. Only when those responsibilities were fully discharged could he feel he was in a position to help his father. Neither, I said, should he invite his father to his house. The demands of a disturbed, now rather elderly man would not be good for the Lomax family. He took my advice, but more recently told me that he does try and help his father when he can.

While psychological definitions can never have that quantitativeness that exists in Science, nevertheless we always regard the state we call violence as being intermediate between that shown by aggression and that shown by thoughts of or commission of murder. Whereas the aggressive child not accepting psychoanalysis can nevertheless he helped by environmental treatment, and helped in such a way that the cure appears permanent, the violent child is one who never seems able to accept the analytic assistance that is offered. His sorrow at an attack, verbal or physical upon another, leads very quickly indeed to a temporary contrition and before tea time a child, who in the morning has been vile in his attitude or tone to a member of the staff or another boy, will be happily playing a game of bridge or chess with the offended party as if nothing had happened. When the attack is renewed, as it probably will be, it is again quickly followed by contrition. Such boys form a relationship to one adult and then to another as the attacks change their target from the first to the succeeding staff members. This makes therapy based upon a steady encouragement and non-analytic relationship nearly impossible. But as the work is shared amongst colleagues so that a consistent attitude is shown to the child, the variations in social or moral advice are wide. Thus the child in shifting his attention from one to another adult is refusing to acknowledge a permanent relationship which could lead him to a happier state from which a fundamental cure may be commenced.

We have had such cases, and as with all other children, we have watched their careers with interest after they have left the school. In general they have not been successes, although by paying some regard to that which we sought to do for them they have avoided conflicts with the law.

They mostly marry submissive women, who appear to have a capacity to tolerate any insult their husbands offer them, and if I imagine what would happen should their wives oppose them through some sudden discovery of courage, I fear that the husband could change from what their wives might call moodiness or depression into a raging violence from which great harm could arise. Clearly needing some expression of love within their lives, these adult boys have chosen wives who are unlikely to precipitate the difficulties I fear, and with that curious wisdom shown so often by the neurotic, have created a situation in which although mental ill health exists, it does not demonstrably flourish.

Quite clearly the violent boy is seeking to project his own terrors and rage onto others. The chief characteristic of such children, and of the difficulties in dealing with them at all, is their unfounded attribution of base motives to those around them. The exaggerations of the violent child may reveal emotions he has not been able to bear within himself and feeling unsure of his own safety, he makes attack the best defence.

On one occasion, I was chatting in the staff sitting room when the door was suddenly flung open and a boy angrily came to me and putting his face within a few inches of mine said, 'You sod! I'll do you! You fucking swine, you'll get what's coming to you!' Before I could recover, he had slammed out of the room. I enquired into his behaviour preceding the outburst and discovered that in conversation with another boy, that boy had told him of some criticism of mine of a purely general nature which the violent boy had then decided applied to him and to him only. It was true that the criticism did in fact apply to him, but it was impossible for him to bear any reflection upon his behaviour. If we pretend that my reaction to it had been one of reciprocal rage, then the boy would have been punished for his impudence. But although acceptance of the insult did very little in itself to remedy the situation, punishment would have made the child bear an even greater grudge than he did.

Eventually this boy did come to me to say he was sorry for what he had said and wished he could understand why he did these things. There followed a period of two months in which I saw him at frequent intervals and we discussed the divorce within his family and the way in which his father neglected his divorced mother financially. He told me how his mother moaned to him about poverty and the superficial layers of the discordance at home were uncovered. When we approached the reason for the boy acting in the particular way which had led to his attending our school, the appointment-breaking period started. Often I interpreted to him the reason for his evading the appointments which at quite another level he wanted so much, and explained to him how the unpleasant-

ness and misery were things he and I had to work through so that
he would no longer seek his retaliation through others. I tried to
show him, again through the fact of the broken appointments, that
he had decided the pain of seeing these things would be too much.
He had convinced himself that the hurt caused by these tensions
at home had been buried and suffocated, but I preferred to trespass
deeper to the very centre of his confusion and to try to make him
grow into the maturity that he really desired.

Another boy who had lost his father in tragic circumstances and
who was being brought up in an institution had so offended all by
his violence that they decided to get rid of him. In view of the
records on his behaviour it was difficult to believe that we were in a
position to help, but because at that time we had one of the very
few vacancies we are prepared to apply to these dangerously
disturbed children, we took him. From his own uncertainty that no
relationships could exist for him, and because of his fear of testing
the permanence of any relationship he followed the offensive pattern
of hatred.

One day I had an interview with his mother, and it was pathetic
to realize her terror of her son. According to her and to other
observers attached to the child guidance clinic, the other three
children in the family appeared to be quite normal and had been
able to withstand the death of the father.

This boy, the eldest of the family had never had a good relationship with his father whilst he was alive. He was a small man
physically, with a squeaky voice and he had accepted that his son
was the biggest factor of direction within his family. From my
observations, although I had little evidence to support my view, I
have no doubt that the boy, sensing in the father a rival to his own
pre-eminence within the family, had quite coldly thought of the
possibility of killing him. When in fact the father did die, the boy
nursed a strong feeling of guilt. While being conventionally sorrow-
ful for his father's death, yet another side of him was triumphant at
his own position as the head of the family. Under these circumstances, his contrition, so characteristic of such boys, swung from
one extreme to the other. Whatever the facts, some of the expletives
the boy used, some of the phrases in his essays, all showed that
lurking in the background there was a feeling on his part that he
had been responsible for the removal of his rival within the family

207

and as in that sense he was a murderer so, as a murderer, he had continually to evade detection.

One day, coming out into the back drive, I met him with a twelve-bore gun that he had stolen from the gardener's locked potting shed. 'I'm going to get you,' he said. I asked what I had done. 'You know what you've done,' was his shouted answer. 'And if you bloody well think you can bloody well get away with it you have another bloody think coming!'

I shall always remember that reply because of the virulence and terror he showed in the repeated word 'bloody'. I asked him if there were not better solutions to his difficulties, to which he replied that he was not going to listen to any more 'clap-trap'. 'Must it always be clap-trap,' I asked him. 'Is there not some sense somewhere that might be able to help you?' He replied, 'You can save all that codswallop for people who like it. As for me I'm going to shoot your bloody head off!'

'Is the gun loaded?' I asked.

'How could it be?' he shouted, his whole attitude changing immediately. 'I've no cartridges'.

It was a fortunate remark on my part for I do not know what I would have said next. Doubtless I would have thought of something and while one can keep an incident of this kind at the level of conversation, one is in control and can probably save the violent person from that which he fears most which is, of course, an execution of his violence.

This boy still sees us from time to time. He is in professional employment but not married, and perhaps his failure to do so shows how much he still fears a permanent relationship of such depth.

CHAPTER XIX

Violence

THERE are those boys whose aggression instead of being directed against others, is turned back upon themselves. Such cases are very difficult to treat because, if a child knows he is being watched, he is more likely to rebel than he would be if he remained in ignorance of such surveillance.

One boy was always falling out of trees, so much so that in the end, after two broken arms, a broken collar bone and a broken leg, we had to forbid him to climb them. Another boy had no fewer than ten bicycles while he was with us, because his possession of each in turn led to an accident. Not only was he injured badly enough to be taken into hospital, but the bicycle was completely destroyed. In the case of another boy we had to prevent him from playing with fireworks, and we told his parents that there was not only the chance, but the probability, of an accident if they could not contain his extraordinary addiction. But during a brief holiday at home he bought some explosive chemicals, and so mishandled them that he blew off two of his fingers. Another such case of self-inflicted violence was of the boy who assured us he could swim well, and contrived to be in the school swimming bath without having passed the preliminary test. Fortunately there happened to be an adult present when this boy dived into the deep end without being able either to swim or float.

Now in these four situations one has as awkward cases of violence as if they had been directed against others. They bespeak a greater inner conflict, and promise of greater difficulties in adulthood if they are not cured. It is usually the boy who inflicts self-injury, wrongly called accident, who is seeking to expiate some dreadful deed committed in the past. When a boy with this curious accident proneness is in bed waiting for a limb to mend, his manner to those who serve him and visit him is good, sweet and charming, but once the cure is complete the same cycle of events needs to be repeated. It is only while he is suffering, or appears in other people's eyes to be suffering, that he can feel the retribution he has earned for some unconscious crime is being accepted.

One such boy had been very reluctant to speak to me privately or to seek any advice, but accidentally I discovered he was keeping a diary. Surreptitiously I was able to read part of this. It started as a sort of daily journal, but it became more personal and more sophisticated. But every incident seemed only to concern his mother. The father was hardly ever referred to; and as the emphasis on the mother continued so a peculiar hobby emerged.

'When my mother was away in hospital one summer and could not come back for several weeks, I became irritated if anybody touched me or talked to me and so snappy that people left me alone. So I was forced to find occupations of my own and this made me frequent chemist's shops. I used to make coloured mixtures, and mixtures that fizzed. Then I came across a formula in a science book which told me how to make gunpowder, and I worked on that until I produced a powder that would explode. I often experimented with rat poison which contained phosphorus, but continued my experiments until I tired of powders and used nitric and sulphuric acids. Very often my compounds would fail to explode, but sometimes they worked. I tried nitrifying the various powders I had made, but with very little success. Then I started to frequent the library, looking up the *Dictionary of Explosives* and other books which seemed to have something to do with the same things.'

As the biography continued, it showed that gradually he had concentrated upon tubular explosive objects; frequently he emphasized his isolation which he had experienced when his mother went temporarily into hospital. Later, as his diary showed, he attributed this to the workings of a malevolent providence. He feared that his mother had been removed as a punishment because of his aggression and

210

unkindness to others. In later parts of his biography which, one imagines, was mostly fictional, he wrote about blowing up walls, and said that he had started on ruined houses. He mined buildings, and all the time was making explosives in bigger and more dangerous quantities. One story which I believe to be true was that he made as much as a pound of explosive material, which he then took to a moorland and detonated. In some way the noise and violence was deeply satisfying and, as he told me when discussing his biographical writing, he had experienced a simultaneous orgasm.

His interest in the analytic sessions was diffident, but nevertheless he was able to trust me and to produce sufficient evidence for me to work on. At one stage he was able to discuss his own homosexual fantasies; he could not speak about this particular matter, but said he could write about it.

'I know why explosives attract me but that makes very little difference to the attraction,' he wrote. 'I know now from analysis that I could keep them under for two or three months, but sooner or later they would have their way. There is no question of going back into the old channel; I am still in it and have very little hope of ever getting out. Another thing I must say while I have the courage, is that I am very homosexual. It must come out sooner or later, so here goes. Ever since I began with explosives I have been homosexual. I repressed it and so I became polite to both sexes and tried to become a recluse. I was often so disgusted with myself that I took terrible risks with my hobby, using hammers and chisels on detonators. Here at school I am still partly the same, never natural. How I envy those who chatter about this and that girl they love, and as the weeks go by I feel more and more hopeless. That is the clue, Shaw, that you have been looking for for so long. I wonder how far we can go in trying to understand what I am really up to.'

I was able to encourage the boy to speak more about his homosexual fantasies. He always took the passive part in those fantasies, desiring the attention of men, but there was no clue in his family background for this abnormality. But it gradually emerged in our analytic sessions that, as is so often the case, he envied the relationship between his parents, and believed that his father's possession of his mother's attention was unfair. Even in his baby days he had plotted ways to end his father's monopoly of his mother and maintain his baby demands.

When the father came home from work the boy would make himself amiable, to use his oft-repeated word, and put himself out to delude the father into believing in his goodwill. At this time he was forming his interest in explosives, and it seems that he looked upon them as some sort of protection against what he considered unconsciously to be the greater danger of homosexuality. One of the difficulties in curing homosexual adolescents is that they tend to protect themselves under layers of concealment. When they feel, as they do at some intermediate stage of the analytic process, that as a result of removing these layers they will be confronted again with the suspected truths, one has to be careful in dealing with a possible transference situation.

Ultimately the boy was brought to understand that his real object had been to denigrate his mother in such a way that his father would not want her and thus devote more attention to himself. This is a frequent cause of homosexuality, and it is usually when the mother is dominant over an introverted father. As the (usually single) boy grows up, he is likely to mistake the sexual attributes and rights of the two parents and in that confusion, reverses their two roles. If he believes that his bossy, directive mother is really a male, he will seek a male girl as his life mate. Failing that, he will choose a real male.

In this boy's case however, the reversal of the sexes' role had been largely of his own choice, through jealousy of his mother's role. At a very early age children should be aware that their rights are different to the father's, and that whatever quarrel exists is a quarrel only in their imagination. Unfortunately our powers of observation are often too slight to be aware when a child becomes confused over this basic truth.

Once this boy had faced the fact that he was a homosexual, and that his explosives had been a defence against that homosexuality, he began to come to terms with the fantasies that had plagued his nights in bed for years.

This boy was unrepresentative of his group. Because he was able to accept the fact of his own jealousy and greed in the infantile sexual sense, he was able to free himself from the actions designed by him as a punishment for all his evil ideas. His after-history has been an extremely encouraging one. He is a humorist, and can recall some of the ridiculous behaviour of his childhood with amusement that he could so long delay a process of growing up, and try to obscure the real basis of his envy and greed.

One of the most difficult situations to deal with is that area of aggression between cruelty and murder. It is noticed only rarely, for children are extremely adroit at avoiding detection. But however much they escape notice when they transgress, the suffering and pain of that wrong is present in them. Because an animal is alive and suffers in a way some inanimate object cannot suffer, it is a constant temptation to the child. In all the convolutions and trickeries of the child who is seeking to escape an accusation of cruelty to animals, runs the secret knowledge that the animal represents a living, human person.

One boy was discovered stealing tame mice from another boy and, in an unspeakably cruel manner, dragging their legs away from their bodies. Only with immense difficulty was he brought to confess to what he had been doing, and the confession was only obtained because he realized the goodwill of the adults who sought to understand his motives. His younger brother had been born just before he came to the school. He was largely unwanted himself, because of his bad behaviour and generally aggressive attitude, and when the younger brother arrived and was treated with all the love from which this boy felt himself to be barred, the torture of the younger brother which he liked to dwell upon in his mind was transferred into action with living things such as pet mice as substitutes for the hated baby. A great danger in these situations is that there is no guarantee that an attack carried out upon an animal substitute will not later be transferred to a human substitute. It may be thought that such an explanation is an unnecessarily complex one, and that the boy who tortured the mice should be punished, and having told him that the punishment would be renewed if the offence was repeated, hope for some change of behaviour on those lines. But such treatment might prevent him killing mice, it would not prevent him from wanting to do so, and might later have serious repercussions on an innocent person.

The boy's father was an ex-regimental sergeant major, who had

had the boy illegitimately late in life. The boy had been present at the marriage of his parents when he was nine years old, although there seemed to be no reason whatever, as both parties were single, for the marriage to have been delayed so long. His mother, who had been in and out of the home all his life as if she were already married to his father, was a simpering, self-effacing, apologetic creature, who was quite clearly in utter terror of her husband. Her terror was partly controlled, and only evinced in occasional bitter comments, but always she tried to trim her sails to what she imagined to be the wind of her husband's wishes. The boy reacted against this bullying father by attacking small creatures.

The boy did not stop at mice. There were several kittens and cats about the school, the pets of various children and staff, and they too, suffered, one of them in a way that was violently sadistic. It was shortly before November the fifth and a firework was inserted anally into a mother cat and ignited. Fortunately the cat was soon discovered in its misery and destroyed. Difficult as it was to restrain our disgust with such a child, we had to concern ourselves only with the real reasons for his atrocious act. There had been another child born within the family early in November. The boy wanted no more babies within his family and by murdering the cat, the baby substitute, was adopting the strict, summary, treatment of a conventional R.S.M. to deal with the situation. It is perhaps needless to point out the probable sexual connection between the cat's condition and the method chosen for its death. Clearly the cat could have kittens and the boy thought, as children often do, that babies will come out of the mother's bottom. Cats are well known for their philoprogenitiveness and the boy's anger that a competitor had arrived within the family, to further complicate the complexities of the family life, prompted him to make the cat take on the punishment he wished to mete out to his mother.

I spoke to him about these matters but his pessimistic acceptance of what I said made me fear for his future.

The next unpleasant incident was when the boy corralled two sheep in a corner of a field and by belabouring them with sticks and cutting them with a knife he managed to kill them. Such an action in a boy now fourteen years of age prompted us to think that at that point we should regard him as having passed beyond our capacity to help, and he should become an in-patient in a mental hospital.

214

When this was put to him, he showed real emotion and concern for the first time. He cried and pleaded with us not to send him away. In a tortured voice he cried, 'This is the only place I've wanted to be at. Let me stay here. Things will get better!'

From that point on there was an improvement; sadly it was an improvement prompted by fear of disciplinary action rather than by shame for his actions, but his sessions continued with increased success. He began to express feelings for those within the school, which hitherto had been noticeably lacking, but he often failed to attend the sessions, and found it impossible to believe that my understanding did not mean condemnation, or that if I refused to condone, I would still not condemn. When the time came for him to leave us, he had managed to pass a sufficient number of 'O' levels to obtain employment in a bank. That employment continues; and we wait in trepidation for whatever may follow.

During his last nine months with us he formed a special relationship with a colleague of mine, which eclipsed and replaced my own. That relationship is maintained, and although the boy is still subject to temptation towards violence, and angry thoughts about legitimate rebukes from his manager, he knows that, with the help of my colleague, he has his difficult condition reasonably under control. Had his analysis fared better, we might have been able to regard him as cured instead of merely improved sufficiently to contain his own misery without inflicting it upon others. One day, perhaps, he will tell us he is going to get married, and then all the skill of my colleague will be required to give advice in what will surely be a tender, subtle and frail situation.

CHAPTER XX

Murder in Green

THREATS of war, and all the other violence around us these days, so easily distract us from the real and persistent existence of aggression among ourselves. Some people deplore the violence of blood sports, and when they hear of a Meet in their district, collectively attend to protest, but very often their demonstrations in themselves are most aggressive to the huntsmen, involving fisticuffs and abusive language. We may ask, therefore, how far is their kindly regard for the stags and foxes an inversion of their own aggression? Unconsciously they may deplore the aggressor within themselves and can only come to terms with it if they project it into others, and the follies of the huntsmen added to the nature of that sport give them a ready target.

More successful from the point of view of sales than this book is likely to be, is the crime novel with its huge readership excited by a narrative often concerned solely with the search for a murderer who, significantly, is the least likely suspect in the whole story. Murder trials reported in the daily press are read with an avid interest not so easily discerned for important political items that impinge upon our own civilization and welfare to a much more significant extent.

The attitude of society to murder is mixed. Excitement at a murder trial is not easily explained by the desire for justice and legality, and the success of the crime novel is certainly not attibutable to a seeking for literary entertainment. With such colouring of society's attitude to aggression and murder it is no wonder that emotion on this subject swings like a pendulum from one extreme limit to the other. In conversation about murder it is clear that many kinds of irreconcilable beliefs are dormant in people. On the one hand we have the angry person demanding capital punishment, and on the other the person who deplores such punishment. The release of a murderer before society feels he has expiated his crime calls forth all kinds of unscientific, uninformed criticism of the Home Secretary, whose department has sanctioned that particular release with full knowledge of all the facts. In subjects that draw such strong feelings we tend to cling to obsolete beliefs as an old tramp clings to his threadbare overcoat, hugging it closer as the seasons change until it becomes nothing more than his winding sheet.

To those who know little of the behaviour of murderers, it comes as a surprise to discover that in most cases the murder is his first act of criminality; in a sense one can say that, paradoxical as it seems, a murderer is not a criminal. Fortunately there are less than 200 murders every year in England but what, perhaps, is not so clearly understood is that nearly every murder committed is of friends, members of the family or relatives. Murder is rarely an act committed for mercenary gain. Certain bank robbers carry revolvers and are prepared to use them, but that kind of murder in this country is infrequent. Yet it is invariably referred to in the press as a sensation, and attracts much greater consideration than it merits. While over past years crimes of violence have increased, the fact is that most murders are committed within the orbit of a family and not against total strangers.

Another difficulty in understanding murder is that much matter important to social understanding in the murderer's act is never revealed in court because it does not conform to the judges' rules of evidence.

We have had several boys at our school who were potential murderers. Such children are not as rare as it is generally believed. Hardly ever is their anger carried into a murderous assault, and in the children we propose to describe, that act never actually occurred, but feelings sufficient to generate it were present. Had those boys remained untreated it is more than likely that they would have been brought into court, accused of murder, before they were thirty years old.

Murder gives to the murderer a promise of a solution to all his early psycho-sexual conflicts. Once the murder is done the killer, although unable to explain the maelstrom of horror behind the tranquil facade he presents to society, is appalled. These whirlpools of feeling were first formed as a slight eddy in infancy. It is often a surprise that, when detected, the murderer proves to have been a man of otherwise good and ostensibly reasonable behaviour. Somewhat isolated socially from his fellows, he has concealed successfully the existence of his tempestuous, dreadful thoughts. More often than not a murder investigation reveals that the murderer's bedroom, particularly if he is single, contains pornographic literature, all kinds of female underclothing, and other objects which have generally been acquired dishonestly and have some not necessarily patent, but generally hidden, sexual significance. From a study of press reports one knows how frequently prostitutes are involved in murders, or are themselves murdered, and it is obvious to all who study the background of such an act that the involvement of sex is paramount, and that the distortion of ordinary sexual concepts has been present all the time. Had the person involved been more fortunate when a child, he might have been recognized as disturbed in this significant manner, and given help.

The sexual murderer is often one who reads pornography which is easily obtained nowadays. Reading pornographic literature has a disturbing effect on the unstable and, although temporarily satisfying or relieving his internal sexual pressures, does appear to have the secondary effect of stimulating the perverted impulses that already exist. This is not so noticeable to the pervert as to those who seek to understand his condition. This is more than unfortunate, because the reader was seeking an outlet for his perversion and, had he been able to find one, the perversion might not have taken an aggressive form.

In the case of Leonard Morris who, when he came to us, was just over thirteen years of age, there were fantasy murders lurking in his mind. Among his problems were house-breaking and a persistent stealing of low-powered motor cycles, and whenever he was caught by the police he gave an astounding display of aggression

218

towards them. His reaction to police, based I believe upon a most concentrated terror, was to attack them in such a way that unless they were quick in their own physical defence they would have suffered serious mutilation. He would attack their eyes and kick at their sexual parts. In the police station he would attack and smash the furniture. We were extremely reluctant to consider taking him at the school; indeed, it was only through strong persuasion from a psychiatrist, who over the years had co-operated well with us and was one of the few who supported us in the foundation of the school, that we felt we had a social duty to try and help this boy.

When we looked at the boy's case history, there were many highly significant factors, perhaps the most important being his circumcision without anaesthetic, carried out in the kitchen at home, when he was three years old. According to the report given to us by his aunt, it was a terrible scene, and since that day he had not only a terror of doctors, psychiatrists and most professional people, but also a deep fear of any kitchen. We were lucky to have the evidence of his aunt, as his own mother had died several years previously, and as she was the only other witness of the circumcision scene we would have been without this valuable information.

At the age of seven years, Leonard weighed ten stones. This adiposity arose from frequent visits to the larder, bespeaking an enormous interest in what went on in the kitchen. When conducting the preliminary interviews with this boy, the clinic found he always volunteered a list of his latest misdeeds, showing negligible guilt. The relationship between himself and his stepmother was very disturbed, and when talking about his father at the clinic he expressed much aggression. This was no doubt based on long-standing emotional insecurity due mainly to the death of his mother, but there was some suggestion that the situation was not entirely stable even before her death. In addition there were vague suggestions from the boy's school of some difficulties in the psycho-sexual sphere; they could provide no details, claiming only that the boy's presence was a bad sexual influence in the school.

His father had lost patience with him: he had no trust left in his son and everything of value, particularly money, food and clothing, was locked up at home. He was also afraid to strike Leonard because, after one severe beating, he found the boy apparently unperturbed and coldly drawing pictures of a guillotine in which the person being decapitated was labelled with the words 'My Father'.

When he was six his mother had died from a carcinomatous condition of the breast. Leonard told me of his anticipation of her funeral and his experience when, from an upstairs window, he watched the coffin leave the house. He also remarked on his father's anger when he refused to go to the funeral, and the months that he spent afterwards wondering if some miracle could happen so that his mother would knock at the door and he would open it to find her standing there. Often he played obsessive games like avoiding the cracks between pavement flagstones, success at avoidance meaning that his mother would be at home when he got there. It took him nearly a year to forgo these tricks; their disappearance was precipitated not by the healing qualities of time or the support of a loving family, but through his father's remarriage to a person whom Leonard had suspected him of sleeping with long before his mother died. This woman was good, but like so many step-mothers she found herself out of her depth when trying to cope with the suspicious behaviour of her stepson. He refused to accept an olive branch after a row, or indeed any overture of a kind that could lead to a deepening affection, and she easily became exasperated with his behaviour.

Leonard had bitten his fingernails almost to disappearance, and his stepmother reacted in a disastrous way by painting his fingers with bitter aloes. The reason is not too difficult to guess as she probably realized her own responsibility in the matter, perhaps unconsciously divining that if she could have provided the loving breast to this bereft child, the the fingers need not be sucked, nor the nails bitten. Defiantly, Leonard sucked off the bitter taste, pretending that he liked the flavour, and thus by outwitting her provoked fresh annoyance. Time went on, the fatness increased, the delinquent symptoms grew more and more severe, and all the time the kitchen was avoided and terror shown of all doctors. At last the situation was such that the boy was forced to go to the clinic, and there, despite his history, it was discovered that he trusted the social workers and the psychiatrist who conducted the first inter-view. Because of their understanding, and Leonard's response, it was thought that he would benefit from being with us.

This fat, truculent, aggressive boy, who had succeeded in alienating all affections, arrived at the school. Nothing we could say or do could impress him with our goodwill. 'I suppose you're laughing at my squint,' he flung at us in the first few moments. His obesity, his squinting and his misbehaviour, made him a target for all the unpopularity and criticism that could be imagined. He feared there were policemen on the staff; any uniformed person seemed to bring forth an astounding conflict of emotion and occasionally, if taken out in a car, whenever the car happened to pass a policeman he would shrink lower down in his seat, to bring his face below the level of the car window. The fear was deeply pathological and as significant as the boy's fatness.

After six weeks he disappeared after dark, but soon we heard he had been caught by the police while riding a stolen motor-cycle. Every evening as time went on our apprehension increased that again he would leave the school premises and steal a motor-cycle. All rational criticism or consideration of his behaviour was out of the question; he knew it was wrong, but it seemed that his compulsion to take the motor-bike was irrevocable.

Time went on, it seemed to us, with very little promise of improvement. Attacks on staff were frequent and were always combined with absurd accusations of their bad intentions towards him. These circumstances accentuated the tragedy of the boy's complete isolation. The position called for really firm handling.

I said to him one day, 'You can be a fool, a lunatic, or a criminal. Are you a lunatic? Your behaviour is so far outside your control, and you seem so unable to bring it within control that you may well be a lunatic. If that is the case you should go to a mental hospital where they can restrain you from adding to the harm you have already done yourself. Are you a criminal? If you are, obviously you should go to an approved school, but once that kind of thing starts the next step will be a Borstal institution and finally, as a man, you will end up in prison. Perhaps you are only a fool and can be helped. You have to choose between those three alternatives.'

In saying things like that to a boy one has to divorce one's tone entirely from condemnation, or they will only sound like threats. In this case, Leonard did ask that he might see me again privately.

Once more I explained the rules of analysis, emphasizing that nothing he said would affect my opinion of him. The function of the analyst is not to judge, condemn, praise nor reward, but solely to effect some degree of understanding. But there could be no guarantee of success and, if he assumed some miracle would be accomplished, he was wasting his time with me. For in fact his work would be much harder than mine; it involved facing certain truths about himself which he had hitherto evaded. I explained, too, that the analytic investigation would be total, including his fatness, his bad behaviour, his dishonesty, and the theft of motorcycles. No matter what cropped up in conversation, we would have to explore it and work it out in detail. Finally, I reminded him that he had to say the first thing that came into his head, no matter how unpleasant or how difficult it was to confess.

The first tragedy he relived within the analytic situation was the death of his mother, but I was suspicious, as always, when a tragic circumstance cannot be withstood. In ordinary families, the sympathy and love which exists before a tragedy should continue, and support the child in its time of need. Not surprisingly, therefore, we soon discovered that before the poor woman's death, he had been a possessive, demanding boy who sought to use his mother as a psychological valet rather than a person with her own rights and duties. She would do all the things he demanded of her and insist on nothing against his wishes. Characteristically, in these advanced cases of aggression, it became clear that Leonard greatly resented his father's involvement with his mother. His jealousy was very strong. The father was a quiet, severe and over-stern man, and because Leonard was plotting and scheming to monopolise his mother, even at a completely unconscious level, he would see his father as an avenging nemesis who would sooner or later detect him in this selfish, parasitic attitude to his mother and take a fearful revenge.

I use strong and emotive words because the depths of Leonard's emotions at that time cannot be exaggerated. Monopolistic parasitism of a mother is something that invariably calls forth guilt. It is wrong to deny a mother the privacy and rest to which she has a right. Even in our babyhood she is entitled to be alone at certain times of the day. The other children in the family may also legitimately claim her attention, but in the mind of Leonard only he should be allowed what he sought, and all competitors had to be denied in case their share reduced his portion.

This is an abnormal type of insolent selfishness, but in this case we were not dealing with a normal boy or even a normal selfishness. A person who later might be capable of killing has obviously been gripped very hard by the urge of self-protection. Only if the person is looked at for what he really is, and not what our wishes and hopes would make him, can we expect to approach the understanding that must be a prerequisite of any effective therapy. I was naturally suspicious of the boy's attempts to blame so much upon the death of his mother, for his selfishness started before that event.

Soon we arrived at what appeared to be a solution. Who in fact killed his mother? Might her death not have been caused by his own insatiable demands upon her breast and her attention? At that point of discussion the boy's tears flowed freely.

'I wonder, Shaw,' he said, 'if that business in the kitchen when my foreskin was cut off comes into this? Could I have imagined that as being a kind of punishment for what I sought to do to my mother? I wonder if I could have worked that in to all that punishing stuff you're telling me about?'

I remarked that the fact that he had thought of it was in itself interesting. Later in the analysis it did appear that, long after the circumcision, Leonard had thought much about it and had wondered whether, rather than being medically justified, it had been a punishment for what he had done to his mother. Here one can see the emergence of a sexual association.

At the same time, we should remember that his fear of the kitchen might also have indicated a fear of the presence of his mother in some unpleasant situation. Not unreasonably, others had ascribed his fear of the kitchen to the operation carried out there, but the over-eating started at that point, and he might have thought he had been punished for taking too much of his mother and that that avenue of aggrandisement was now forever barred by the castrating, circumcising, judging doctor-policeman. So how else could he get food except by sneaking about, picking here and there at every opportunity.

Thus we established the fact that his feeling of selfishness, jealousy, envy and greed directed towards his mother had become sexualized and was associated by his mother's death. It was difficult to establish whether he knew if his mother had breast

223

cancer, but at that point it was interesting to observe from his drawings the frequency with which crabs were depicted. *Cancer* is the Latin word for crab, and I pointed this out to him.

Slowly he said: 'I often wondered if it was something to do with her breasts that killed her, because something was said between my father and aunt which I think referred to this, but I was never certain and I didn't dare ask.'

We proceeded to the next matter which heralded one of the bigger sources of guilt with this boy. The art master had told me that frequently his drawings were coloured green; there would be green skies, green houses, green people, and in a most irrelevant and inartistic way this colour was always obtrusive. I asked Leonard to show me some of his drawings, and I pointed out the ubiquity of the green colouring.

He said, 'I know bloody well what that means, but its very difficult to tell you.' He made me swear I would not tell anyone, although he has released me from that vow today.

'When my mother died, some of the green pills the doctor used to give her were left over, and I pinched them'.

'Why did you do that?'

'I don't know. But when my father remarried, he'd been with that stepmother of mine long before he married her because I'd caught them together several times.'

I said, 'But we were talking about the green pills.'

'Yes, they were little things in a sort of gelatine tube,' he answered. 'I know that my mother had to take them to stop the pain, but at the time I pinched them, Shaw, really and truly I thought they had killed her. I thought that by giving her the wrong kind of pill the doctor had killed her.'

I explained it was not the doctor who had killed his mother, but that he, Leonard Morris, believed he had done so, by sucking her dry and vampirising her attentions to such an extent that there was nothing left of her but an empty shell.

'This selfishness as an infant, Leonard, was so intense in you that you could not bear to live with it. Because you believed it was responsible for your mother's death, you blamed it on to the inefficiency of the doctor; but you cannot escape guilt in that way. We have to face the fact that you were acquisitive and selfish, and when we face it you will be able to understand that all babies are

224

like this and that you still have that baby in you which will not allow you to grow up.'

Such an analysis is not completed in a few minutes. The idea took over two months to convey, and that particular aspect of the boy's information had taken nearly a year to discuss. The cure of an incipient, aggressive, violent potential murderer is never quick and I wonder whether the cure of such a person is ever possible if it is delayed much past the onset of adolescence.

We had now understood the reason for the drawings being coloured green. I asked him what he had done with the tablets. 'This gets even worse', he said. 'You know how much I hated my stepmother because she's such a bloody bitch?'

'I know that you think she's a bloody bitch, and I know you do hate her, but it may be that part of your hatred is because she will not lend herself to your exacting and selfish demands in the way your real mother did.'

In general he agreed to the truth of this. In this sort of situation, understanding is not on an intellectual plane so one does not expect understanding to be very clear or complete.

Leonard continued to evade discussion of the use to which he had put the green capsules, but at last, with shame and with tears in his eyes, he told me how from time to time he had put some into his stepmother's tea, expecting they would kill her. At a certain level of his subconscious mind he believed they had killed his mother. He felt that, as his stepmother had failed completely as a mother, the only thing to be done was to remove her entirely so that perhaps a third choice would be better for his own selfish ends. His subsequent guilt was almost as great as if the attempt had worked.

When a true wish arises to make reparation, a child's cure is almost certain. I was glad when at last Leonard said, 'I wish I hadn't put the pills in her tea. What can I do to put that right?'

'The fact that you seek to put it right, and understand you should make some reparative act, is sufficient. Quite obviously you can't take the pills out of the tea that has been drunk, and it would confuse issues at home further if you went to your stepmother and told her of this matter. But as you have expressed the wish to put things right that you made wrong, I am content that you have done all you can in the psychological situation. I don't think, however, you are going to get away as easily as that, because there are a

H

number of other things you have done wrong, and it is from that wrongdoing you now suffer.

For six months we investigated the punishing circumcision which fundamentally he believed to be a castration, the avenging doctor-judge, his compulsive theft of motor-cycles which still persisted. Work in the art room provided the first clue: motor-cycles began to come into his pictures always executed with enormous care. Leonard first drew perfectly symmetrical circles, and these circles and their colouring were given an attention and care beyond anything else in the painting. It was characteristic that the picture must be completed in the same period that had seen its commencement, and he could never leave it and return to it later. Once conceived, it had to be completed, just as the decision to steal a motor-cycle, once conceived, could not be withstood for more than an hour or two. Leonard showed me some of his paintings describing their completion and monopoly of time taken by the two circular parts of the motor-cycle. During one analytic session he painted such a picture and I pointed out to him the vast amount of time he was spending on the least complex part of the creation, and so our attention became focused upon the two round things, for that is what he called the two motor-cycle wheels when he first mentioned them.

So we talked about the two round things. A mother has two breasts, and these had been invaded by the biting, clawing, cannabilistic crab whose name was not really cancer, but Leonard. His mother had died, and that was why he had to go on in an unending search for two substitute round things that would give him back the love he had lost. Then Leonard spoke in muffled tones and with a broken voice that indicated absolute sincerity of a depth that can never be described.

'That bloody motor-bike pinching business; what pleasure have I ever got out of getting into all that trouble? I've never known why I do it. People have read me lecture after lecture and punished me endlessly. I fill myself with terror in case I am caught doing it, but now for the first time perhaps I begin to have some idea why I have done it.'

It is very difficult to eradicate character defects that have been founded in early infancy and in this case the foundation of the murderous selfishness was even before the kitchen circumcision. In order to excavate so deeply one needs not only to have a knowledge of human motives and the co-operation of the boy, but something which in our present state of knowledge one can only describe as good fortune.

Although two years had now passed, Leonard's behaviour within the school was far from perfect. He had lost his fear of kitchens and was not stealing food. The tendency to steal motor-bikes no longer existed because he understood the true source of love and no source of love could be found in two fake round things that he had acquired illegally. His attention of an aggressive, truculent kind within the school had been transferred from men to women, and he was making demands of a most exacting kind upon their maternal patience. Our women workers are used to all sorts of demands on their understanding, but on many occasions the patience needed with Leonard could only be shown by an angel. In an outburst of temper he would shriek filthy abuse at them, and such abuse, when given in front of other boys or tradesmen at the back door of the school, are not insults that can easily be absorbed. It is only when one understands the feeling behind such remarks that the insult loses its sting.

But he now showed a keen understanding of his social crimes, and had a desire to make amends. It was at this point, when most people would be tempted to feel that he had been cured, that another challenge arose, perhaps the biggest of all.

Although Leonard had been seeing me now for over two years he suddenly developed a violent dislike for me. When he had given his attention to women on the school staff I had changed from being the providing mother, and as my dominant personality was still necessary to him, I became his hated, stern father, taking revenge for his attacks upon the school 'mothers'. He was very unpleasant in his remarks about me; sometimes of a highly sexual and improper kind, certainly always of a selfish, grasping kind, to other children and colleagues.

He once said to me, 'You may think you are bloody clever, but perhaps it will take that grin off your face if I tell you I've been thinking of killing you.' I asked him how he would kill me. 'First of all I would cut off your cock. Then I'd cut your head off and throw both into the stream in the woods.'

Then came a denunciation of my knowledge and an expression

227

of intense jealousy of my capacity to create and to understand. Such denunciations were interspersed by contrite tearfulness, in which he begged to be excused for his attacks on me, acknowledging the unfairness of them. In the midst of this mixed contrition he said, 'Sometimes I think I haven't got through the hatred for my father, and you are just a stand-in for him. In one sense he pinched my two mothers, and what's sauce for the goose is sauce for the gander. If he does it to me, why shouldn't I do it to him?'

We returned again to the subject of the former thefts of motorcycles and I asked him if he still thought of stealing such things. He replied that he had often thought of stealing my car, to which I said, 'What would you do with it if you stole it?'

'Oh, I'd sell it,' he answered, 'and get the money and have a hell of a good time.' In trying to say 'money' he made a slip of the tongue and used the word 'mummy'. I knew then that the challenge would become very real, and I often saw him loitering near me during the day. He would generally offer me some service, but I recognized that as merely a decoy, for his real aggression was now directed against me.

This was not a surprising situation, considering the unique nature of our relationship. This boy had been seeing me for over two years and during all that time the relationship had become one of utter truthfulness and frankness. In a situation of that unusual kind, unusual results arise. Fortunately in Leonard's case he was able to continue seeing me without breaking appointments or making his private sessions impossible.

One day he said. 'Something terrible's happened. I can't tell you what it is.' I asked him if he could write it, and presently a letter arrived.

'Dear Shaw, I can't say this to you in words but perhaps it might get it off my chest if I write it. I keep on having dreams that I am fucking (here he mentioned the Christian name of the Matron.) I wish I could stop it. She is very nice to me and in reality I wouldn't ever fuck her because she is much older than me, but I keep on pretending I'm doing it in bed. She undresses and I invite her into my bed and I'm undressed and we go all through the movements, but just before it should be coming to an end, I go back to the beginning and start all over again. Shaw, what does this mean?'

We discussed the letter and I was able simply and easily to show

228

him that this, far from being retrogressive or something of which he should be ashamed, showed so clearly how much he desired a mother's love. He was now adolescent, and in this period it is not unusual if love becomes sexualized. This was a revelation, not that he wanted to have intercourse with the Matron, but that he wanted her in the way that a boy desires a mother.

By the time we had completed the third year of these interviews he had passed through a phase of fantasying he was cutting off women's breasts, excising their sexual parts and, just as he had done when he had cut off my sexual parts and head in his fantasies, throwing the parts into a muddy stream. Here was his last attempt to convince himself that love was filthy and useless, showing a total devaluation of something he felt he could not have.

Eventually Leonard came to understand the proper basis of family love, that a mother's love is to be given to her children, but a wife's is to be given to her husband. The giver decides upon the time and nature of the gifts, and the recipient can be ennobled by them. Explanations of this kind to a Leonard cannot be communicated easily in words; they must be conveyed by the actions of adults towards him, by their tolerance of his ways. One has to feel and know by experience and learn by words, that to give and to receive are both good and the ultimate expression of simultaneous giving and receiving results in the creation of life.

After four years we really felt that a radical resolution of Leonard's difficulties had at last been accomplished. His whole manner had changed from that of a sulky, truculent lout to one of a co-operative young man, and his weight was normal for a boy of his years—all the obesity had gone.

We have not given space to describe the sad educational state Leonard was in when he came to us, and its gradual improvement, but he went on to university and is now a practising accountant. He works abroad, and although we have not had the pleasure of meeting his family, the tone of his letters is such that suggests it is a family that will never experience other than happiness.

CHAPTER XXI

Sadism or Murder

DESPITE his marked ability, Martin North was dismissed from his grammar school at the age of twelve. The headmaster justified the dismissal on the grounds that the boy was never serious over his work, and was a constant nuisance in many small ways, refusing to conform and demanding an excessive share of individual attention. Martin was odd in a way the headmaster found it difficult to pin down. He was a strange, timid child who lacked the temperament for a life of conformity. There was no one, strong reason and, as with so many children whose misbehaviour is difficult to define, one can suspect a very deep degree of maladjustment.

Martin's mother had taken him to the clinic, who had experienced the same difficulty in trying to define the nature of the boy's maladjustment. Owing to the peculiar intangibles in the quality of the boy's behaviour, none of the complaints lent themselves to explanation. Yet both the headmaster and the clinic were clearly striving to say something they knew to be of great importance.

After several interviews at the clinic, Martin's mother carelessly remarked that, when she thought of her son's toddler stage, nothing would ever make her go through that period again. This indicated that at this early aggressive level he had been mismanaged, and that perhaps his difficulties started in babyhood. Although there was nothing in his early history which suggested any physical cause, his motor co-ordination was poor, and when we first saw him he was overgrown and clumsy in movement, which added to his odd

230

manner. His mother said his buffoonery was increasing, and the clinic wondered whether Martin, despairing of trying to make his mark in any better manner, had decided to make his mark as a fool.

The activities he showed at this stage were extremely erratic. He rushed at everything, giving the general impression that behind him there was great pressure and he could spare no time to think or plan an action. As the interviews at the clinic progressed, and Martin was given an opportunity within their play therapy system to reveal other conflicts, it was shown that he had developed many bad relationships with adults, relating to an early infantile conflict with his mother. These matters were pointed out to Mrs North, who agreed that with all other children she had met, nieces, nephews and the children of friends in the district, there had never been the contentions with them that she had experienced with her own son.

There was some delay before we could find him a vacancy, and during this period we had three interviews with his mother. She told us something she had not said at the clinic, that when going through her son's bedroom she had come across books on sex and torture, and the presence of various articles in his room which he could only have stolen. She was so shocked at her discovery that she had not told anyone about it. She had thought for some time the boy had been stealing, but because the articles he stole were so bizarre, and so irrelevant to the needs of any child, she had not felt she could possibly mention it either to him or others.

She then came to a point which she said occasioned her far more concern than any other matter about which she had already spoken. She feared deeply that he might physically assault her. I asked if he had ever made a threat, but she said she had no evidence to support her feelings but she had formed the conclusion that if she went too far in her criticisms of him, for example to complain of the books in his bedroom, he would reply by some violent action.

Conversation with this intelligent mother was rewarding, and before Martin came to us we had some degree of understanding of the type of misbehaviour we were likely to experience.

Martin quickly started private conversations with me and produced much matter of a shocking scatalogical and dirty nature. When he told me he had 'rude' dreams I asked him what a rude dream was like. He replied, 'Well, that might be a boy letting down his trousers and showing his arse.' He continued, 'I wanted to do a

231

girl, and after a bit I found my chance, and I did a girl on some waste ground by the Methodist Church. I haven't told anybody about those things.'

On another occasion he said: 'My mother is frightened of mice and snakes and my dick.' He immediately followed this remark with two pornographic rhymes which recounted that part of a drain had been thrown at his mother's genitalia and his mother had grabbed his testicles. To me it was surprising that I had come across a tangled relationship with his mother so soon in my private conversations with the boy. This had been predicted by the clinic's hint of infantile aggression, and it was remarkable how accurate that prediction was. Despite all his nonsense, he appeared to be most apprehensive of doing wrong, and there was no doubt that he felt genuine and normal guilt.

The next significant thing he mentioned was that at the age of nine he and a fourteen-year-old and committed fellatio. The next few sessions were occupied with long, rambling tales of anal excitement, pornographic preoccupations and a boring recital of dirty jokes.

After he had been with us for three months, many valves started to disappear from boy's bicycles. Martin told me it was he who had been taking these valves, and he readily accepted my advice to leave the valves in a public place so that the owners could make their bikes workable again. He said, 'I've got to go on pinching things like that, although stealing valves from bikes makes me no happier, nor anyone else for that matter.'

He then went on to speak of fantasies of showing his penis in public, being frightened to do so but compelled to in spite of his fear. 'I'm frightened to show my penis at home because if I did I would get a beating, so instead of that I do all kinds of annoying things which I know are in some way connected with me trying to show them my cock. A year ago the girl I f—— went up to my brother and I wondered if the two were going to do it. When I thought that, I waited until my brother got home and then I took the valves from his bike.'

It seemed obvious that a mere discussion of his extraordinary interest in sexual perversion would take us little further. He could not find sufficient patience to listen to what I was saying. The first occasion on which I felt he might listen was after an enormous outburst of one of his characteristic tempers. Instead of attacking another person or embarking upon the filthy language which usually characterized his violence, he bashed his head continually against the drain-pipe at the back door. Fortunately I happened to be passing. He stopped immediately, picked up a nearby stone and threw it through a window.

Next day he asked to talk to me about this incident. 'I am certain,' he said, 'that the drain-pipe, the stone, the bike valves and the girls and showing off my penis to different people all have something to do with my bad temper.' He told me he had tried to blow off steam by hitting a tree with a stick and throwing at bottles on a rubbish dump. I asked him if he could express these complications in a drawing, but when the drawing was shown I could only see a maze of sexual symbols quite detached from any anatomical meaning.

As our conversations continued I felt we were not modifying his perverted conception of sex, but merely giving him opportunities for verbally expressing it. It was clear, too, that Martin was using his analytic sessions as an excuse for destruction of school or other boy's property and general misbehaviour. It was necessary to take some action to impress upon him strongly that whatever the reasons for his condition, in the ultimate analysis he was a moral failure. However understanding we might be at the school, when he involved other people in his violence or theft he must expect to pay the penalty which ordinarily would be exacted elsewhere. We had to tolerate his exhibitionism but we arranged that, if anybody could not avoid smiling at it, the smile should try to express casual interest rather than amusement. Quickly senior boys and then others copied our attitude, and he soon realized that he would not attract special attention by his bizarre sexual exhibitionism.

His first reaction to this treatment was to start speaking in baby language. My colleagues and I decided to take the collective attitude to him that if he spoke in a language that boys of his age did not use, he could not be understood, and if he was not understood, he could not expect the satisfaction of his demands. Because one technique appears to fail, that is no reason why one should hesitate too long before trying another. The child's welfare is paramount, and when it is felt that different techniques might

233

promise results even if they disobey the rules of analysis, those techniques are promptly brought into use.

The next ploy was that his conversation became limited to the subject of thunder, lightening, gales, flood, fire and storm. When ploughing through the eighth hour of such conversation, I pointed out to him that as eight sessions had now been occupied in this fashion it was time we got on to something else.

'Do you know what snowing is?' he asked suddenly. I replied, 'Yes, I think so.' He contradicted me. 'No, you don't! When it's snowing, it's the angels tossing off!'

For all those sessions, and in his conversations outside the analysis, he had been trying to express this sexual theme through an interest in meteorology. Again we tried to trace the sexual theme to its origin, and again we failed. His stream of pornography persisted, and although he was learning to understand that these factors had a significance to him that as yet he did not comprehend, he showed no depth of psychological insight.

During his eighth month with us there suddenly emerged a friendly attitude to adults and boys at the school. Considering that he was generally in some trouble or had recently been angrily complaining of his treatment, this change was surprising. Nevertheless his marked refusal to accept the truth of his eccentricities, and the apathy he showed whenever I mentioned important emotional points, was ominous. The obviously sexual determinants in his behaviour continued and when these matters were presented to him in a way that made evasion impossible, he answered with nonsense.

About a month later he remarked to me that he wanted to see faeces emerging from another's anus, and said it would be good fun to lie flat on the floor on his back with his face covered with a glass dome with people defecating on to the top of that dome. He added that it would be particularly good to have women doing it, and then remarked in an utterly casual off-hand manner that he wanted to have sexual intercourse with his mother.

Later he exaggeratedly referred to the number of fir trees that had been cut down in the wood, and the number of cups that had recently been broken when a tea tray was dropped accidentally in the kitchen. His verbalization was so chaotic that the sense of his sentences was difficult to follow. He then expressed ideas about

234

castration, in which the fir tree being felled was a phallic mutilation and the cups that were broken were vaginal mutilations. Speaking with a most rapid elocution he then suddenly referred to his assault up on windows.

'I'm certain that window-breaking is something to do with the glass dome over my head when I watch women doing a shit,' he said, 'and the boot polish I pinched the other day is something to do with the thing that comes out of a woman's bottom.'

The total situation was so chaotic that I felt considerable alarm; here were disturbed and crazy thoughts being produced as if from an erupting volcano.

I began to receive a number of reports from male staff members that, as they passed, Martin would grab at their testicles. After some reflection we decided to charge him for assault within the school court system whenever these matters occurred. This was not because we felt any disciplinary sanction would remove the boy's with to do what he did, but it would emphasize that he had responsibility for his actions. We thought that only by continued emphasis of his personal responsibility he might be encouraged to do more to help himself.

We were becoming stricter in discipline with Martin now because he was, surprisingly, so happy with us, and appeared to rely upon us to such an increasing extent, that we were confident he would accept it in a way that would clearly have been impossible at the beginning. But during our analytic sessions I was careful to avoid any connection whatever with the discipline which was being imposed upon him. He would complain to me of its unfairness and I would attempt to explain its purpose, but at all times I avoided any suggestion that I was responsible for it. At last, Martin appeared to understand that our patience was determined and likely to continue. Out of that understanding he astonished me one day.

'Shaw, I think I've just been mucking about with you and your analysis. I had a dream last night, and since then I have been thinking that if only I could start a diary, I might be able to write down the things I can't really say to you.'

I was tremendously encouraged at such co-operation never before shown by this boy, and very cautiously I accepted the idea and encouraged his to proceed. But I was not expecting the immense autobiography that followed. I still have this, and it is no less than

235

330 foolscap pages, in which the boy gives the whole of his life and all his feelings about other people. It reminded me rather of *Ulysses* which is just one day in a man's life, but even the genius of James Joyce does not equal the importance of the discovery that Martin North made of himself when he wrote, not a literary creation, but an understanding of his tortured sexual fantasies.

All his unhappy chatter about sexual symbols, pornographic books, books about torture, and thefts, admitted of easy explanation when one of his first autobiographic revelations was a coherent account of his fantasies of killing girls. When giving me this instalment of his autobiography he wrote at length.

'I am giving you something now which I can hardly believe is in myself,' he argued, 'but I know it's there from the dreams I have and the things I think about. I could kill a girl.'

I asked him then if he felt it proper to include that sort of reference in the next instalment. He did, and he wrote then of cutting off the breasts and sexual parts of the girls he had killed and, by a highly complex ritual, incorporating those parts in himself. 'You must think I'm loco,' he said, when showing me that part of his writing.

'Far from it,' I replied. 'You are not the first person who has been dissatisfied with not being everything in himself, and certainly you will not be the last.' I explained that his envy meant he was dissatisfied with being a male only. For some reason he was prepared to steal the female parts of girls and ritualistically incorporate them in himself.

Unfortunately fantasies of this kind can be expressed actively and all of us can recall cases of well-known murders where the female victim has suffered mutilation. Any prostitute can confirm that one of the many hazards of her occupation is the client who will make a sadistic attack directed towards her breasts or sexual parts.

Martin's autobiography next related fantasies of castrating men, which tied in with the symbolic castrative attacks upon staff members when he would grab at their testicles. As can be expected, the person identified as the chief target for his castration was his father. As a result of that symbolic attack on his father, and the appropriation of his father's penis, he could be not only a boy, but a man at the same time, and possess the almost terrifying potency and power between his legs which he believed was lacking in him. He feared retaliation however; on the one hand the father would submit to the degrading castration; but, on the other, his revenge for the boy's fancied act would be of such an order that the boy would be torn limb to limb.

The next two years were a great burden on the patience of people who came into contact with him. But they were a burden on Martin as well, and we persevered together.

All of us have difficulties and must deal with them, but a fourteen-year-old must deal with them at a fourteen-year-old level just as a man of thirty must deal with them at a compatible level. But Martin North had been trying to deal with his problems at the utterly egotistic level of a child less than a year old. At that age we can express little and therefore any difficulty is beyond the understanding. The bewilderment of the onlooker is only equalled by the subject's own.

I advised Martin to continue with his diary. He did so, and it evolved through the years into an easy composition of some artistic and creative merit, quite free from the sexual symbolism of the first parts. Even though we were now sailing in calmer waters, we continued to read the diary with care, for we always guard against judging cures by what appears on the surface.

Martin's behaviour became so amiable and co-operative that he affected the whole school with his example. He was an enormous help with new boys, and his counsel to them was always quite free from any threads connected with his own past difficulty. Academically he made full use of his very great gifts, and did so with a rather charming modesty.

The last part of his diary I had was received six years after he left the school, in which he announced his engagement to a girl he subsequently married. His letter expressed to me what I can only describe as a sacred gratitude.

A delinquent act is often an expression of guilt. When sometimes a strong conscience or super-ego succeeds in preventing the delinquent act, then psychic punishment can take over. Psychic punishment in some children is very strong, and always present in those who are guilty of an aggression which in adulthood could lead to murder.

Norman Oswald came to the notice of the probation department through his embezzlement of his Scout Troop's funds. It was clear that the embezzlement had not been in order to obtain money, because all he had done with it was to throw it into a canal. It had been done in order that he should be punished. To seek punishment in such an irrational manner, meant there must be some irrational quality in his guilt, and the Probation Officer wisely advised the juvenile court that this should be a clinic case. During the interval between the discovery of his embezzlement and the visits to the clinic, the boy's mother had discovered in his bedroom pornographic books, books on torture, and various items of women's underclothing.

The thefts astonished her for, as will be seen later she had no suspicion of their sexual nature. When I saw her for the first time she was an unhappy woman, confounded and dismayed. She had had to confess to the existence of a mystery in her son's life, and accept that she did not really know him. She burst into tears when she told me of the horrific pictures which she had found in his bedroom, hidden among the piles of underclothing. Some months later I learned the true reason for her tears.

When he came to the school Norman showed little sign of his difficulties, but gradually we noticed that younger boys found him interesting for various periods. With his fertile imagination he created a world of fantasy with criminal characters, and the adventures of fiction usually ended with him as the hero. He lived in this fantasy world, and in telling others these stories his happiness was increased. Those who interrupted him, or staff who criticized his literary abilities, were denounced by him with unqualified savagery. We were not surprised when after a while the stories took on sexual undertones which soon became offensive. This was now morally disturbing and, in our opinion, disruptive to the school. The matter was mentioned to Norman with the suggestion that he should see me. He accepted the invitation, and in my study he spoke to me in a provocative tone.

'I suppose you know I collect dirty books?'

'Have you any?' I answered. 'Perhaps I get my fun in other ways. Sex can be fun, and good, but perhaps the books you mention are not very funny.'

A few days later he asked me if he might see me for analysis and he produced one of the most wicked paintings I have ever seen. This painting was an illustration of a pair of women's old-fashioned knickers, on each leg of which was a grinning face. The visage staring out from each leg can only be compared to that of a gloating demon, and the horrors of all the disturbed pictures of Weirtz, Dadd and Gilray were outclassed by the terrors of this boy's pictorial imagination. He feigned indifference, but not very deeply, for after that in a spate of confessions he told me of all the fantasies that came unbidden into his head.

In reply to a question about another terrible drawing he burst into tears and screamed: 'I know I'll do a sexual murder if I go on like this. Can no one stop me? Can't you do something about it, Shaw?'

I asked why he was so convinced that he would commit a sexual murder.

He replied. 'You don't know what I think and dream about. When I think of what I want to do to women I know there's something terribly wrong with me. I put my hand right up their cunts, right into their bodies and turn them inside out, just as you'd turn a vest inside out. If I told you half the things I think about you'd kick me out of the room.'

I assured him that I would do nothing of the kind, and there is no purpose in this narrative in repeating more of the dreadful horror of the fantasies this boy had visited upon himself. He was able to see that the help offered might be of assistance, and like other children in this condition he was able to co-operate and tell me of his sadistic and sexual thoughts in his dreams.

'It's all mixed up and I can't make out its meaning, and yet when I wake up things seem easier in daylight, but after what you've been telling me, Shaw, I see now that all those stories with the sexy bits I have been telling the other boys were really only a continuation of what I did in my thoughts at night and in my dreams. Then I get a dirty book and my cock goes stiff, and I think of killing girls all over again, even in the daytime.'

At this point he suddenly stopped. His lips closed in a firm line, and he asked, 'What are you writing down in shorthand?' I told him I was making notes of his remarks so that I could be of more help, but at that point he suddenly swung from his chair and, seizing a smaller one, threw it at me. A stream of abuse poured

239

from him as he tore open the study door and left the room, slamming it after him. A day later he wrote to me, 'You have no right to write down what I say if it is a secret.' I found him in the school and produced the pages of shorthand notes; without explanation I took him to the boiler room and burned the papers. He then accepted that he could trust me.

From interviewing his mother, and from reading the case papers, I had never anticipated what the boy now started to talk to me about. He told me his mother was not married to the man she called her husband (a fact I had confirmed by referring to Somerset House), and had a succession of lovers, sometimes conducting two amours at the same time. She was unaware of Norman's knowledge of this fact, and she did present such an ordinary appearance that it was difficult to accept there was another side to her life which Norman himself had seen. Having no one to turn to in his sexual perplexity he had tried to solve it himself but, owing to the stress of the circumstances, had failed.

At an infantile level he had decided he could not share his mother with her visitors any longer. He believed she belonged to him and he could not bear the fact that others could oust him from her love. The way in which this appeared to be so important fitted with the boiler room scene, for it was after that incident that he told me how, coming across a tie which belonged to one of his mother's visitors, he had taken it, knowing the man had partially undressed in the sitting room before going to his mother's bedroom, and with ceremony and ritual he had burnt it on the kitchen boiler. My act, which was accidental, in burning something of importance to both of us on the school boiler, had reminded him of that occasion and reactivated an emotion about which he then felt he could talk.

From the success of that discussion sprang all his other revelations which eased a path for an understanding of the follies of his own attempted solution of a problem that should never have been inflicted upon any boy. I explained to him how, refusing to share his mother with others, he had decided to monopolise her so she could never be taken by the other men. The obvious way of doing this was to steal the parts of her which were most important to him; and, failing in that, he had returned to the fantasy idea of killing her, as a technique to prevent her being taken by the men of whom he was so intensely jealous. Such an interpretation was evolved

240

only after months of discussion of his mother's sexual misbehaviour and of details of her sexual life. Part of this was doubtful as fact, but most of it fitted with the life of a woman who supplemented her income by prostitution.

At four or five years of age he had tried hard to find out in detail what men and women did together in bed. Obviously such an attempt is bound to produce wounds and scars that only heal with difficulty. Had Norman pursued his sadistic attitude to women, undoubtedly in adulthood he would have ended by killing them.

It was a surprise to me how quickly his symptoms disappeared and his attitude to others changed. Eventually he succeeded in making a contribution within the society of the school. From the content of his drawings, produced in art class, it was clear that the terrors had left him. It was obvious, too, from his dreams, which later were ordinary heterosexual dreams of boyhood adolescence, that he had found normality. Our main task now was to show him that his experiences had been abnormal and improper, and that for him to assume that this experience was commonplace would be terribly wrong.

We told him that love would come to him with an unforced marriage and that no amount of looking back to his past would in any way contribute to the love that we all hoped would come to him in the future. After some years he married. The marriage prospered at first, but after two years he wrote to tell us of difficulties. He came to see us; later his wife came, and we were delighted that we were part of the instrument that helped to remove some degree of marital discord. It is long ago now that the marriage faltered and might have broken up, but it has prospered and succeeded for over twenty years.

The accounts of children whose sadistic ideas and actions show clearly how they might have committed murder, make us regret that those who actually commit murder have not been diagnosed early enough in their childhood for prevention of the final rejection of society. Too great an optimism would be unwise, because of those who could be cured many would not accept treatment or understand the basis of analytic help. But even if only a few of those who subsequently plunge into the dreadful tragedy of murder were saved, that early diagnosis would have led to triumph.

CHAPTER XXII

The Future

THE diagnosis of maladjustment is not in itself a cure. That discovery is a puzzle presented by an enigmatic child as a challenge to the sagacity of the adult. At Red Hill School, after thirty-three years my colleagues and I have learned many hard lessons both in achievement and disappointment, but we will go on because we realize that these children can only be helped by understanding. A highly disciplined regime is costly in effort and absolutely ruinous in disappointment. A boy is not basically inadequate, but needs space and time to learn of his own inadequacy.

Disagreement between the members of our staff and different boys is inevitable when so many star performers work under the same roof but, properly understood, disagreement can create achievement. The hardest tumble is to fall over one's own mistakes and, in the daily expression of our work we make many, but if we realize one of the true objects of a mistake is to learn from it, then even error has its place in man's experience.

There are thought to be several protections against temptation and one of the most popular is punishment, but this is often a cowardly attempt to change another's behaviour. Our object is to remove the temptation and not deal with the result of it. Equally we must believe in the essential goodness of the child so that we may uncover the hidden source of the factors that led to his despair.

We may be glad that there are ten Commandments or sorry that there are as many as ten, but in any attempt to help those who transgress, the effort has to be based upon a real and deep belief that the sufferer needs help that is based on love. Pity is useless. Confession from a child helps him to understand and lighten his burden. When he realizes the origin of his difficulties, then he can often deal with his own weaknesses.

We have succeeded in the past; our hope is that we may continue to succeed for the future.

GEORGE ALLEN & UNWIN LTD

Head Office
40 Museum Street, London, W.C.1.
Telephone: 01-405 8577

Sales, Distribution and Accounts Departments
Park Lane, Hemel Hempstead, Herts.
Telephone: 0442 2361/2

Auckland: P.O. Box 36013, Northcote Central N.4
Barbados: P.O. Box 222, Bridgetown
Bombay: 15 Graham Road, Ballard Estate, Bombay 1
Buenos Aires: Escritorio 454-459, Florida 165
Beirut: Deeb Building, Jeanne d'Arc Street
Calcutta: 17 Chittaranjan Avenue, Calcutta 13
Cape Town: 68 Shortmarket Street
Hong Kong: 105 Wing On Mansion, 26 Hancow Road, Kowloon
Ibadan: P.O. Box 62
Karachi: Karachi Chambers, McLeod Road
Madras: Mohan Mansions, 38c Mount Road, Madras 6
Mexico: Villalongin 32, Mexico 5, D.F.
Nairobi: P.O. Box 30583
New Delhi: 13-14 Asaf Ali Road, New Delhi 1
Toronto: 81 Curlew Drive, Don Mills
Philippines: P.O. Box 157, Quezon City D-502
Rio de Janeiro: Caixa Postal 2537-Zc-00
Singapore: 36c Prinsep Street, Singapore 7
Sydney N.S.W.: Bradbury House, 55 York Street
Tokyo: P.O. Box 26, Kamata

SALLIE TROTTER

No Easy Road

The author was the first woman social worker ever appointed in Britain to work inside an all-male prison—Wandsworth, in fact—with more freedom than had hitherto been offered to anyone not strictly of the prison staff. She was made responsible for the welfare and rehabilitation of 1,500 men, none of them first offenders. This book is the product of an experience that is quite unique.

The first part is an account of her experiences within the prison walls, of the prison and its staff, and of the criminals themselves; also of the day to day routine and problems raised by her unusual situation as a woman among so many tough and possibly dangerous men. The second part considers the theories of others with regard to treatment of the criminal and the author's own attempts to analyse them. The third part is devoted to Sallie Trotter's own ideas, for instance on rehabilitation, the moral issues, and the factors that turn a man into a criminal.

It is a serious book, but the author brings a completely fresh mind to bear on problems which have for too long been a male monopoly, whether the writers have been former officials and inmates, or outside critics and reformers. This new viewpoint seems to have been highly successful in the prison itself, and it certainly makes her book wholly absorbing. She has many valuable ideas to contribute and many interesting stories to relate, and the way in which her own personality emerges is particularly striking.

HARRIET WILSON

Delinquency and Child Neglect

'This is a lively and stimulating book and is well worth reading by every teacher in a densely populated area.' *Education*

'A valuable and careful sociological study . . . not only a solid but an attractive study.' *New Society*

OTTO L. SHAW

Maladjusted Boys

'Anything that Otto Shaw writes or says is bound to be of great value. Here is a story that will convince by its evident fruits those who are increasingly dissatisfied with the claims of conventional educationalists and penologists. There are excellent chapters dealing with the home and maladjustment, the delinquent, the obsessional child, truancy, parents, staff, religion, sex and mass media.' *British Journal of Psychiatric Social Work*

'. . . teachers and social workers who are intimately concerned with this problem will find this book of great professional interest, but it deserves a far wider readership.' *Teachers' World*

'. . . We can be grateful to Mr. Shaw, not only for the work he is doing, but also for making a readable book of it.' *New Society*

PAULINE NORRIS

Prisoners and their Families

'A source book of the utmost importance to penologists, welfare officers and lawyers . . . should be taken very seriously by anyone concerned with the law or its administration.' *Sunday Times*

'This most competent and meticulous study will provide incontrovertible ammunition for all those concerned to reform a wretchedly unsatisfactory aspect of our national life.' *The Times Educational Supplement*

'This book is of major significance. It needs to be considered seriously by everyone concerned with sentencing, and by all social workers who may work with prisoners' families.' *Social Service Quarterly Autumn*

JOHN F. WATSON

Which is the Justice

'See how yon' justice rails upon yon' simple thief.
Hark in thine ear; change places; and, handy-dandy,
which is the justice, which is the thief?'

King Lear's observation of human nature is paralleled and upheld
by these reflections of a London juvenile court magistrate of long
standing. The author draws on a wealth of experience in the courts,
but more especially on his personal contacts outside them, and the
result is a narrative that is sometimes amusing, occasionally critical,
but always human in its approach.

John Watson freely admits that, confined to boarding school, he
committed not a few of the offences for which young people were
later to be brought before him. It was surely a fortunate day when,
at the age of nineteen, he became a voluntary worker in Wormwood
Scrubs Prison, where he had a rare opportunity to help conduct a
fascinating social and educational experiment. Prison visiting and
teaching led him to further voluntary work among borstal boys, and
then at thirty-two he became one of the youngest magistrates ever
appointed at that time.

Throughout his book the author stresses the differences in the
nature of the relationships between children and their parents,
children and magistrates, and parents and magistrates. He also
believes strongly that all the judiciary, lay as well as professional,
should receive training in penology. His experiences in Germany,
where he went to advise the Control Commission on problems
arising from an upsurge of juvenile crime, give us an insight into
conditions in that country in the immediate post-war years, and into
the significance of the environment on social behaviour.

But the leading characters are always boys and girls in trouble,
the temptations that assail them in modern society, and the mistakes
and injustices of which they are the main victims.

LONDON: GEORGE ALLEN AND UNWIN LTD